Handbook of Transportation and Marketing in Agriculture

Handbook of Transportation and Marketing in Agriculture

Editor

Dr. S.K. Chattopadhyay

2011

Gene-Tech Books®

New Delhi - 110 002

ISBN 81-89729-95-0
ISBN 978-81-89729-95-0

Published by : **GENE-TECH BOOKS®**
4762-63/23, Ansari Road, Darya Ganj,
NEW DELHI - 110 002
Phone: 41562849
e-mail: genetechbooks@yahoo.co.in

Printed at : **Chawla Offset Printers**
New Delhi – 110 052

PRINTED IN INDIA

Preface

The scope of agriculture today is not merely limited to production of crop yield, but is extended to the transportation, marketing and proper supply of agricultural products. In an arena where commercialisation has become the byword, an efficient network of transportation systems and markets have become crucial to enhance the reach of agriculture. Considering such a scenario, it becomes important for the contemporary farmer to not just limit himself to enhancing crop yield, but extend his attention the proper supply of his products.

The present text has been aimed to guide farmers and agronomists on the essentials of the transport system and marketing challenges and opportunities in agriculture. Acquainting them with the infrastructure necessities the responsibilities and problems faced in these arenas, the book delineates for the readers the ways in which agriculture has been responding to the impulses of change, especially through its expansion within the context of these two sectors. Emphasis has been placed upon discussing both transportation methodologies and techniques as well as urban and rural marketing practices concerned with agriculture.

S.K. Chattopadhyay

Contents

1

Principles of Agricultural Transportation

The agricultural industry's current infrastructure deems transportation a necessary component of most operations. Due to ongoing consolidation, increasing transportation distances is required for agricultural products to reach centralised development and processing points. Economic considerations associated with agricultural transportation normally consist of direct costs associated with freight charges dictated by load size, hauling distance, difficulty in reaching pickup or delivery destination, and any special handling that may be required. Items such as shrink, death loss, and requirements of special insurance may also be considered.

Simultaneously, indirect costs resulting from other factors contribute to the realised expense of transportation. Short-falls in terms of personnel and equipment have the potential to contribute additional costs to the transportation process. Limited documentation and quantification exist within scientific literature regarding the influence of indirect costs. In addition to obtaining competitive freight rates and services, a transporting agent should ensure that the product will arrive in excellent condition. Of particular concern are products of a perishable nature, such as frozen and chilled foods, as well as processed and packaged foods, drinks, and juices. Important considerations include:

— Effective packaging and labelling;

— Temperature, humidity, and other environmental controls;

— Well-maintained transportation equipment; and

— Proper loading, in-transit monitoring, and unloading.

Under the best circumstances, product quality can only be maintained, not improved, during transportation. Initial product quality should be the highest possible. Products in top-quality condition:

— Have a longer shelf life;

— Allow more time for transportation, storage, and marketing;

— Satisfy importers, brokers, and consumers;

— Increase repeat sales and profits; and

— Help expand markets.

The transporting agent should keep in mind that products must be protected from:

— Rough handling during loading and unloading;

— Compression from the overhead weight of other product containers;

— Impact and vibration during land, ocean, and air transportation;

— Rolling, pitching, yawing, heaving, swaying, and surging during ocean transportation;

— Loss or gain of moisture to or from the surrounding air;

— Higher or lower than recommended temperature; and

— Cross-contamination or odours from other products or residues.

By selecting and packing only top-quality products, transporting agents can help ensure good arrival condition. Effective packaging, environmental controls, and proper transportation equipment are essential.

Packaging and Labelling

Proper packaging of agricultural products is essential to maintaining quality during transportation and marketing. Packaging serves to enclose the product and facilitate handling. Labelling provides required information and a further opportunity to position the product in the market through attractive graphics. Shipping high-quality, high-value, perishable products in poor-quality packaging can lead to damage, decay, low prices, or outright rejection by the buyer. Improper labelling can also lead to delays and product loss.

Packaging must withstand:

- — Rough handling during loading and unloading;
- — Compression from the overhead weight of other containers;
- — Impact and vibration during transportation; and
- — High humidity during precooling, transit, and storage.

Packaging materials are chosen on the basis of the product and environmental considerations. Factors to be considered are method of packing, temperature, humidity, desired atmosphere around the product, packaging strength, cost, availability, buyer specifications, graphics, labelling, freight rates, and government regulations. Packaging manufacturers, foreign buyers, wholesale markets, retail stores, packaging magazines, and consultants are an important source of information on current packaging trends and desires. All packaging should be recyclable or reusable, and the necessary amount of material should be used to protect the product.

The options of incinerating packaging waste or shipping waste to landfills are being reduced throughout the United States and Europe. Mandatory recycling programmes, packaging bans, and solid waste reduction programmes have been established in many countries. Packaging also should be standardised to facilitate unit loading on standard-size, reusable pallets in use in the United States, Europe, and other countries. Pallet handling and leasing companies have been established in response to economic as well as environmental concerns.

Boxes should be sized and filled in accordance with the importer's or buyer's desires. Boxes that are very wide and weigh more than 20 kg (44 lb) encourage rougher handling, product damage, and container failure. Excessive weights and damaged packaging are common complaints of importers of U.S. meat products who receive boxes weighing up to 45 kg (100 lb). In the Netherlands, for example, a single worker does not have to lift over 15 kg (33 lb) unassisted, in accordance with labour regulations and occupational safety concerns. Overfilling causes product damage and excessive bulging of the box, which leads to reduced compression strength and container failure. Underfilling also may cause product damage. The product may be bruised as it moves around inside the box during transport and handling or during crushing of the available headspace.

Widely used packaging materials include:

— *Fiberboard:* Pallets, slipsheets, bins, boxes (glued, stapled, interlocking), lugs, trays, flats, dividers, and partitions.

— *Wood*: Pallets, bins, crates (wirebound, nailed), baskets, trays, and lugs.

— *Paper:* Bags, sleeves, wraps, liners, pads, excelsior, and labels.

— *Plastic:* Pallets, bins, boxes, trays, bags (mesh, solid), containers, sleeves, film wraps, liners, coatings, dividers, and slipsheets.

— *Polystyrene:* Foam boxes, trays, lugs, sleeves, liners, dividers, and pads.

— *Fiberboard Boxes:* Fiberboard boxes are the most widely used packaging, due to their versatility and recyclability.

There are many fiberboard box styles and sizes. A minimum 19.3 kg/cm2 (275 lb/in2) bursting-test-strength or 7.86 kg/in (44 lb/in) width edge crush test fiberboard is recommended for boxes intended for export. The strength is needed for the handling, transport conditions, and high humidity the boxes must endure. Many boxes are now certified with an edge crush test instead of the bursting strength test. This information is available from the packaging supplier and stamped on each box. Foreign buyers or importers should be consulted about the size, pack, and box style desired.

Fiberboard boxes for products that are precooled in the box, packed wet, or packed with ice are wax-impregnated or coated with water-resistant material. Wax-treated fiberboard is generally not considered recyclable, so polyethylene and other coatings have been developed instead. Water-resistant coatings may be needed because the compression strength of untreated fiberboard can be reduced by more than one-half in conditions of high relative humidity common in refrigerated environments.

In addition to maintaining box strength, coatings help to reduce the loss of moisture from the product to the fiberboard or weakening of the fiberboard from moisture from the product. All glued boxes should be made with a water-resistant adhesive that also is recyclable. Specially coated modified atmosphere fiberboard packaging has been developed to slow product respiration rate and eliminate the need for ice and wax coatings in packages of fresh broccoli and other products. Film wraps of individual commodities and film wraps of fiberboard boxes of product have also been developed with the same purpose in mind. Proper product precooling and maintenance of refrigerated product temperatures are required for modified atmosphere packaging to work as intended.

Holes are provided in fiberboard boxes of some products to provide ventilation of product heat (respiration) and allow circulation of cold air to the product when a modified atmosphere is not required. Handholds provide a means of handling boxes during loading and unloading. All holes must be designed and placed in a manner that does not substantially weaken the box. Wood Crates--Wood crates and wirebound wood crates are popular with some shippers due to their material strength and resistance to high humidity and moisture damage during precooling, transit, and storage.

The crates are constructed in a manner that allows a lot of air circulation around the packed product. There is concern over whether wood crates are recyclable or reusable. Machines are available to grind up wood crates for conversion into mulch or other materials, but some countries in Europe have discouraged their use. Fasteners or wire in wood crates to be recycled should be made of steel with a maximum diameter of 10 mm, to allow grinding of the crates and extraction of the fastener particles with magnets.

Top-to-Bottom Stacking

The majority of fiberboard boxes and wood crates are designed to be stacked top-to-bottom. Compression strength and product protection are sacrificed when boxes or crates are stacked on their ends or sides. Misaligned fiberboard boxes can lose up to 30 percent of their strength, while boxes that are not stacked top-to-bottom (stacked either crosswise or off-center) can lose up to 50 percent of their top-to-bottom compression strength. Various materials are added to boxes to provide additional strength and product protection. Fiberboard trays, dividers, or partitions, and double-or triple-layer sides and ends in boxes provide additional compression strength and reduce product damage.

Pads, wraps, sleeves, and excelsior are used to reduce bruising. Pads also are used to: provide moisture, as with asparagus; absorb moisture as with retail packages of meat, poultry, and seafood; provide chemical treatment to reduce decay, as with sulfur dioxide pads for grapes; and absorb ethylene, as with potassium permanganate pads used in boxes of bananas and flowers, or oxygen in the case of some modified-atmosphere packaging.

Plastic Film Liners or Bags--Plastic film liners or bags are used to retain moisture, provide for a modified atmosphere, or maintain product integrity, such as in a cluster of grapes or tomatoes. Plastic with various size perforations, depending on commodity requirements, is used to let oxygen in and carbon dioxide out. Special films are used to seal the products and provide for a modified atmosphere either by allowing the product to consume oxygen, releasing carbon dioxide and therefore slow product respiration and ripening, or by flushing the package with a modified atmosphere or by vacuum packaging. This is done for bananas, strawberries, cherries, tomatoes, meat, poultry, seafood, and many other products that benefit from a modified atmosphere.

Paper and Polystyrene Foam Liners--Liners help to insulate the product from hot or cold temperatures when they are shipped in unrefrigerated air cargo holds and uninsulated air cargo containers. Wet paper is used to provide moisture to fresh cut herbs and flowers. Shippers should check with the Foreign Agricultural Service (FAS) or Animal and Plant Health Inspection Service (APHIS) for packaging materials restrictions in foreign countries, especially those made from plant parts such as wood, straw, or leaves. Some of these items are prohibited in other countries or require special documentation or quarantine treatments. Countries with phytosanitary or environmental restrictions on packaging materials include Australia, New Zealand, and the European Community. Soil also is restricted by many countries.

Packing Methods

Types of packs include:

— *Volume Fill:* Products are placed by hand or machine into the box until the desired capacity, weight, or count is reached.

— *Tray or Cell Pack:* Products are placed in moulded trays or cells which provide separation and reduce bruising.

— *Place Pack:* Products are wrapped and carefully placed in the box. This provides reduced bruising and a pleasing appearance.

— *Consumer Pack or Prepack:* Relatively small amounts of the product are packaged, weighed, and labelled for retail sale.

— *Flexible Packaging:* Each product is individually wrapped and sealed in film to reduce moisture loss and decay, and in some cases, provide for a modified atmosphere by letting oxygen in and carbon dioxide out through the design of the film layers, at a rate that slows product respiration and ripening. For some commodities the film may be treated with fungicides or other chemicals.

— *Modified Atmosphere:* Individual commodities, consumer packs, boxes, or pallet loads of commodities are sealed with special plastic film or bags and flushed with nitrogen to slow respiration, ripening, or aging of the product. In each case the packaging is formulated for a specific product.

Packing Fresh Fruits and Vegetables

The packing of fresh fruits and vegetables is of concern due to their highly perishable nature. Growers, processors, packers, shippers, and repackers should:

— Ensure adequate sanitation during harvesting and packing to avoid contamination of produce with pathogenic organisms that can cause food-borne illness;

— Use a chlorinated wash to remove dirt, debris, and organisms present in harvest operations;

— Sort out bruised, cut, decayed, insect-infested, odd-sized, immature, or overripe items;

— Use the minimum amount necessary of fungicides/ bactericides to limit decay on certain products, strictly in accordance with label instructions and foreign country restrictions;

— Use the minimum amount necessary of officially approved wax or resin coatings to reduce moisture loss on certain products, strictly in accordance with label instructions and foreign country restrictions;

— Use the minimum amount necessary of officially approved pesticides for certain products to eliminate insect pests, strictly in accordance with label instructions and foreign country restrictions;

— Remove field heat (precool) as soon as possible after harvest, and maintain the cold chain;

- Use grade standards or buyer's specifications in packing;
- Place only uniform sizes or amounts in each box;
- Place only products with a uniform level of maturity in each box; and
- Clearly mark the grade, size, weight, or count on the box, along with any other required label information, such as country of origin, exporter, importer, gross and net weights in kilograms, total number of packages, size of package in centimetres, handling marks (international pictorial symbols), cautionary marks, port of entry, pesticides, and fungicides used, or wax or resin coatings used, in a language accepted by the destination country.

Damaged fresh products can ruin an entire shipment and reduce importers' confidence in the grower and shipper. Products in this condition:

- Spread decay to other products in the load;
- Produce more ethylene gas and heat, which cause further ripening and decay; and
- Lose more water resulting in shrivelling and wilting.

Packing methods for fresh produce include:

- *Field Packing:* Products are placed in fiberboard boxes or wood crates during harvesting. Some products are wrapped. The filled containers are then taken to a precooling facility to reduce field heat.
- *Shed Packing:* Products are processed or packed indoors or under cover at a central location. The product is brought from the field to the packing shed in bulk in field crates, bins, or trucks. The products are precooled either before or after they are placed in shipping containers.
- *Repacking:* Products are taken out of one container, regraded, and placed in another. This is often done to make smaller boxes for the retailer or consumer packages.

— *Fresh-cut Processing:* Products are washed, trimmed, shredded, peeled, cut, and otherwise processed into salad mixes or ready-to-eat items under sanitary and temperature-controlled conditions using Hazard Analysis Critical Control Point (HACCP) or similar systems of quality control. These items are then placed in modified-atmosphere consumer and foodservice packages which are then grouped in fiberboard boxes for distribution under constant refrigeration.

Packing Meat, Poultry, and Seafood Products

Through careful sanitation, modified-atmosphere packaging technology, temperature control, and loading of marine containers at meat packing plants, extended shelf life of 70 days or more for chilled beef and lamb has been possible since the late 1980's. This has provided higher revenues for the meat exporter as compared to frozen product shipped by sea or chilled product shipped by air. Recently instituted HACCP procedures may help additional firms get into the export market with extended shelf-life, quality-assured chilled and frozen products.

Standardised Boxes

Due to the large number of different box sizes in use, box and pallet standards have been developed by the fresh produce, frozen food, floral, and grocery industries in Europe and the United States to reduce handling damage and packaging waste. Standardised boxes can:

- Reduce box inventory for manufacturers and growers;
- Provide unit loads and more stable mixed pallet loads;
- Reduce transportation and marketing costs; and
- Use 90 to 100 percent of the pallet surface with no overhang and little underhang.

The following are standard pallet sizes:

- Standard Grocery Manufacturers Association (GMA) pallet used in the United States--1219 by 1016 mm (48 by 40 in).

— International Standards Organisation (ISO) pallet used in Europe--1200 by 1000 mm (47.24 by 39.37 in).

— Europallet, also widely used in Europe: 1200 by 800 mm (47.24 by 31.5 in).

The following five box sizes that fit well on all three of the above pallets are recommended for international trade, especially in Europe.

— 600 by 400 mm

— 400 by 300 mm

— 400 by 200 mm

— 300 by 200 mm

— 200 by 150 mm

Unit Loads

Shippers, carriers, and receivers prefer handling palletised unit loads instead of individual boxes, one at a time. Most distribution centres are set up to store palletised loads in three-tier or higher racks.

Unit loads provide for:

— Reduced handling of boxes;

— Less damage to the boxes and the products inside;

— Faster loading and unloading of transportation equipment;

— More efficient distribution center operations; and

— Reduced pilferage of products.

Unit loads may include some of the following features:

— Standard size reusable or recyclable wood pallets or slipsheets;

— Fiberboard, plastic, or wire vertical interlocking tabs between boxes;

— Boxes with holes for air circulation, which align when the boxes are stacked squarely on top of one another, corner to corner;

- — Recyclable glue between boxes to resist horizontal slipping;
- — Plastic netting around the pallet load of boxes; and
- — Fiberboard, plastic, or metal cornerboards with plastic or metal strapping around the cornerboards and boxes.

Pallets

Wood pallets must be strong enough to allow storage in racks. Pallets also should be capable of being reused a number of times. Provisions for forklift and pallet jack handling are necessary. The design of the bottom of the pallet should not block air circulation. Block-style 1200 by 1000 mm pallets are standard in European pallet pools and should be used for any exports to Europe. The Europallet, 1200 by 800 mm, also is popular in some European countries. Australia uses an 1100 by 1100 mm pallet.

One-way pallets are increasingly being rejected by importers and receivers due to recycling and disposal costs. Product received in Europe on pallets other than the 1200 by 1000 mm and 1200 by 800 mm pallets used in those countries may be required to be re-palletised at the port of entry, leading to additional handling costs, product damage, and pallet disposal costs. Pallets must have an adequate number of top deck boards to support fiberboard boxes. Otherwise the boxes may collapse between deck boards, crush the product, or cause the entire load to lean or fall off the pallet. A sheet of fiberboard with holes for air circulation can be used to help distribute weight across the pallet.

Boxes must not overhang the edges of the pallets. Overhang can reduce the strength of fiberboard boxes by one-third. This condition can lead to collapse of the entire load, crushing of the product, and difficulty in loading, unloading, and storage in racks. On the other hand, boxes that use less than 90 percent of the pallet surface and do not align with the pallet edge can shift in transit. Pallet loads of boxes that are not strapped or netted should have at least the top three layers of containers cross-stacked to provide stability. Some shippers use film wrap, tape, or glue on the top layers in addition to cross-stacking. The boxes must be strong enough to be cross-stacked without collapsing. Film wrap should not be used on boxes of products that need ventilation.

Use of Slipsheets

Slipsheets, made of sheets of fiberboard or plastic, are used by some shippers instead of pallets to reduce transportation costs. Slipsheets eliminate the cost of buying, disposing, or returning pallets. A special forklift with a clamping device is needed to transfer slipsheet loads to and from the warehouse pallets at the shipper's and receiver's distribution center and into the trailer, container, or railcar. If this special forklift is not available, the unit loads must be transferred box by box onto pallets, leading to costly delay and product damage.

Slipsheets made of recyclable fiberboard or plastic must be strong enough to be clamped and pulled onto the forklift tines or plate for lifting. Fiberboard slipsheets should be treated with a recyclable coating for use in wet conditions. Slipsheets used in transportation equipment should have holes for air circulation under the load. The use of slipsheets in refrigerated transportation equipment with shallow floor channels is not recommended due to the need for adequate air circulation under the load. Unit loads of boxes on slipsheets should be netted, stretch-wrapped, or otherwise secured with cornerboards and strapping.

Labelling and Branding

Labelling of boxes may provide required information for export certification, identify and advertise the products, and assist receivers in storing and retrieving the boxes. Fiberboard boxes can be preprinted with colourful graphics. Wood packaging has glued, stamped, or stenciled labelling. Some high-quality fruits and vegetables are individually branded with small colourful trademark stickers. Some shippers also provide selection, storage, recipes, posters, and other point-of-sale material for the retailer or consumer.

All boxes and consumer packages should be clearly labelled, bar coded, and branded in the language accepted by the destination country. The following information should be included on boxes along with any other data required by the foreign country:

- — Common name of the product;
- — Net weight, count, and/or volume;
- — Brand name as well as name and address of the packer or shipper;
- — Country of origin;
- — Size and grade, when standards are used;
- — Recommended storage temperature;
- — Special handling instructions; and
- — Name of officially approved fungicides or bactericides used in packaging.

Each country has labelling requirements that must be followed. Labelling of consumer packages is mandatory under most national regulations. For example, the United States requires that in addition to the product name, net weight, and name and address of the manufacturer, packer, or distributor, processed items must have a nutrition label and all ingredients listed in descending order of prominence. The Food and Drug Administration (FDA) classifies fruits and vegetables with wax or resin coatings as processed products which must be properly labelled with names of the coating displayed at the point of retail sale or on the individual items. Many processed products also are labelled with a "sell by" date or "best if used by" date.

Environmental Controls

Removal of field heat by the process of precooling to a recommended storage temperature and relative humidity is absolutely necessary to maintain the quality of fresh fruits, vegetables, plants, and cut flowers. The quality of most products will rapidly deteriorate if field heat is not removed before loading into transportation equipment. The rate of respiration and ripening increases two to three times for every 100° C (18° F) above the recommended storage temperature. Refrigerated transportation equipment is designed to maintain temperature and should not be used to remove field heat from products packed in shipping containers. The refrigeration units also are not capable of raising or controlling the relative humidity.

A high temperature difference between the refrigeration unit evaporation coil and the product will increase the loss of product moisture. This will cause the evaporator to frost and the products to shrivel or wilt and weigh less. Most fruits and vegetables have a water content between 80 and 95 percent.

Precooling Factors

Precooling extends product life by reducing:

- Field heat;
- Rate of respiration (heat generated by the product);
- Rate of ripening;
- Loss of moisture (shrivelling and wilting);
- Production of ethylene (ripening gas generated by the product); and
- Spread of decay.

The success of precooling is dependent on:

- Time between harvest and precooling;
- Type of shipping container, if product is packed beforehand;
- Initial product temperature;
- Velocity or amount of cold air, water, or ice provided;
- Final product temperature;
- Sanitation of the precooling air or water to reduce decay organisms; and
- Maintenance of the recommended temperature after precooling.

Precooling should occur as soon as possible after harvest. Harvesting should be done in early morning hours to minimize field heat and the refrigeration load on precooling equipment. Harvested products should be protected from the sun with a covering until they are placed in the precooling facility. Many products are field or shed packed and then precooled. Wood wirebound or nailed crates and waxed or coated fiberboard boxes are used for packed products that are precooled with water or ice after packing. This process is being modified in response to the demand for recyclable boxes.

Precooling of products packed in boxes and stacked in unitised pallet loads is especially important as air circulation around and through the packaging may be limited during transportation and storage. Precooling is particularly important for products that produce a lot of heat.

Precooling Methods

The choice of precooling method depends on the nature, value, and quantity of the product, as well as the cost of labor, equipment, and materials. Precooling methods include:

- *Room Cooling:* Boxes of products are stacked in a refrigerated room. Some products are misted or sprayed with water during room cooling.
- *Forced-Air Cooling or Wet Pressure Cooling:* Air is drawn through stacks or unit loads of boxes of products in a refrigerated room. For some products, water is added to the air.
- *Hydrocooling:* Products are flushed with ice water in bulk tanks, bins, or boxes.
- *Vacuum Cooling:* Heat is removed from products packed in boxes by drawing a vacuum in a chamber.
- *Hydrovacuum CoolingL:* Moisture is added to products packed in boxes before or during the vacuum process to speed the removal of heat.
- *Package-icing:* Slush or crushed ice is injected into each box of product. Some operations use bulk bins.

Portable ice plants, hydrocoolers, vacuum coolers, forced-air coolers, and package-icing machines are available for use in the fields. This equipment is useful for remote or small-scale operations that cannot justify investment in a fixed precooling facility. Mounted on skids, dollies, or tractor trailers, the equipment can follow the harvest from field to field and be shared by many growers. Hydrocooling and vacuum cooling are the fastest cooling methods. Cooling times of half an hour are possible. Products and packaging must be able to withstand direct water contact in hydrocooling. In vacuum cooling, the products should have a large surface area, low density, and high moisture content. The boxes and wrapping must allow ventilation of heat.

Forced-air cooling can take 1 or 2 hours, depending on the amount of packaging, while room cooling may take 24 to 72 hours. Packaging must allow ventilation of heat for these methods to be successful. Package-icing provides effective cooling and a high relative humidity for products and packaging that can withstand direct contact with ice.

Many tropical fruits, vegetables, plants, and cut flowers require much less cooling than products that are cooled to 0° C (32° F). All products should be precooled as near as possible to the recommended storage temperature and relative humidity. Product temperatures should be taken in sample boxes by inserting an electronic thermometer into the product. The data should be recorded for future reference.

Mode of Transportation and the Carrier

The design and condition of the transport equipment, and the loading method used, are critical to maintaining product quality. The mode of transportation and the carrier should be chosen carefully.

Selection factors

The mode of transportation and type of equipment used should be based on:

— Destination;

— Value of the product;

— Degree of product perishability;

— Amount of product to be transported;

— Recommended storage temperature and relative humidity;

— Outside temperature conditions at origin and destination points;

— Time in transit to reach destination by air, land, or ocean transport;

— Freight rates negotiated with the carriers; and

— Quality of transportation service.

The reliability and quality of transportation services provided by different carriers must be carefully considered along with the rates charged. Services and schedules are subject to change. Shippers should contact air and ocean port authorities at their origin and destination locations to receive the most current information on available services. Local trade publications also are excellent sources of information, as many carriers and their agents advertise their schedules and destinations. Refrigerated trailers and containers are recommended for products shipped in large volumes with transit and storage lives of 1 week or more. After transit, there must be enough remaining product life for marketing. Carriers using trailers and containers may offer door-to-door service, which reduces handling, exposure, damage, and theft of the products.

Air cargo containers also can be used to provide door-to-door service. Products transported by air are generally high in value, highly perishable, but shipped in lower volumes. Freight costs are higher by air, but transit time is reduced considerably. Many products are shipped in unrefrigerated air containers or on air cargo pallets. This requires close coordination at the origin and destination airports to protect the products when flights are delayed. Cold storage facilities are needed at airports to ensure product quality. Refrigerated air containers, insulated blankets, or gel pack refrigerants should be used when possible.

Products that can be shipped in refrigerated trailers and van containers are sometimes shipped by air to take advantage of brief market opportunities, such as the beginning of a season when prices are high and supply is limited. Often an importer who is first to receive a certain product is able to build goodwill and increase sales throughout the season.

Available Equipment

The following transportation equipment is available:

- *Air Cargo Containers:* For air and highway transport.
- *Air Cargo Pallets With Netting:* For air and highway transport.
- *Highway Trailers:* For highway transport only.
- *Piggyback Trailers:* For rail, highway, and roll-on/roll-off ocean transport.
- *Containers:* For rail, highway, and lift-on/lift-off ocean transport.
- *Breakbulk Reefer Vessels:* Handling palletised loads in refrigerated holds.
- *Bulk Vessels:* Handling dry and liquid products in holds.
- *Railroad Boxcars:* Handling palletised or individual shipping containers.

Refrigeration and Ventilation Systems

The following systems are available:

Mechanical: Diesel-generated electric power is used over the road and aboard ocean vessels. Van containers are plugged into electrical power at depots and aboard ships.

Cryogenic: Liquid or gaseous nitrogen or carbon dioxide, which is released into cargoes of frozen food and occasionally chilled food under controlled conditions. Some products, such as leafy green vegetables, are not compatible with carbon dioxide refrigeration.

Dry Ice: Solid blocks of carbon dioxide in special trays or compartments are used in air cargo containers, pallet containers, and within individual shipping containers of frozen product. Shippers must check with airlines prior to using dry ice, as it is considered a hazardous material. If permitted, the containers and accompanying documents must be properly marked to show the amount of dry ice used. Some products, such as leafy green vegetables, are not compatible with dry ice. Direct contact with dry ice will injure fresh products.

Wet Ice: Ice is used within individual shipping containers or on top of a load of containers, either as a supplement or instead of mechanical refrigeration. Many airlines refuse to handle shipping containers with wet ice due to the risk of expensive damage from leaking containers. Airlines that do permit wet ice require that it be placed in sealed polyethylene bags inside a leakproof container with a moisture absorbent pad.

Top-ice is used for certain fresh products to supplement mechanical refrigeration and help maintain a high humidity. Most refrigeration units on trailers and containers cannot control relative humidity and actually remove moisture from products as a natural part of the cooling process. Top-ice on loads should be applied in rows instead of a solid mass, especially in bottom air delivery equipment. Air circulation should not be blocked. The thermostat on top-iced loads should be set at 2° C (35° F) to prevent freezing of the ice into a solid mass which would block air circulation. Products that can be top-iced also can be package-iced, provided the correct packaging materials are used.

Gel Refrigerant: Frozen containers of chemical eutectic gel are used to maintain temperature within shipping containers. This is the refrigeration system preferred by most airlines.

Ventilation, Ethylene Scrubbing, Humidity Control: Fresh air exchange in the refrigeration system or vents in dry or insulated containers can be used to protect products from a buildup of heat, moisture, carbon dioxide, or ethylene. Leafy green vegetables are sensitive to carbon dioxide, while many products are sensitive to ethylene. In lieu of ventilation, potassium permanganate pads can be installed in the trailer or container at the refrigeration unit to absorb ethylene. These ethylene scrubbers also can be placed inside individual shipping containers. Moisture absorbents and kraft paper liners are used to control condensation on products during transportation through different climates. Some refrigeration units are capable of maintaining humidity at optimum levels.

Multitemperature: A mechanical or cryogenic system provides two or three temperature conditions in separate compartments of a trailer or container which can be used to carry loads of frozen, chilled, and dry products in one vehicle. Advance planning is required when loading multitemperature trailers. The conditions provided by three compartment trailers may include -18° C (0° F), 0° C (32° F), 10° C (50° F), or ambient temperature for products not requiring refrigeration. The frozen compartment is usually located at the front of the trailer closest to the refrigeration unit. Movable bulkheads are placed between the compartments. Separate evaporators or ventilation between compartments provide temperature control for the nonfrozen products. Side doors are needed to access the forward compartments when the trailers are inspected at ports of entry or used to make multiple deliveries on a single run.

Modified or Controlled Atmosphere: Nitrogen and some carbon dioxide gas is added to pallet bags, or to the cargo compartment of refrigerated van containers, displacing oxygen. This reduces product decay, respiration, and ripening of certain products. Controlled-atmosphere systems monitor and replenish the nitrogen, scrub carbon dioxide, and adjust the level of oxygen according to specific product requirements. This allows products to be shipped at a higher level of maturity. Controlled atmosphere also allows for longer transit times enabling shippers to use less costly land and sea transport instead of air transport for highly perishable products and to allow the transport of riper fruit. Products shown to benefit include apples, asparagus, avocados, bananas, cherries, kiwifruit, mangoes, pears, and strawberries.

Modified or controlled atmospheres of reduced oxygen, and elevated nitrogen and carbon dioxide, are provided to specially equipped containers of certain fruits, vegetables, meat, and seafood after loading is completed. The atmospheres are tailored for each commodity. Three controlled atmosphere systems are available: gas injection, membrane air separation, and pressure swing absorption. Ethylene scrubbers can be added to these systems. For modified and controlled-atmosphere gas injection systems, containers are equipped with channels at the doorway. A plastic curtain is sealed in the channels to reduce air leakage. Gas ports in the side of the container are used for the injection of the desired atmosphere and discharge of the existing air. In the case of controlled atmosphere, an electronic controller, a scrubber for absorbing excess carbon dioxide, and an air exchange port to allow in more oxygen are provided.

Trailers are generally considered too leaky, and transit times too short to benefit from modified or controlled atmospheres. Instead, shippers may use a gas injection system of modified atmosphere, which is applied either to pallet loads enclosed by a plastic bag or applied to individual modified-atmosphere shipping containers. The pallet application is primarily used for strawberries. The packaging application has been used for tomatoes and broccoli. The above systems are proprietary and, applied under a service agreement, available at select ports and shipping points around the world. In the case of container loads, the service applicators must check the container for excessive air leakage prior to the application and correct major problems.

The membrane air separation system is either built into the refrigeration unit or clipped on to it. The pressure swing absorption system is installed separately in the container in addition to the refrigeration unit. These systems generate nitrogen, reduce oxygen, and add or remove carbon dioxide as needed. These systems can be programmed by the shipper and are able to overcome some air leakage.

Membrane air separation is also available to service individual holds in refrigerated vessels or a number of porthole containers in the hold of a vessel. Research continues to be conducted on using controlled atmosphere systems to reduce or eliminate insect infestations. Warning labels must be applied to containers and vessel holds with controlled atmospheres to caution employees that the atmosphere will not support human life. The cargo area must be ventilated properly before personnel can enter to unload the cargo.

Equipment Features

Long-distance transportation through tropical and frigid climates requires rugged, well-designed equipment to withstand the transit environment and protect the products. Desirable features in refrigerated trailers and containers include:

— Adequate refrigeration capacity to hold frozen food at extreme ambient temperatures;

— Adequate air circulation for uniform product temperature and high relative humidity throughout the load;

— A solid return air bulkhead at the front of the trailer to ensure air circulation throughout the load;

— Vertical ribs on side walls and the rear door to assist in air circulation;

— Adequate insulation and provisions for heating in areas with extreme cold weather;

— Deep floor grooves or channels to provide an adequate cross-sectional area for air circulation under loads placed directly on the floor;

— Supply-air temperature sensing of the operation of the refrigeration unit to reduce product chilling and freezing injury;

— Provisions for ventilation to prevent ethylene or carbon dioxide buildup;

— Provisions for application of controlled or modified atmospheres; and

— Adequate suspension to reduce the amount of shock and vibration transferred to the shipping containers and the products inside.

The capacities and dimensions of air cargo containers, air cargo pallets, refrigerated trailers, and refrigerated van containers vary among carriers due to differences in equipment design and manufacture. Carriers should be consulted for specifications, availability, and rates well in advance of shipping. Many carriers provide valuable assistance and information on loading and operating their equipment.

Room for air circulation must be provided in transport equipment loaded with agricultural products. The nature of the product, packaging type, and loading method affect air circulation, as well as the total weight and volume occupied by the load. Maximum cargo weights are limited by carriers to comply with restrictions on particular transport and handling equipment, or limits enforced by Government agencies to protect roads and bridges. Due to light product density or load limits, many loads do not use the maximum rated-weight capacity of the transport equipment.

Most carriers check their transport equipment before delivery to the shipper for loading. Good equipment condition is critical to maintaining product quality. The shipper also should check the equipment to ensure it is in good working order and meets the needs of the product. Carriers provide guidance on checking and operating the refrigeration systems. All transportation equipment should be checked for:

— *Cleanliness:* The load compartment should be regularly steam cleaned.

— *Damage:* Walls, floors, doors, and ceilings should be in good condition.

— *Temperature Control:* Refrigerated units should have been calibrated recently and capable of supplying continuous air circulation for uniform product temperatures.

Shippers should insist on clean equipment. A load of products can be ruined by:

- — Odours from previous shipments;
- — Toxic chemical residues;
- — Insects nesting in the equipment;
- — Decaying remains of agricultural products; and
- — Debris blocking drain openings or air circulation along the floor.

Shippers should insist on well-maintained equipment and check for the following:

- — Damage to walls, ceilings, or floors, which can let in the outside heat, cold, moisture, dirt, and insects;
- — Operation and condition of doors, ventilation openings, and seals; and
- — Provisions for load locking and bracing.

For refrigerated trailers and containers, the following additional checks are important:

- — With the doors closed, the cargo area should be checked from inside for light--door gaskets must seal. A smoke generator also can be used to detect leaks.
- — The refrigeration unit should cycle from high to low speed when the desired temperature is reached and then back to high speed.
- — The location of the sensing element that controls the discharge air temperature must be located. If it measures return air temperature, the thermostat will have to be set higher to avoid a chilling injury or freezing injury to the products.
- — A solid return air bulkhead should be installed at the front of the trailer.
- — A heating device should be available for transportation in areas with extreme cold weather.

— Equipment with a top air delivery system must have a fabric air chute or metal ceiling plenum in good condition.

Products requiring refrigeration should be thoroughly precooled prior to loading into transportation equipment. Product temperatures should be taken with an electronic probe thermometer and recorded on the bill of lading for future reference. The load compartment in the equipment also should be precooled to the recommended transport or storage temperature for the product. Ideally, the loading area should be enclosed and refrigerated, with dock seals at the trailer or container doors.

Proper loading practices are critical to maintaining temperature and relative humidity, protecting the products from impact and vibration forces in transit, and preventing insects from entering the load. Special care must be taken when shipping mixed loads—the products must be compatible.

Methods of Loading

Basic loading methods include:

— Bulkloading, by machine or hand, of unpackaged commodities;

— Hand loading individual boxes with or without pallets; and

— Unit loading of palletised or slipsheet loads of boxes with pallet jacks or forklifts.

Mixed Loads

Many products are often transported in mixed loads or stored with other products. They must be compati. .e in terms of:

— Recommended temperature and relative humidity;

— Production and sensitivity to ethylene; and

— Production and absorption of odours.

Many products are subject to chilling injury when transported or stored at lower than recommended temperatures. This damage often becomes apparent after the products warm up. Products injured may show pitting, discoloration, water-soaked areas, decay, and failure to ripen.

Many products are recommended to be transported or stored at temperatures only 1° C to 3° C (2° F to 6° F) above their freezing points. Thermostats on some trailers and van containers are set 1° C to 3° C (2° F to 6° F) higher than the recommended temperature of 0° C (32° F) for chilled products. Most tropical products that freeze are first damaged by chilling injury. Most products need to be transported and stored at a high relative humidity. Some products are more susceptible to moisture loss than others. Moisture loss results in wilting and shrivelling. To reduce moisture loss, products must be adequately precooled before transit. Some products also are waxed, film-wrapped, package-iced, or top-iced. Relative humidity during transit and storage must be maintained as much as possible.

Never transport or store fruits and vegetables that produce a lot of ethylene with products that are sensitive to it. Ethylene can cause premature ripening of some products and will ruin others, such as plants and cut flowers. Cucumbers and celery turn yellow, while lettuce will turn brown, in the presence of ethylene. Potassium permanganate pads can be used to absorb ethylene during transit and storage. Never transport or store odorous products with products that will absorb the odours. Never load fruit, vegetables, or other food products with nonfood products that provide any risk of contamination through transfer of toxic chemical residues.

Similar-sized shipping containers should be loaded together in mixed loads for increased stability. Heavier shipping containers of products should be loaded first and distributed evenly across the floor of the trailer or container. Lighter shipping containers can then be placed against or on top of the heavier products. Load lock bars, load gates, and pallets placed in a vertical position can be used to separate and secure stacks of different-sized shipping containers.

To facilitate inspection of mixed loads at ports of entry, a representative sample of each commodity should be available near the door. This can minimize the unloading of cargo for examination. The longer the transit time, the higher the risks in transporting mixed loads of agricultural products. Therefore, it is essential that guidelines be followed closely to maintain quality in distant markets.

Providing for Air Circulation

Inadequate provisions for air circulation will ruin a load, even in well-designed transportation equipment. When possible, boxes should be kept off shallow floors and away from flat sidewalls by using pallets, racks, and dunnage. Room for air circulation must be provided under, around, and through the load to protect the products from:

— Heat gain from the outside air during hot weather;

— Heat generated by the produce through respiration;

— Ethylene produced by certain products;

— Heat loss to the outside air during extreme cold weather; and

— Chilling injury or freezing injury during operation of the refrigeration unit.

Temperature Monitoring

Shippers should follow the carrier's recommendations on loading and setting the temperature of the equipment's load compartment to avoid chilling or freezing injury to fresh products. Discharge air may be colder than the set-point temperature if the refrigeration system operates on return-air temperature sensing. The temperature should be clearly marked on the bill of lading. Drivers and shipper should check product temperatures with a pulp thermometer and record the temperatures during the loading process.

Many carriers advise setting the thermostat temperature 1° C to 3° C (2° F to 6° F) higher than the recommended temperature of 0° C (32° F) for chilled products. This depends on the design of the transportation equipment. Newer equipment with supply-air temperature sensing and good air circulation can be operated closer to the recommended temperature. For most tropical fruits and vegetables and plants that have recommended temperatures in the 10° C to 21° C (50° F to 70° F) range, the thermostat is set at or near the recommended temperature.

It is now possible to monitor refrigeration unit operating conditions from a central control room on a ship or by satellite transmission. Refrigeration units for trailers and containers may have an electronic recorder which can monitor up to three different points in the load. This data can be downloaded and analysed on a computer. Mechanical temperature recorders which place data on a circular chart also are used.

In addition to trip insurance, all loads should have a small portable air-temperature recorder (supplied by the shipper) placed between packages in the area where the warmest temperatures occur. Recorder companies recommend placement on top of the load, near a sidewall, one-third of the way in from the rear doors, and away from any direct discharge of refrigerated air.

Railcars should have two or three portable recorders. In loads with top-ice or humidity above 95 percent, the recorders should be waterproof or enclosed in a plastic bag. Models are available for frozen food applications. Shippers and receivers must follow the recorder company's instructions on documenting the load, starting the recorder, reading the results, and returning it for calibration and certification. The temperature recorder chart and/or instrument number should be clearly marked on the bill of lading. These steps are essential for settling claims over temperature management during transportation. In the European Union temperature recording is mandatory. It also is necessary in the case of cold treatment quarantine shipments in which fruit is held at specific temperatures to kill fruit flies.

Cold Treatment

Shippers should avoid loading at night. Insects attracted by light can enter the load and cause problems upon inspection at destination. The loading area should be enclosed to prevent insects from reinfesting treated and packaged products. The Animal and Plant Health Inspection Service (APHIS) operates a preclearance programme in which product is inspected and certified to be free of injurious insect pests and plant diseases. Such shipments are marked and sealed to prevent tampering and infestation.

Fumigations for pest control inside loaded transportation equipment are usually done under APHIS supervision in accordance with the necessary treatment schedule for a particular product and insect. Cold treatment of certain products during transportation also is used to kill insects. This involves strict temperature control throughout the load for up to 2 weeks. APHIS maintains a list of refrigerated vessels and refrigerated containers certified as capable of maintaining intransit cold treatment temperatures.

Bracing the Load

Loads should be secured with some of the following materials to prevent vibration and impact damage in transit:

— Aluminum or wood load locks;

— Fiberboard honeycomb fillers;

— Wood blocking and nailing strips;

— Inflatable kraft paper air bags;

— Cargo nets and straps; and

— Wood load gates constructed of 25 by 102 mm material.

Air Cargo Equipment

Air cargo containers are loaded by hand or with forklifts when using fiberboard LD-3 container inserts. Polystyrene foam triangular inserts, wood blocking, and fiberboard dunnage are recommended to brace boxes and provide a level platform on the sloped surface of LD-3 containers. Refrigerated air cargo containers should be used when available. Air cargo pallets are loaded by hand or with forklifts. The loads should be secured with straps, tape, or cross-stacking of the boxes. A weatherproof or insulated cover can be placed over the load along with the required cargo netting, provided the pallet load is protected from sunlight.

For refrigerated trailers and containers the following loading practices are recommended:

— Precool the trailer or container to the recommended transport or storage temperature. Turn off the refrigeration unit during loading if the loading area is not refrigerated; otherwise, the evaporator will frost due to the warm air drawn in by the unit.

— Thoroughly precool unit loads, as air circulation to some of the shipping containers may be limited. The containers should have openings for cooling and ventilation of product heat.

— Avoid loading tightly against flat sidewalls. Use centerline loading for unit loads.

— Secure unitised loads with dunnage between the walls and load.

— Do not block air circulation at the rear door.

— Secure the rear of both hand-stacked and unitised loads with straps, load gates, or load lock bars to prevent the load from shifting against the rear doors.

Trailers and Containers With Top Air Delivery

For refrigerated trailers and containers with air delivered to the top of the load by chutes or ceiling ducts, these additional practices are necessary to maintain product quality:

— Hand-stacked loads should be evenly spaced, with lengthwise air flow channels created on every other layer, to ventilate product heat (respiration).

— Header stacks must be provided at the front bulkhead of the trailer or container in hand-stacked loads to connect all the lengthwise channels and allow the air to return to the evaporator.

— Loads of frozen food or nonrespiring products can be loaded solidly without air channels in the middle of the load.

— Fiberboard boxes must be strong enough to counter the reduced stacking strength due to the boxes being offset to provide airflow channels.

— Pallets should be used with hand-stacked loads to provide adequate air circulation in equipment with flat or shallow grooved floors.

— The load should not block the ceiling air chute or plenum.

Trailers and Containers With Bottom Air Delivery

For refrigerated trailers and containers with air delivered to the bottom of the load through the floor channels, these additional practices are necessary to maintain product quality:

— Hand-stacked and unit loads of boxes should have bottom-to-top ventilation slots that align in the stacks. Otherwise, small vertical air flow channels are needed between boxes as a result of the slight bulge in the box sides.

— At least 13 mm (5 in) of space should be provided at the ceiling for return-air circulation.

— The load should cover most of the floor surface to force more air through the load. Pieces of fiberboard can be used to cover any remaining floor space next to unit loads or stacks of boxes. Only the floor area next to the doorway should be open to permit return air flow.

During transportation of refrigerated loads in trailers and containers, the carrier should check the operation of the refrigeration unit and temperature of the load compartment regularly.

Before completely unloading a shipment for storage, receivers usually check the load to determine if it meets specifications for quality, grade, and packaging. The receiver also will note whether the load was adequately braced and the correct temperature was maintained. Product temperatures in sample shipping containers throughout the load should be taken and recorded, using an electronic probe thermometer.

The air-temperature recorder should be read, if one was placed in the load. Shippers and carriers should be notified of any problems with the product, packaging, loading method, or transportation equipment, so corrective action can be taken. If there is a problem with the load, the receiver, carrier, or shipper can request an inspection by a licensed inspector. Unresolved disputes over product quality or payment can be referred to arbitration or other legal avenues.

Unloaded products need to be protected from direct sun, condensation, ethylene, and contamination. Products needing refrigeration or protection from hot or cold temperatures should be placed in the recommended storage conditions as soon as possible. Otherwise, the efforts of growers, shippers, and carriers to maintain product quality will have been in vain.

Uniform air circulation in the storage room at the proper temperature and relative humidity is important to remove product heat that occurs from respiration, and from outside heat that enters through door openings and building surfaces. Doors to refrigerated storage area's should be protected with plastic strip curtains to reduce heat gain during operations. Warm air will quickly reduce relative humidity in the cold storage area. To maintain temperature and relative humidity, the storage room refrigeration system should have a large evaporator surface area, an adequate number of fans, and a humidifier. Temperature control should be by an electronic thermostat. The system must be carefully balanced to avoid free moisture or excessive air flow.

Electric forklifts and pallet jacks should be used with horticultural products to reduce ethylene. Periodic sanitation of the storage room walls, ceilings, floor, and refrigeration units is necessary to reduce decay organisms and odours. Carbon filters can be used to absorb odours and volatile gases, while potassium permanganate pads and air exchange can reduce ethylene.

References

Ashby, B.H., *et al., Protecting Perishable Foods During Transport by Truck,* HBK-669. USDA, AMS, September, 1987.

Atlantic Mutual Companies, *Buyers Guide To Marine Cargo Insurance,* New York, NY, 1990.

Cassell, Clark C., *The World is Your Market - An Export Guide for Small Business,* Edited by William Delphos. Braddock Communications, Washington, DC, 1990.

Fuell, L. D., D. C. Miller, and M. Chesley, *Dictionary of International Agricultural Trade,* USDA, FAS, June 1988.

Friedheim, Amy, *Ocean Liner Freight Rates and Services,* USDA, AMS, May 1991.

Hardenburg, R. E., A. E. Watada, C. Y. Wang, *The Commercial Storage of Fruits, Vegetables, and Florist and Nursery Stocks,* HBK-66. USDA, ARS, September 1986.

Lassanyi, Mary E., *Directory of Export and Trade Assistance,* USDA, NAL, November 1991.

Lipton, W.J. and J.M. Harvey, *Compatibility of Fruits and Vegetables During Transport in Mixed Loads,* MRR-1070. USDA, Fresno, CA, 1977.

Marine Office of America Corporation. "Air Cargo Insurance & Transportation." Unpublished paper, 1991.

Maryland Office of International Trade, Department of Economic and Employment Development. Maryland Exporters' Guide. Baltimore, MD, January 1988.

McGregor, Brian M. Tropical Products Transport Handbook. HBK-668. USDA, AMS, September 1989.

Nicholas, C. J. Export Handbook for U.S. Agricultural Products. HBK-593. USDA, AMS, March 1985.

Sea-Land Service, Inc. "An International Shipment." Unpublished paper, February 1982.

Society of American Florists. Care and Handling of Flowers and Plants. SAF, Alexandria, VA, 1985.

2

Transportation of Horticultural Crops

Transport vehicles should be well insulated to maintain cool environments for pre-cooled commodities and well ventilated to allow air movement through the produce. During transport, produce must be stacked in ways that minimise damage, then be braced and secured. An open air vehicle can be loaded in such a way that air can pass through the load, and provide some cooling of the produce as the vehicle moves.

Travelling during the night and early morning can reduce the heat load on a vehicle that is transporting produce. Mixed loads can be a serious concern when temperature optima are not compatible or when ethylene producing commodities and ethylene sensitive commodities are transported together. High ethylene producers can induce physiological disorders and/or undesirable changes in colour, flavour and texture in ethylene sensitive commodities.

Open Vehicles

Bulk loads of produce should be carefully loaded so as not to cause mechanical damage. Vehicles can be padded or lined with a thick layer of straw. Woven mats or sacks can be used in the beds of small vehicles. Other loads should not be placed on top of the bulk commodity.

Cooling open loads is desirable whenever possible. A truck ventilating device can be constructed for an unrefrigerated open vehicle by covering the load loosely with canvas and fashioning a wind catcher from sheet metal. The scoop should be mounted at the frornt of the bed and should reach somewhat higher the height of the cab. High transportation speeds and/or long distance transport run the risk of causing excess drying of the crop.

Bulk Loads

This ventilating system was designed for hauling bulk loads of fresh fava beans in Iran. The wind catcher and ducts were constructed using wooden crates. After removing their end panels the crates were wired together into the pattern shown below. Air flows upward through the load during transport, helping to keep the produce from overheating. This system has also been used in pick-up trucks, and for hauling bulk greens and green beans. Best results are obtained when transporting during the early morning hours, before sunrise.

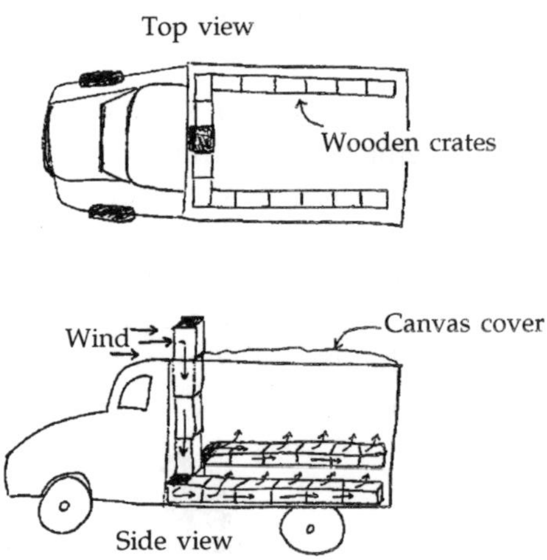

Figure 1.

Refrigerated Trailers

For optimum transport temperature management, refrigerated trailers need insulation, a high capacity refrigeration unit and fan, and an air delivery duct. The illustration below shows these and other desired features in a top-air delivery trailer. The condition of the inside of a refrigerated trailer affects its ability to maintain desired temperatures during transport. Handlers should inspect the trailer before loading.

Stacking patterns

In order to reduce the conduction of heat from outside the vehicle into the load of produce, stacking patterns should reduce the amount of contact between the produce and the floor and walls of the vehicle.

Illustrated below is pyramid stacking of bags inside a refrigerated trailer.

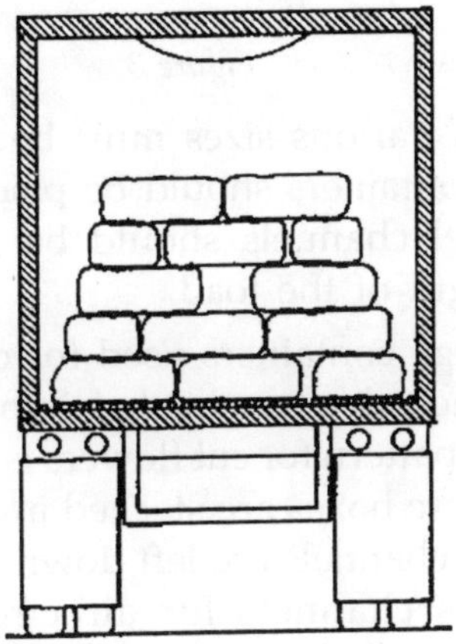

Figure 2.

Bushels of produce can be loaded into a refrigerated trailer using a pattern of alternately inverted layers that leave plenty of space between rows for air circulation.

Produce transported in cartons should also be stacked so as to allow adequate air circulation throughout the load. The diagram below illustrates cross-wise offset loading of partial telescopic containers. On the floor of the truck, pallets or other supports should be used to keep the cartons out of direct contact with the floor.

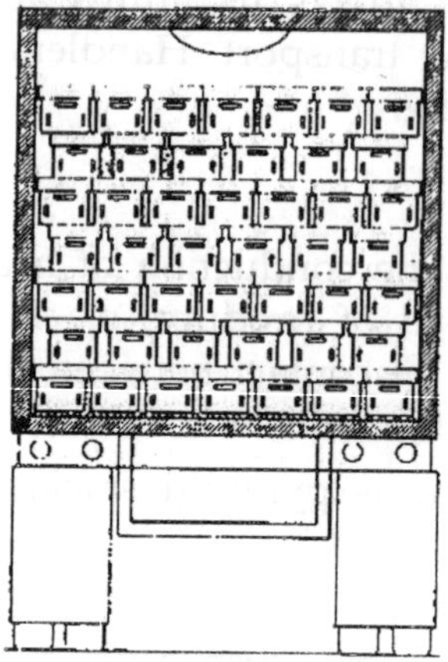

Figure 3.

When cartons of various sizes must be loaded together, the larger, heavier containers should be placed on the bottom of the load. Parallel channels should be left for air to move through the length of the load.

Often the large containers used for cut flower packaging must be handstacked when loaded into a transport vehicle. The best loading pattern for cut flowers is known as the pigeon hole pattern, where boxes are stacked in alternating solid and open layers, and channels are left down both side walls. This pattern provides channels for air circulation lengthwise through the load, and allows every box to be in direct contact with refrigerated air.

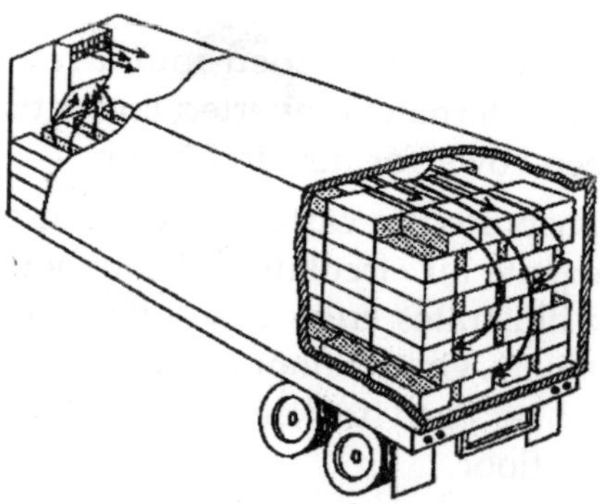

Figure 4.

Stacking Patterns

Containers should be loaded so that they are away from the side walls and the floor of the transport vehicle in order to minimise the conduction of heat from the outside environment. In the diagrams below, the numbers of cartons refer to how many cartons would be in contact with the walls and floor of the truck when fully loaded.

Only the load on the bottom right is fully protected from heat transfer. The use of pallets keeps the cartons off the floor, while centre-loading leaves an insulating air space between the pallet loads and the outside walls.

Load Bracing

There should always be a void between the last stack of produce and the back of the transport vehicle. The load should be braced to prevent shifting against the rear door during transit. If the load shifts, it can block air circulation, and fallen cartons can present great danger to workers who open the door at a destination market. A simple wooden brace can be constructed and installed to prevent damage during transport.

Handling at Destination

When handling produce at its destination, again it is important to avoid rough handling, minimise the number of handling steps, and maintain the lowest feasible temperature. If produce is to be stored before sale, then wholesale and retail markets need clean, well insulated storage rooms. Since a variety of commodities is usually being handled simultaneously at this point, it is important to remember not to mix those with different temperature requirements or store ethylene sensitive commodities near ethylene generating commodities. Stacking of non-uniform containers should be done with care to prevent collapse of weaker packages.

Before produce is sold to the consumer, the handler may wish to sort for quality, or at least to discard any damaged or decayed produce in order to give the product more market appeal. If ripeness or maturity is non-uniform, sorting at destination can provide the seller with a higher price for the better quality produce. If the produce handled is a climacteric fruit crop that was harvested before it was ripe (bananas, tomatoes, avocadoes, mangoes), the handler at destination may want to ripen the produce before it is sold to the public. Sometimes commodities such as bananas are left at ambient temperatures and allowed to ripen naturally.

Covering the bananas with a plastic sheet will help ripening be more uniform throughout the lot. Placing a simple air vent (a pipe or a tube of some sort) into the centre of the pile of ripening fruit can help reduce overheating during ripening and increase subsequent shelf life. The introduction of ethylene gas or ethylene-releasing compounds into a special storage environment (known as a ripening room or cabinet, depending upon size) is a more effective way to ensure uniform ripening. When displaying horticultural crops, single or double layers of produce are most likely to protect the commodities from compression damage and overhandling by the consumers.

Temperatures of the display tables or refrigerated supermarket displays should be suited to the commodity on sale. For example, while peppers and tomatoes look pleasing when displayed with lettuce, peppers and tomatoes are chilling sensitive, while lettuce is not. Misting commodities that can tolerate surface water with coot clean water can help maintain a high relative humidity around the product.

Outdoor marketplaces suffer from a lack of temperature control and high air circulation, which can lead to dessication of crops, which will be seen as shrivelling and wilting. These marketplaces can often benefit by the increased use of shading and protection from prevailing winds. Finally, the handler at destination can help reduce losses in the future by maintaining good records of the sources of losses suffered at the wholesale or retail level. Identifying whether losses were due to mechanical damage, decay/disease, immaturity or overripeness allows the handler to provide better quality feedback to produce suppliers.

Unloading

A loading dock can ease the work associated with handling horticultural produce at destination. Containers can be transfered more rapidly and with less bending and lifting. For large trucks, a loading dock 117 to 122 cm high (46 to 48 inches) functions well, while for small trucks or pickups a height of 66 to 81 cm (26 to 32 inches) is recommended.

Figure 5.

A simple device for easing the work of unloading transport vehicles can be constructed using a two pulleys and a strong rope. One pulley can be mounted inside the truck at the front of the bed, the second outside on a portable post or on a stationary object like the side of a building. Containers can be hung directly by their handles or placed into a sling.

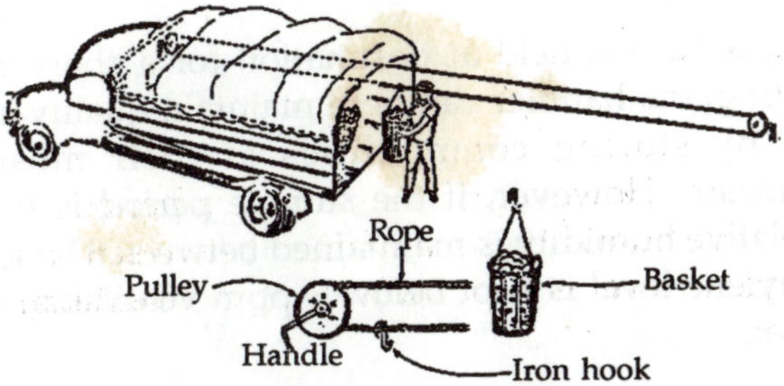

Figure 6.

A simple set of stairs can be constructed to ease the work of loading and unloading produce. The stairs illustrated here can be folded and pushed back under the back of the truck when the vehicle is in motion. The steps can be made of wood or steel matting and steel bars can be used for supports. Using a ramp is a simple and safe method for unloading produce. The ramp should be wide enough to prevent accidents and strong enough to carry the full weight of the handler plus the package she/he is carrying. Providing handtrucks or small carts can also ease the work associated with unloading.

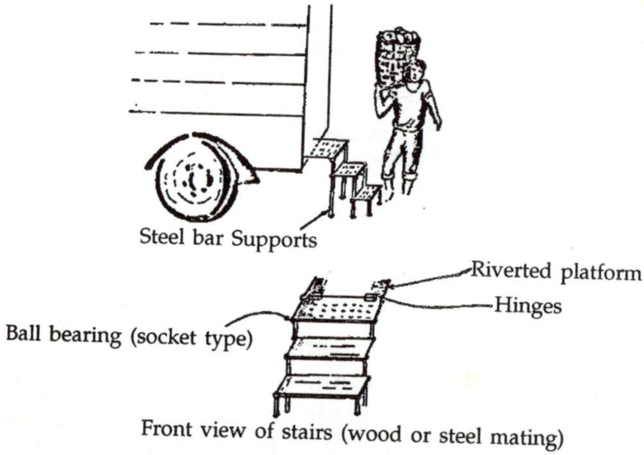

Figure 7.

Storage Temperatures

When produce is held at destination for a short time before marketing, the handler can help maintain quality and reduce losses by storing commodities at their most suitable temperature. However, if the storage period is five days or less, relative humidity is maintained between 85 and 95%, and the ethylene level is kept below 1 ppm ventilating or using a scrubber.

Repacking

Some produce may require washing, trimming, bunching or

sorting at the wholesale or retail market level. The layout of the work station used for handling produce at destination should be organised to minimise non-productive movement. In the illustration below, a dump table is located next to a sink for washing produce, and the drain board is positioned directly next to the sink.

Once produce has dried, cartons can be packed and placed onto a cart located right next to the repacking table. With this layout, a single operator could easily perform all the handling steps or several handlers could work side by side. Some produce may have to be repacked by the wholesaler or retailer due to changes in quality or uneven ripening. The tomato sorting table illustrated below has work stations for up to five who select either ripes, pinks or breakers and allow the green tomatoes to run off to the end of the line. Rejects (culls) are placed in pails under the table.

Ripening

Some commodities may require ripening before sale at the wholesale or retail level. Ripening rooms are often used for tomatoes, citrus fruits and bananas. The use of diluted ethylene gas mixtures is safer than using pure ethylene which is explosive and flammable at concentrations of 3% or higher.

For tomatoes, technical grade ethylene gas is introduced into the room at a concentration of about 100 ppm for about 48 hours. Approximately 0.25 cubic feet/hr of ethylene gas is required for each 1000 cubic feet of ripening room volume. A small fan can be used to ensure a uniform continuous flow of ethylene into and through the room. Forced-air ripening is increasingly being used to provide more uniform temperatures and ethylene concentrations throughout the ripening room.

Ripening can also be initiated by using ethylene generated by passing ethanol over a bed of activated alumina. This method is safer than using pure ethylene gas. Ethylene-releasing compounds such as ethephon {(2-chloroethyl) phosphoric acid} are sometimes used to ripen tomatoes destined for processing. When using ethephon as a spray, the amount of ethylene released will increase as pH and/or relative humidity increase.

The following illustration is a degreening room designed for use with citrus in pallet boxes. The ceiling of the room is relatively high, allowing boxes to be stacked at least four high. A false ceiling is added to provide for adequate air movement throughout the room.

Several small ripening rooms may be more useful than a single large room for small scale handlers, since the amount of product handled at destination may vary from time to time. In this case, flow through systems can be designed to allow the use of one or more rooms at the same time. Flowmeters can be located in one place for ease of monitoring, or can be strung out in a line. Locating all the flowmeters in one place requires the use of more tubing than if flowmeters are located in each ripening room.

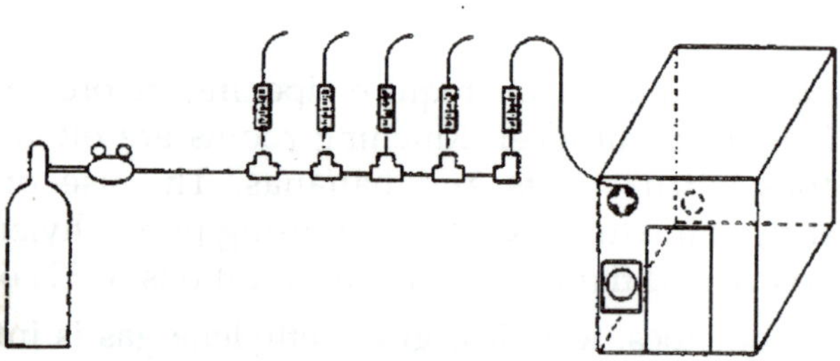

Figure 8. Flowmeters in one location

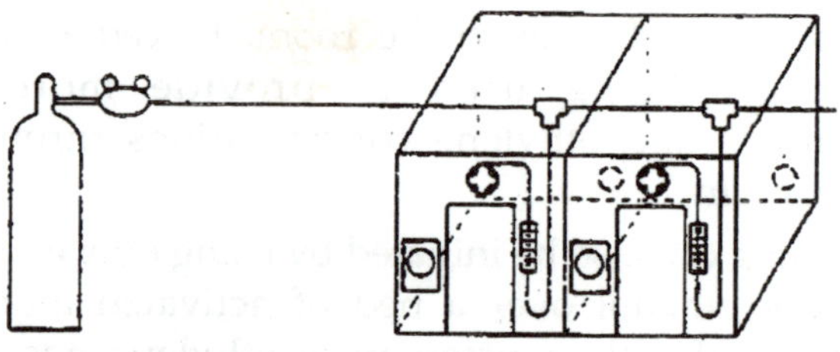

Figure 9. Flowmeters located in each ripening room

Small-scale handlers can now lease portable ripening facilities from a variety of companies in the United States. The self-contained, portable system illustrated below features a 20 pallet capacity, high capacity air flow and is simple to operate. All that is needed is a loading dock and a supply of 220V electricity.

Small-scale wholesalers and retailers can ripen fruits in bins or large cartons by placing a small quantity of ethylene-generating produce such as ripe bananas in with the produce to be ripened. Cover the bin or carton with a plastic sheet for 24 hours, then remove the plastic cover.

A simple way to ripen fruits at home in small amounts is to use a ripening bowl. Fruits that require ripening should be placed into the bowl with a ripe apple or ripe banana (or any other high ethylene-generating product). The bowl shown below is made of clear molded plastic and has ventilation holes around the top. Using this method, ripening will take from one to four days. Home ripening is also possible using another, extremely low-tech practice-- place fruits to be ripened into a paper bag with a ripe piece of fruit, close loosely and check in a few days.

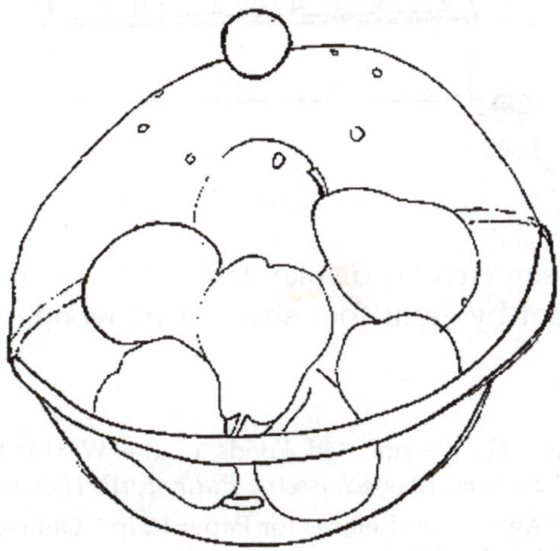

Figure 10.

Wooden Display Table

This wooden display table is designed to be used for commodities such as cruciferous crops or leafy green vegetables that tolerate cooling with ice. The table can be used in the horizontal position or as a tilted display. Four to five lbs of crushed ice per square foot of display space are required for cooling per day. A catch pail should be provided for melt water. To minimise ice needs, the display tray should be insulated and kept out of the direct sun.

High relative humidity can be maintained during display by misting leafy vegetables and water tolerant crops with clean, cold water. A simple sprinkler device can be constructed by perforating a pipe with tiny holes and connecting it to a hose. If this display is used outdoors, shade should be provided.

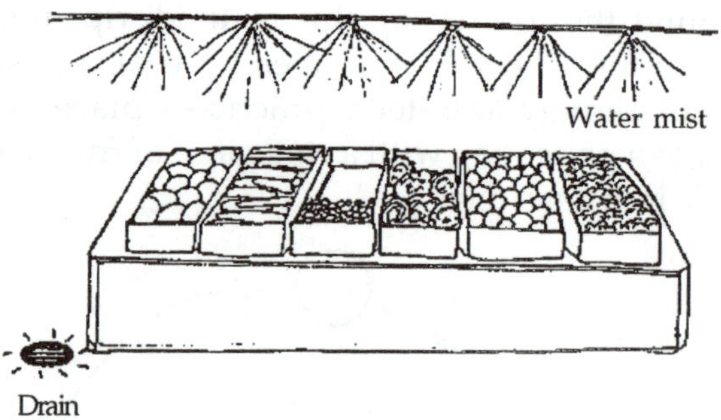

Figure 11.

A simple semi-circular display table can be constructed from one four foot by eight foot sheet of plywood.

References

Campbell-Platt, G., "Fermented Foods of the World: Dictionary and Guide," *Stonam, Massachussetts: Butterworth Heineman*, 1987.

Hunsigi, G., "Agricultural Fibres for Paper Pulp," *Outlook on Agriculture* 18 (3): 96-103, 1989.

Lurie, S., "Postharvest heat treatments of horticultural crops," *Hort. Rev*, 1998.

3

Transportation of Livestock

The transporting of livestock and poultry by truck, train or plane is an important part of the domestic livestock industry and is necessary for its survival. The evolution of the livestock transportation systems mirrors the development of the system of movement. At first, river transport was the main means of movement into the interior of the country. People, livestock and poultry all floated along together.

The first known records of livestock transportation occurred in about 1607 on an English ship named the Susan Constant, which was transporting Jamestown bound colonists. As time passed and the New World developed, supply ships from England carried livestock as regular cargo. Purebred stock was imported to Plymouth and Philadelphia. By about 1700, the exports of cattle and packed meat regularly left the port of Philadelphia which was bound for the West Indies. Livestock fatalities during sea shipments would often be 50% or more, which was attributed to poor feed supply, overcrowding, and rough seas.

Chicago's meat exports had risen to almost 10% by 1848. Supposedly the first shipment of live cattle to Chicago by rail car was in 1867 on the Kansas Pacific Railway. About twenty carloads of longhorns from Texas left the rail yard at Abilene, Kansas on the Kansas Pacific Railroad destined for the Chicago Stock Yards. This event changed the face of the livestock industry. Cattle from Texas were driven to rail yards for transport to major feeders, processors, and packers. Cattle trails were carefully chosen to minimize distance and maximize feed to sustain and fatten cattle. Cowboys were hired to gather, drive, and hold cattle at major buying stations.

Cowboys reported route trail fatalities of about 3%. As the railroads expanded, processors multiplied and refrigeration technology developed, the refrigerated rail car was patented in 1867. The need to drive cattle ended and the cattle drive trail disappeared by 1889. The improvement of refrigerated transport gave birth to the dressed meat market. The distribution of dressed meat exploded, causing the need to ship live cattle by rail to slowly decrease and to become economically unfeasible.

By the early 20th century, railroads dominated the dressed meat market and the commodity trucking industry was in its infancy. By the middle of the 20th century, the refrigerated trailer was developed for commercial trucking and then the shipping of processed meats was done primarily by the trucking industry. The rail roads had fallen in to disrepair nor could they offer as many options for shipping and receiving of cattle and other livestock. Shipping live cattle by truck was much more economical, humane and offered more options in routing cattle to auctions, feeders, and processors. The trucking industry helped to create an interconnected road system throughout the United States.

As cities developed a demand for fresh meat was created. Industries developed in response to this need. An example of one such industry was the driving of live turkeys from northern Vermont to Boston, Massachusetts a distance of over 200 miles! This industry soared from 1824 until 1900. While turkey drives may seemed quaint or humorous, until the invention of refrigeration, every city in America had to have such a supply system for it fresh meats. The cattle drives of the west were really the movement of cattle from an area of oversupply to a rail head where the herds were loaded on trains and shipped to cities. As the railroads expanded into the areas of supply, the trail drives went the way of the turkey drives - they flew out the windows.

Railroads were the backbone of the animal transport system in the country for nearly a century. Animals were collected in distant locations and shipped via rail to central markets for slaughter. Chicago wasn't called the hog butcher of world by mistake. Special trains also carried show animals from one show to another. It was not uncommon for show flocks and herds to travel a circuit that over a four month time frame would take them from coast to coast.

After World War II the road system of the country began to expand. Interstate roads as we know them didn't come into existence until the 50's and were not fully developed until the 70's. The development of the interstate road system spelled doom for the railroads as the major livestock carriers. Trucks now became the major movers of livestock because they could go more places than trains. The Interstate road system changed where we slaughter and process animals. Before the development of the interstate road system animals were shipped into major cites to be processed. Today, slaughter plants are located near the supply of animals. This allows for animals to be processed and their carcasses or now boxed parts to be shipped country wide via trucks and in the case of specialised products such as horse meat via plane to Europe and beyond.

While livestock are shipped in many types of vehicles, the work horse of the commercial industry is the semi or "Pot" trailer. These are 40 feet long by 8.5 feet wide. They have multiple decks so that more animals can be hauled at a time. When attached to a truck they can legally haul weight of 80,000 pounds including the weight of the truck and trailer.

Many farmers and producers have bumper hitch and "gooseneck" trailer of varying sizes that they use to haul animals. These trailer are built so that they are only a foot or so above the ground. This allows for easy entry onto the trailer by any passengers. Because they are built low the need for expensive loading ramps is eliminated. These trailers are usually backed up to a race and the animals led or moved (chased) onto the trailer. Sometimes hogs, because they do not like to step up, will be loaded onto a hydraulic lift trailer, which lays on the ground. After loading the hydrolic trailer is raised to the level of the trailer the animals are to be loaded onto, allowing the hogs to walk on. Like large semis these trailer also have dividing gates. These gates are helpful in confining animals in a space that better fits the number of animals. Animals need to be limited as to the space they can move while travelling. This will be of real benefit in case of sudden stops or turns. Animals allowed too much space could be thrown or injured in a accident.

As the livestock transportation business becomes more sophisticated, speciality vehicles are being developed to meet specific needs. The sheep semi trailer is an example of this. The sine industry is also developing specialised vehicles. Old school buses are often times used in the transport of day old chicks or turkeys. The birds are actually confined to special boxes for shipment. School busses are also used or for the movement of young pigs from one location on a farm to another. School buses offer includes draft free transportation and are roomy so that a number of animals can be hauled.

Today, the commercial transportation of livestock and poultry is regulated by state and federal governments. There are laws as to how long animals can be transported without stopping and unloading the animals to allow them to drink and to rest. Other concerns when shipping animals are the density that the animals are loaded onto a truck at. Animals should have enough space to enable them to stand up if they fall. Animals loaded too loosely can be injured if the vehicle makes a sharp turn or sudden stop. Divider panels in large vehicles are useful in maintaining proper animals densities. A vehicle should be well ventilated to prevent the buildup of ammonia and exhaust fumes. Ventilation is more critical than temperature when transporting animals in cold weather. Truck exhaust fumes should be directed above or away from the animals. Good ventilation minimizes heat stress during hot weather.

The loading and unloading of livestock is a stressful time. Loading facilities should be designed to aid in the movement of animals as much as possible. Cattle and sheep will follow one another more easily than hogs do and they respond well to chutes in which they enter a trailer in single file. Hogs are best loaded from ramps in which they can maintain visual contact with each other. Often times "Judas Goats" are used to load sheep. These are specially trained animals that will be placed in a pen of sheep. The goat will lead the sheep up the loading ramp, and into the truck. Because of the nature of the sheep, which is to follow, they will march right behind the goat. Once the deck is full however, the goat deserts his "friends" and runs back down the loading chute ready to lead another unsuspecting flock to their doom. Judas animals are not used when loading hog and cattle. Hogs do not follow well enough and cattle can be moved easily with out animal help, and there are fewer of the animals needed to will up a trailer.

Effects of Transport

Poor transportation can have serious deleterious effects on the welfare of livestock and can lead to significant loss of quality and production.

Effects of transport and movement include:

— *Stress:* leading to DFD beef and PSE pork;

— *Bruising:* perhaps the most insidious and significant production waste in the meat industry;

— *Trampling:* this occurs when animals go down due to slippery floors or overcrowding;

— *Suffocation:* this usually follows on trampling;

— *Heart failure:* occurs mostly in pigs when overfed prior to loading and transportation;

— *Heat stroke:* pigs are susceptible to high environment temperatures and humidity;

— *Sun burn:* exposure to sun affects pigs seriously;

— *Bloat:* restraining ruminants or tying their feet without turning them will cause this;

— *Poisoning:* animals can die from plant poisoning during trekking on hoof;

— *Predation:* unguarded animals moving on the hoof may be attacked;
— *Dehydration:* animals subject to long distance travel without proper watering will suffer weight loss and may die;
— *Exhaustion:* may occur for many reasons including heavily pregnant animals or weaklings;
— *Injuries:* broken legs, horns;
— *Fighting:* this occurs mostly when a vehicle loaded with pig stops, or amongst horned and polled cattle.

Transportation Methods

Moving Cattle

The most appropriate methods of moving cattle are on hoof, by road motor vehicle or by rail wagon. Moving cattle on the hoof (trekking) is suitable only where road and rail infrastructure does not exist, or when distances from farm to destination are short. This method is slow and fraught with risks to the welfare and value of the animals. Rail transport is useful for short-haul journeys where loading ramps are available at railheads and communication is direct to destination. Road motor transport is by far the most versatile, the method of first choice and the most user friendly. The most satisfactory method of transporting cattle is by road motor vehicle. Moving by rail truck requires more careful management and trekking is satisfactory for well-planned distances.

Sheep/goats

Of the food animals these are the easiest to transport and generally travel well on hoof, rail or road. Double-deck trucks are also suitable.

Pigs

Pigs are difficult animals to transport, and the only satisfactory method is by road, although rail can be used under careful circumstances.

Poultry

Broilers and other poultry such as turkeys or ducks are best transported by road. Flocks of birds should be subdivided in small numbers in crates. Recommended are plastic crates, which can be stacked on top of each other on a vehicle and which can easily be washed after use. The lid of the crates is for loading and the opening at the side for removal of the birds.

Ostriches

The skin and meat of ostriches is particularly valuable, so careful transport by road vehicle is the only suitable method of transport. Having selected the preferred method of transport of slaughter animals, it is necessary to take into account numerous factors in order to ensure the health and welfare of the animals.

Mode of Transport

Many factors should be considered when selecting the mode of transport. Cost is always important, but must be measured against the quality of, and potential losses incurred in, transport.

- Herding by road was the only form of transport available in the not-too-distant past, and it is still the main method of moving cattle on the farm, and often from farm to farm. Where saleyards or railway loading points, are close by, it is still the cheapest way to move animals. When animals are moved at their natural pace, and if the distance is not too great, stress as well as loss (e.g. bruising, shrinkage) is minimal. A comfortable distance for beef cattle to walk in a day is 10 to 12 kilometres.
- Transport by rail has been a major factor in allowing the centralisation of the industry and in opening new markets. Rail transport should continue to fulfil this role for a long time to come, although it has become less important in the transportation of slaughter stock.

— Road transport is taking over a major portion of livestock transportation due to the ease and convenience of transporting cattle by road. It is an important means of reducing stress to livestock. Animals in transit undergo "shrinkage". This is due to reduced water intake, and to poor food consumption which is characteristic of animals in transit. Shrinkage can amount to 4 to 6 % for trips of less than 70 km, but can be as high as 8 to 9 % for distances exceeding this. Road transport reduces travelling time, and partly overcomes shrinkage.

When deciding on the mode of transport, convenience, and cost, must be the major criteria. Allowing animals to walk to their destination, time permitting, is cost-effective, and reduces stress. The only limitation is distance. Although many animals can travel great distances on the hoof, this is not advisable where the abattoir is the destination. Should a farmer decide to herd animals over distances greater than 30 km, care should be taken to plan the route well. Rest and watering points must be identified over the whole route, and the distances travelled each day must not be excessive.

Rail transport is usually cheaper than is motor transport, and should always be considered for all forms of livestock. A limitation of rail transport is that the farmer has to pay for the full use of a truck, whether it is full or empty. Farmers need to plan the moving of a consignment of animals well ahead of time in order to request the required number of trucks. Cattle trucks containing livestock are carefully monitored, and taken to their destination as quickly as possible. In spite of this, delays do occur. For this reason, rail transport is not always ideal for moving animals to the abattoir.

Road transport is the mode of choice in most cases, because of convenience and efficiency. Animals can be moved to their destination within a matter of hours. There are usually no long delays between requesting the transport, and the actual moving of the animals.

Role of Truck Design

The following should be taken into account when evaluating the suitability of a vehicle, or railway truck, for cattle transport:

— *Floor space*: This should not be less than 1,4 m^2 per adult bovine. A small calf will require 0,3 m^2. Where there is a height factor to consider, the roof height should not be less than 1 600 mm. Should the animals have too much room, they can be thrown around inside the vehicle when it is moving off, or coming to a rapid halt. With the correct number, animals tend to lean against one another, and against the sides of the vehicle. This prevents excessive movement. Partitioning in large vehicles is therefore essential.

— *Floors*: These should be solid and impervious, and, most important, must be fitted with grids or cleats to prevent slipping. There must be no spaces between the floor and the side panels.

— The sides of the vehicle, and the partitions, must be strong enough to hold the heaviest animal. Preference should be given to sides with solid surfaces, and openings should not allow legs or heads to become stuck. The minimum height for both sides and partitions is 1 800 mm.

— *Ventilation must be adequate*: This should not prevent the inclusion of adequate protection against bad weather, sun, rain and wind. Exposure to exhaust fumes must be avoided because this can cause discomfort, and suffocation.

— *Gates warrant attention*: A small loading gate has the advantage that animals cannot turn around, until on the vehicle. Cattle, however, often crash against the sides of a narrow gate, thus injuring themselves. Off-loading gates could span the full width of the truck. This would be possible by designing tip-up gates. The gate used for loading animals ideally, should be narrow, but only if it is to be used in conjunction with a loading crush.

Stress and Transport

The stress associated with transport can cause animals to become ill. Pregnant cows are particularly susceptible. Symptoms very similar to those associated with milk fever are often precipitated. This is related to calcium metabolism, and can be treated in the same way as milk fever. Prevention is achieved by restricting feed intake for two to three days before loading. Feeding hay, at maintenance levels only, is recommended. Transit fever is another disease encountered. This is a form of pneumonia caused by a Pasteurella species. A vaccine is available to treat animals which are due to travel.

Injury to animals is a major source of concern, not only because the public image of the meat industry is adversely affected by media reports of animal maltreatment, but also because the producer suffers major losses due to injury, and bruising. Financial losses associated with injury can be minimised through animal knowledge, and improved truck design.

It is not advisable to transport cows during the last trimester of pregnancy. Should the need arise to transport cows and suckling calves, it is advisable, in order to prevent injuries, to transport them in separate trucks. However, with trips exceeding two days, cows and calves should be grouped together, since the consequences of excessive stress to the calf could exceed potential losses due to injury.

Carcass quality

The tenderness, flavour, and colour of meat is adversely affected by excessive exercise, or stress to the animal, prior to slaughter. Meat also loses its ability to retain fluids, making it unsuitable for sausage making. The red meat industry is rapidly losing its market share to the broiler industry. Poor meat quality contributes to this trend. The producer can help prevent further erosion of his sales by giving this aspect attention. This can be done by:

— Minimise animal movement prior to slaughter. The meat of animals accustomed to walking will not be adversely affected by a normal amount of exercise. Unnecessary running, or additional exercise, however, will have detrimental effects.

— Avoid stress at all costs. This can only be achieved by good stockmanship, with careful handling and selection. There is no doubt that certain animals are more susceptible to stress. These must be culled from the herd because their progeny have a high probability of having the same problem, and they tend to distress more docile animals in their group when being taken for slaughter.

TYPES OF VEHICLES

Any vehicle used for the transport of slaughter livestock should have adequate ventilation, have a non-slip floor with proper drainage and provide protection from the sun and rain, particularly for pigs. The surfaces of the sides should be smooth and there should be no protrusions or sharp edges. No vehicle should be totally enclosed.

Ventilation: Transport vehicles should never be totally enclosed, as lack of ventilation will cause undue stress and even suffocation, particularly if the weather is hot. Poor ventilation may cause accumulation of exhaust fumes in road vehicles with subsequent poisoning. Pigs are particularly susceptible to excessive heat, poor air circulation, high humidity and respiratory stress. Well-ventilated vehicles are necessary. The free flow of air at floor level is important to facilitate removal of ammonia from the urine.

Floors: Non-slip floors in all vehicles are necessary to reduce the risk of animals falling. A grid of cross slating made from wood or metal is suitable. The grid can be removable, so the vehicle can be used for other purposes. Other forms of non-slip surfaces such as grass or sawdust are not suitable. Additional balance for animals is provided by partitioning the interior of the vehicle with either wood or metal poles or solid boards. Broken floors will cause leg and other injuries. Vehicle floors should be level with off-loading platforms, otherwise animals will injure themselves climbing off or be manhandled in order to remove them.

Floor space: Livestock require sufficient floor space so that they can stand comfortably without being overcrowded. Overloading results in injuries or even death of livestock.

Table 1. Approximate floor space for transporting different classes of animals

Classes of stock		Flor area/animal (m^2)
Mature cattle		1.0 - 1.4*
Small calves		0.3
	Porker	0.3
Pigs	Baconer	0.4
	sow/boar	0.8
Sheep/goats		0.4
Ostriches		0.8

Allowances should be made for breed and body size. If the floor area is too large for the number of animals, partitions should be used to avoid animals being thrown about.

Sides: The sides of vehicles should be high enough to prevent animals, particularly pigs, from jumping out and injuring themselves. Insides could also be padded at hip level with, for example, old tyres to reduce bruising of cattle and ostriches. Also there should be no gaps through which a leg might protrude and be broken. Narrow entry doors can lead to considerable bruising of hips. Rail trucks should be fitted with spring coupling to cushion jerky movement.

Roof: A roof is not necessary on a transport vehicle for bovines and small ruminants provided the animals are not exposed for hours in the hot sun. Vehicles for pigs should have roofs unless the pigs are to be transported in the early morning or late evening. Poultry should be protected from sun and rain. Transporting in cages or crates will protect them from physical injury. They should be large enough to allow all the birds to sit down and move their heads freely. Ventilation should be adequate.

At the small-scale level in more primitive conditions animals are often transported under very unsuitable conditions, which may cause a great deal of pain or even death through suffocating, heat stress, dehydration etc..

Pre-loading Precautions

There are a number of simple procedures that can be implemented prior to the loading of livestock, which will considerably reduce the risk of injury and stress.

— Pre-mixing of cattle or pigs leads to greater familiarity and these animals travel better than animals that are strangers. Cattle should be mixed in a pen 24 hours before loading. Victimised or wild animals can be weeded out during this period. Fighting amongst pigs that are strangers is common, resulting in skin damage, wounds and stress. Mix pigs from different pens together before loading, smearing pigs with litter or excreta from the same pen so that they smell similar.

— Most animals can be fed and watered before transporting. This has a settling effect. However pigs should not be fed before transport as the feed ferments and the gas causes pressure on the heart in the thoracic cavity, leading to heart failure and death.

— Do not mix horned and hornless animals in the vehicles as this causes bruising and injury. Different species should also not be mixed - sheep, goats and calves under 6 months can be mixed and individual animals can be transported in a loose sack tied at the animal's neck. Feet should not be tied, and animals should be turned every 30 minutes or so. Pigs should not travel with other species unless separated by a partition. Bulls should not be carried together with other stock unless separated by a strong partition.

— Animals that are diseased, injured, emaciated or heavily pregnant should not be transported, and unfit, heavy, penfed animals should not travel far as they cannot stand up to the rigours of transport.

— Vehicles should be fitted with a portable ramp to facilitate emergency offloading in case of prolonged breakdowns.

Transport Operations

A number of factors must be taken into account during the journey in order that the animals do not suffer, become injured or die.

— *Trekking:* Only cattle, sheep and goats can be successfully moved on hoof, and here certain risks are involved. The journey should be planned, paying attention to the distance to be travelled, opportunities for grazing, watering and overnight rest. Animals should be walked during the cooler times of the day and, if moving some distance to a railhead, they should arrive with sufficient time to be rested and watered before loading. The maximum distances that these animals should be trekked depend on various factors such as weather, body condition, age etc., but the distance given in Table 2 should not be exceeded when trekked.

Table 2. Maximum distances for trekking

Species	One day journey	More than one day	
		First day	Subsequent days
Cattle	30 km	24 km	22 km
Sheep/goats	24 km	24 km	16 km

— *Time of the day:* High environment temperatures will increase the risk of heat stress and mortality during transportation. It is important to transport animals in vehicles during the cooler mornings and evenings or even at night. This is particularly important for pigs. A combination of high humidity and high environment temperatures is especially deadly to pigs. Heat can rapidly build up to lethal levels in a stationary vehicle. Wetting pigs with water will help keep them cool.

— *Duration of journey:* Where possible, journeys should be short and direct, without any stoppages. If the vehicle stops, pigs will tend to fight. Cattle and sheep/goats should not travel for more than 36 hours and should be offloaded after 24h for feed and water, if the journey is to take longer than that. Pigs should have access to frequent drinks of water during long journeys, particularly in hot and humid conditions.

— *Driving:* Vehicles should be driven smoothly, without jerks or sudden stops. Corners should be taken slowly and gently. The second person should be in attendance to spot downer animals so that the vehicle can be stopped and the animal lifted. Train drivers should avoid "fly shunting" of trucks with livestock.

— *Wind chill:* Wind blowing on wet animals being transported in cold weather causes a wind chill factor, where the body temperature is considerably reduced, resulting in severe stress or deaths.

References

Ashby, B.H., *et al., Protecting Perishable Foods During Transport by Truck,* HBK-669. USDA, AMS, September, 1987.

Atlantic Mutual Companies, *Buyers Guide To Marine Cargo Insurance,* New York, NY, 1990.

Cassell, Clark C., *The World is Your Market - An Export Guide for Small Business,* Edited by William Delphos. Braddock Communications, Washington, DC, 1990.

Fuell, L. D., D. C. Miller, and M. Chesley, *Dictionary of International Agricultural Trade,* USDA, FAS, June 1988.

Friedheim, Amy, *Ocean Liner Freight Rates and Services,* USDA, AMS, May 1991.

Hardenburg, R. E., A. E. Watada, C. Y. Wang, *The Commercial Storage of Fruits, Vegetables, and Florist and Nursery Stocks,* HBK-66. USDA, ARS, September 1986.

Lassanyi, Mary E., *Directory of Export and Trade Assistance,* USDA, NAL, November 1991.

Lipton, W.J. and J.M. Harvey, *Compatibility of Fruits and Vegetables During Transport in Mixed Loads,* MRR-1070. USDA, Fresno, CA, 1977.

Marine Office of America Corporation. "Air Cargo Insurance & Transportation." Unpublished paper, 1991.

Maryland Office of International Trade, Department of Economic and Employment Development. Maryland Exporters' Guide. Baltimore, MD, January 1988.

McGregor, Brian M. Tropical Products Transport Handbook. HBK-668. USDA, AMS, September 1989.

Nicholas, C. J. Export Handbook for U.S. Agricultural Products. HBK-593. USDA, AMS, March 1985.

Sea-Land Service, Inc. "An International Shipment." Unpublished paper, February 1982.

Society of American Florists. Care and Handling of Flowers and Plants. SAF, Alexandria, VA, 1985.

4

Transportation of Fish

Transportation of live fish requires oxygen for respiration and removal of the toxic gases and by-products that accumulate, such as CO_2 and ammonia. Certain fish, like catfish, can obtain oxygen through the damp surface of their gills or through the body skin. Other fish, like the climbing perch, have accessory air-breathing organs. But most finfish are transported live in water supersaturated with oxygen and kept at a temperature low enough to reduce their metabolism. Some tropical fish may not support temperatures below 10°C.

Fish is often starved before transportation to reduce its metabolism and increase the packing density. Crustaceans are transported live in wet packages using wet sawdust or other ways to keep the atmosphere surrounding the live animals humid and cool.

There are two basic transport systems for live fish - the closed system and the open system. The closed system is a sealed container in which all the requirements for survival are self-contained. The simplest of these is a sealed plastic bag partly filled with water and oxygen. The open system consists of water-filled containers in which the requirements for survival are supplied continuously from outside sources. The simplest of these is a small tank with an aerator stone. These systems will be reviewed with respect to the problems of fish preparation for transport, types of vehicles and equipments, problems of water quality and its changes during transport, and chemical aids used during fish transport.

There is ample literature on fish transport and associated problems; however, the literary sources overlap and give partly differing interpretations of the recommended ways of transport. These are the reasons why this survey aims at comprising mainly those published results which have been fully verified in practice and which are, therefore, reliably instructive. The basic factors and principles associated with any live fish transport systems, or influencing them, are evaluated before the actual ways of fish transport are commented on.

Principles of Fish Transport

Fish survival in a good state of health during transport is influenced by a number of factors, or combination of factors.

Importance of Fish Quality

The quality of fish transported is a decisive criterion. The fish to be transported must be healthy and in good condition. Weakened individuals should be eliminated from the consignment, particularly when the temperature during shipment is high. When the fish are of poor quality, even a great reduction of fish density in the transport container fails to prevent fish losses. Weak fish are killed at a much higher rate than fish in good condition when the transport time is longer. A need for adapting the fish to a lower water temper-ature may also arise before transport.

Natural ice is used to cool the water; the ice of carbonic acid should be avoided. As a guide ratio, 25 kg of ice will cool 1 000 litres of water by 2°C. If the water contains fish during the cooling process, the temperature drop should not be faster than 5°C per hour. Direct contact of fish with ice should be prevented at the same time. The total temperature difference should not be greater than 12-15°C, with respect to the species and age of the fish.

The fish to be transported, except for the larval stages should be left to starve for at least a day; if the digestive tract of the fish is not totally cleaned, the possible time of transport is reduced to a half, though the conditions may be the same.

The fish with full digestive tracts also need more oxygen, are more susceptible to stress, and produce excrements which take up much of the oxygen of the water. However, when fish larvae are transported, their time of survival without food should be taken into consideration. The transport time of the larvae of herbivorous fishes should not last longer than 20 hours and that of many aquarium species should be shorter than 12 hours.

Oxygen Consumption

The most important single factor in transporting fish is providing an adequate level of dissolved oxygen. However, an abundance of oxygen within a tank does not necessarily indicate that the fish are in good condition. The ability of fish to use oxygen depends on their tolerance to stress, water temperature, pH, and concentrations of carbon dioxide and metabolic products such as ammonia. The crucial factors underlying oxygen consumption by fish in relation with oxygen metabolism during transport are fish weight and water temperature. Heavier fish and those transported in warmer water need more oxygen. For instance, if the water temperature increases by 10°C, oxygen consumption is about doubled.

From the point of view of fish transport, for each 0.5°C rise in temperature, the fish load should be reduced by about 5.6%; conversely, for each 0.5°C decrease in temperature, the load can be increased by about 5.6%. Oxygen consumption also increases with fish excitement by handling. Excitement increases oxygen demand three to five times and, for instance, salmonid fry need up to several hours to return to the normal level of oxygen metabolism which is, in fact, usually after the end of the transport. In water provided with an unlimited amount of oxygen, a fish at rest will consume a minimum amount of oxygen. In a fish transport system, the fish will require more than the minimum amount since they are not at rest.

The amount of oxygen a fish consumes also depends on the amount of oxygen available. At high levels, the fish will consume at a steady rate. When water oxygen levels are low, fish consume lower amounts of oxygen than when oxygen levels are high, despite the degree of activity. Fish transport systems often contain water with oxygen levels that do not provide enough oxygen required to satisfy the fish bodies. To offset this predicament, the fish will shift its metabolism to use the stored oxygen of the body. This condition is likened to that of a man who is at rest and suddenly performs strenuous activity before a proportionate amount of oxygen is taken in. For the man and the fish, an oxygen "debt" is created which must be repaid when favourable oxygen conditions are experienced.

The first hour after loading is a particularly critical time for fish in respect to their oxygen needs. They are excited and require a large amount of oxygen with a short time for adjustment. Significant differences in oxygen demand exist also within fish families. As asserted, for instance, by Uryn, when water temperature increases (4-14°C) during transport, the fry of Coregonus lavaretus consume 2.4 times more oxygen than the fry of C. albula. Fish size is also important. A large fish consumes less oxygen per unit weight than does a small one. Oxygen levels of water for most warm water fish should be above 5 mg.1-1 for normal conditions. This level should prevent oxygen from becoming a major stress factor.

Some conversion coefficients of oxygen demand are indicated by the FRG recommendation: 25 kg of rainbow trout at an individual weight of 250 g have the same oxygen demand as 20 kg of 12 cm stock trout (1 100 fish), or 17 kg of 8 cm stock trout (3 200 fish), or 12 kg of forced fry at the length of 4 cm (ca. 23 000 fish). Taking the oxygen demand of carp as 1, the converted oxygen demand levels for other fishes are as follows:

trout	2.83	bream	1.41
pike-perch	1.76	pike	1.10
roach	1.51	eel	0.83
perch	1.46	tench	0.83

According to Shevchenko, the oxygen consumption of Coregonus peled per kg of weight per hour at a temperature of 10°C is 100 mg; in sturgeon this value is 68 mg, in pike 50-60 mg, and in carp weighing 500-600 g it is 45 mg.

During fish transport in closed systems with pressurised oxygen atmos-phere, oxygen content in water usually is not a limiting factor because there is enough pressurised oxygen in a closed bag. Oxygen deficit may occur in exceptional cases when the density of fish is too high or the transport is longer than the fish can stand.

The dead fish compete with the living ones for oxygen: they increase bacterial multiplication requiring much oxygen, and this multiplication may further produce toxic metabolites. The slime produced by the fish is another substrate for bacterial growth resulting in a decrease of the water oxygen content; this process is intensified when water temperature is higher.

A high oxygen content of water has no unfavourable influence on the fish, e.g., the limit for rainbow trout is 35 mg per litre which is not attainable in practical conditions, as asserted by Heiner; the fish are able to regulate the volume of oxygen entering their bodies. This holds generally with possible exceptions; for the time being there are no data on the effect of a longer exposure to a high oxygen content at a higher temperature in the larval stages of fish unable to keep oxygen content of their blood at an optimum level. In closed systems, slight shaking of the bag supports the penetration of atmospheric oxygen to water.

During long steps when the bags with fish are left without movement, the fish may die though the oxygen reserve in the bag is still high. This applies mainly to dense stocks of salmonids, requiring much oxygen; no such problems are encountered when cyprinids, except their sac fry, are transported, because these fish move the water in the bag by their own movement, thus driving it into sufficient contact with the oxygenated atmosphere.

pH, Carbon Dioxide and Ammonia

Water quality is a function of the load of fish concentration and the length of time for which the fish are transported. The source of the water used during transport must have been tested before dispatching a mass consignment of fish. The water pH level is a control factor because the proportions of toxic ammonia and CO_2 contents are direct functions of pH.

With increasing transport time, CO_2 production through fish respiration shifts water pH towards acidity. Water pH levels about 7-8 are considered as optimum. Rapid changes in pH stress fish, but buffers can be used to stabilise the water pH during fish transport.

The organic buffer trishydroxyl methylaminomethane is quite effective in fresh and salt water. It is highly soluble, stable and easily applied. This buffer has been used on 29 species of fish with no deleterious effects. Levels of 1.3-2.6 g/litre are recommended for routine transport of fish.

Elevated carbon dioxide concentrations are detrimental to fish and can be a limiting factor in fish transport. A product of fish and bacterial respiration, CO_2 acidifies transport water. Although this reduces the percentage of unionized ammonia in the water, it also reduces the oxygen-carrying capacity of fish blood.

Fish may succumb if CO_2 levels are high, even though oxygen levels are seemingly adequate. Trout appear to tolerate carbon dioxide at levels less than 15 mg 1-1 in the presence of reasonable oxygen and temperature, but become distressed when carbon dioxide levels approach 25 mg 1-1.

Fish transported in tanks are exposed to gradually increasing concentrations of carbon dioxide. Unless aeration is adequate, CO_2 levels may exceed 20-30 mg 1-1, in general, for each milliliter of oxygen a fish consumes, it produces approximately 0.9 milliliters of CO_2. If the CO_2 level increases rapidly, as with heavy fish loads, fish become distressed. However, elevated concentrations of CO_2 can be tolerated if the rate of buildup is slow. Adequate ventilation is a necessity for transport units. Tight covers or lids on the units can result in a buildup of CO_2 which will stress the fish. Aeration of the water will reduce concentrations of dissolved CO_2, if there is adequate ventilation.

As Pecha, Berka and Kouril assert, the critical CO_2 concentrations in closed systems range about 140 ml/litre for thermophilous fish and about 40 ml/litre for those preferring cold conditions.

Kruzhalina, Averina and Vol'nova give a closer specification of these critical CO_2 concentrations in closed fish transport systems and suggest the following levels: 60-70 ml/litre for salmonids, 40 ml/litre for mature sturgeons and 20 ml/litre for sturgeon fry, 140-160 ml/litre for mature herbivourous fishes, 100 ml/litre for herbivorous fish fry and 80 ml/litre for the larvae of the herbivourous species.

All these data hold for closed systems; in open systems CO_2 is released from water by any system of aeration. When the fish concentration in the container of a closed system decreases, the critical CO_2 concentration loses much of its importance.

Another important factor is chlorine concentration in water, although - like carbon dioxide - chlorine is also removed from the water by aeration. The concentration of 0.5 mg/litre is considered as dangerous, though even lower chlorine levels, e.g., 0.2 mg/litre disturb the fish respiration mechanism considerably.

Ammonia (NH_3) builds up in transport water due to protein metabolism of the fish and bacterial action on the waste. Decreasing metabolic rate of the fish by lowering the water temperature, and thus lessening fish activity, reduces the production of NH_3. The production of NH_3 by bacterial action can be decreased by shipping fish only after food has been withheld long enough to void the stomach and intestine.

Temperature and time of last feeding are important factors regulating ammonia excretion. For example, trout held in water at 1°C excrete 66% less ammonia than those held in 11°C water, and fish starved for 63 h before shipment produce half as much ammonia as recently fed fish. Fish larger than 10 cm should be starved at least 48 h; those 20 cm and larger should be starved 72 h. No maximum permissible values can be given because the toxicity of ammonia is so greatly affected by water temperature and pH. However, critical concentrations of toxic ammonia are scarcely obtained under standard fish transport conditions.

Effect of Temperature

Water temperature is an important factor. When water temperature is low, the pH remains higher and fish metabolism decreases. The generally applicable zones of optimum temperatures for transported fish are 6-8°C for cold-water fishes and 10-12°C for warm-water fishes in summer, 3-5°C for cold-water fishes and 5-6°C for warm-water fishes in spring and autumn, and 1-2°C for all in winter.

Naturally, these temperature ranges do not apply to the early stages of fish fry. The early fry of cyprinids cannot be transported at temperatures below 15°C, early fry of salmonids at temperatures higher than 15-20°C, and the temperature of 10°C, is considered as optimum for the early stages of the fry of coregonids.

Density and Activity of Transported Fish

Consideration should also be given to the factor of space. As to fry, the ratio of the volume of the fish transported and the transport water should not exceed 1:3. Heavier individuals, e.g., parent fish can be transported in a fish: water weight ratio of 1:2 to 1:3, but with smaller organisms this ratio decreases to 1:100 to 1:200.

In the FRG recommendation, the following ratios between fish weight and the volume of water in the transport tank (with good aeration of water at a temperature of 8-12°C during shorter transports lasting (1-2 h) are table carp 1:1, stock carp 1:1.5, table rainbow trout 1:3, stock trout 1:4.5, stock pike 1:2, herbivorous fishes 1:2.

Table 1. Percent unionized ammonia in water at 0 to 30°C and pH 6 to 10.

Temperature (°C)	pH				
	6.0	7.0	8.0	9.0	10.0
0	0.008	0.08	0.82	7.64	45.3
2	0.01	0.10	0.97	8.90	49.3
4	0.01	0.12	1.14	10.3	53.5
6	0.01	0.14	1.34	11.9	57.6
8	0.02	0.16	1.57	13.7	61.4
10	0.02	0.19	1.83	15.7	65.1
12	0.02	0.22	2.13	17.9	68.5
14	0.03	0.25	2.48	20.2	71.7
16	0.03	0.29	2.87	22.8	74.7
18	0.03	0.34	3.31	25.5	77.4
20	0.04	0.40	3.82	28.4	79.9
22	0.05	0.46	4.39	31.5	82.1
24	0.05	0.53	5.03	34.6	84.1
26	0.06	0.61	5.75	37.9	85.9
28	0.07	0.70	6.56	41.2	87.5
30	0.08	0.80	7.46	44.6	89.0

The conditions of fish transport are also influenced by overexertion and fatigue of fish. When fish are placed in transport containers, they usually exert a large amount of muscular activity. When muscles are actively used, there is not enough blood (thus oxygen) to supply their needs. An alternate system shifts into use where energy is provided in the absence of normal amounts of oxygen. Lactic acid accumulates in the muscles and blood and causes the pH of the blood to drop.

Oxygen utilisation is reduced by the lower pH of the blood. Following a few minutes of strenuous muscular activity, lactic acid accumulation may not be reduced for 24 h. Excitability and recovery from the side effects excitement vary with the species. More oxygen is consumed within the first 15 min. in the transport unit than during any subsequent

15-min period. For this reason, additional oxygen, as much as twice the flow normally required should be provided during loading and the first hour of hauling. The oxygen flow can be reduced to normal level 6 mg 1-1 after this acclimation period, when the fish have become settled and oxygen consumption has stabilised.

A lower individual weight of fish means a much lower total weight of the fish that can be kept in a transport container (Figure. 1); this is due to the higher oxygen consumption and greater demand for space (the space factor increases considerably).

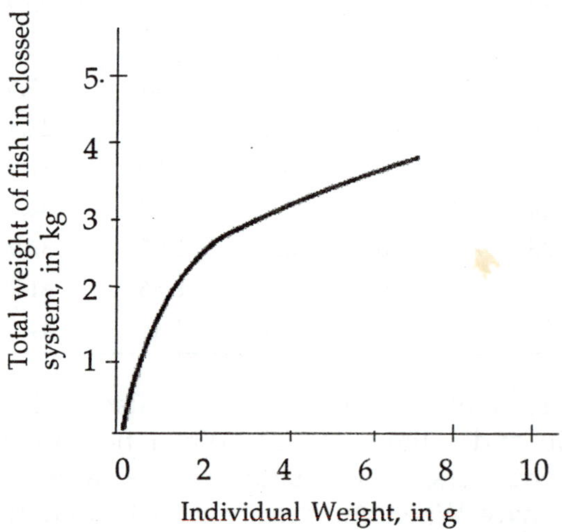

Figure 1. The dependence of cyprinid stock density in closed systems on the individual fish weight, in water temperature 20°C and transport time 5 h.

Stock density of the fish in container also depends on the length of transport time (Figure. 2). The pattern of this dependence is characterised by hyperbolic curve, not straight line.

Higher temperatures mean a lower total stock weight. The time of shipment experts its influence mainly on the larval stages of cyprinids; transport longer than 24 h always means some risk, although all conditions are otherwise good.

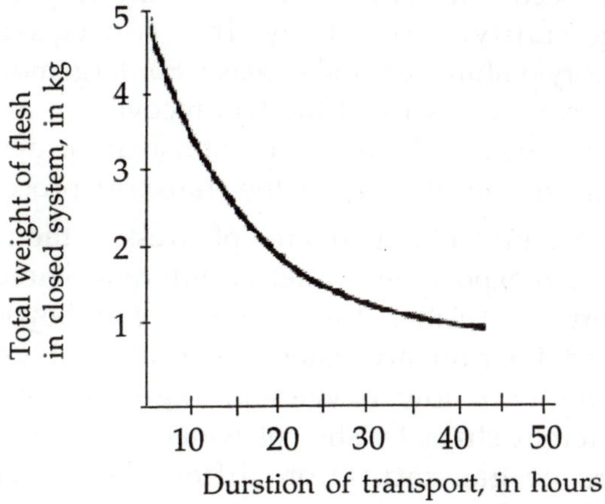

Figure 2 The dependence of the stock density of cyprinids in a closed system on shipment time; individual weight 10 g, transport time 5 h, water temperature 20°C.

Salmonid stock densities in the transport container are always lower than the standard densities for cyprinids, owing to a higher oxygen consumption and a lower critical CO_2 concentration.

Biochemical Changes

Shipment conditions also influence the composition of fish blood and the parameters of blood serum biochemistry. Increased temperature and a lower fish weight-to-water concentration ratio mean a higher number of erythrocytes and a greater haemoglobin concentration of fish blood. No such changes occur at lower temperatures and a lower fish proportion in relation to water volume. Haematological conditions changed by transport were also recorded by Carmichael in advanced fingerlings (15-24 cm) of largemouth bass. When fish were transported at higher densities, the levels of corticoids and glucose in the plasma increased and were retained when the transport was finished.

Although mortality as a direct consequence of transport was low, the secondary effects of stress were responsible for delayed mortality, caused by the consequences of osmoregulatory disfunction and disease. For largemouth bass, the author recommends to let the fish recover for at least 64 h. It should also be noted that release of fish at the destination can be the most critical stage of the transport process.

The fish are under some degree of stress in the transport unit and sudden exposure to water of different characteristies or low quality will further stress the fish, often beyond what they can stand. Poor-quality water may mean freshly pumped ground water with low oxygen or high carbon dioxide content. Different characteristics of water often mean a pH, temperature or gas saturation difference between the transport unit and the receiving water.

Closed Systems of Fish Transport

The closed systems are represented by polyethylene bags and other sealed transport units. They are used mainly for the transport of the early fry, but also brood fish. The transport of fry in polyethylene bags with oxygen is particularly widespread in the world, being used as a very effective method. It substantially reduces the total volume and weight of transport water, enables public transport to be used for fish-transport purposes, makes it possible to prolong the transport time, and is economically advantageous.

Polyethylene Bags

The bags used for fish transport in water with oxygen atmosphere are produced in a number of modifications. They are manufactured from a thin (soft) or thicker (hard) transparent polyethylene foil and usually have the shape of sack or sleeve. The bags of the traditional shape (sacs) usually have the dimensions of 0.8-1.1 × 0.35-0.45 m. The upper end is usually fully open. The bottom either has a seam in the middle or consists of a rectangular piece of foil; the latter variant is better because it helps avoid losses of the fish squeezed in the corners. For safety reasons, the bags are sometimes duplicated: a thin (soft) bag is inserted in another thin bag, or a thin bag forms a lining in a thicker (harder) bag.

The other type of bags has the form of a sleeve. Its width usually is 0.4-0.5 m. The final length of the sleeve depends on where the sleeve is cut. One of the ends has to be completely closed, sealed: a suture is welded, or the folded end of the sleeve is fused in, after tightening with a rubber seal or a plastic adhesive tape, or binding with a rope. The welding is done with a special device, whereas for the fusing (sealing) the flame of a candle will suffice.

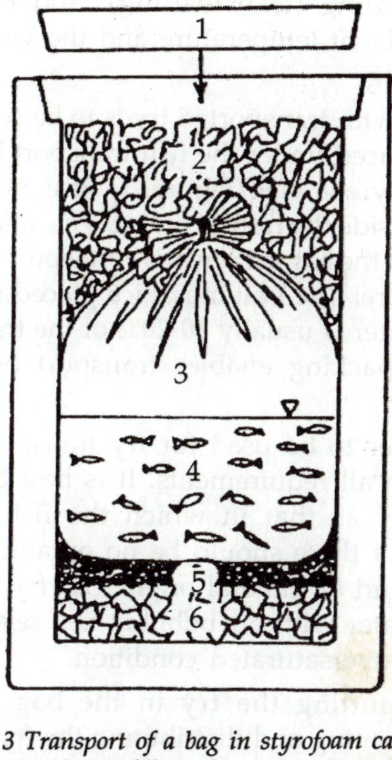

Figure 3 Transport of a bag in styrofoam case.
1 - lid, 2 - insulation filling, 3 - oxygen atmosphere, 4 - water with fish, 5 - insulation lining, e.g., foam rubber, 6 - ice

Another possibility is to bind a knot on the end of the sleeve. It is important to make the knot as tight as possible. One sleeve equalling about 2.5 times the length of the future bag suffices, after binding a simple knot, to make a duplicated bag. During transport the bags with fry are placed in outer cases protecting the bags against mechanical damage, mainly punching or tearing in contact with the ground. The case keeps the bags in the desired position, enables easier handling and/or provides thermal insulation of the bags.

These cases can be cardboard boxes, suitable plastic containers, wide polyethylene cans, polystyrene boxes. The kind of outer casing depends on the number of bags transported, length and method of transport, requirements for further handling (transloading), and on the differences between ambient temperature and the temperature of water inside the bag.

If water with transported try is to be cooled, bags with ice should be placed under the fish-transport bags on the bottom of the polystyrene box (Figure. 3). It is not recommended to put the ice inside the transport bag. The amount of ice depends on the size of the bag with water, transport time and difference of temperature. The volume of ice placed under the bag with transport water is usually 10-20% of the transport water. This method of packing enables transport by public transport routes.

The water to be used for fry transport in a bag should comply with all requirements. It is best to use water of the same quality as that in which the fish were kept before transport, but there should be no organic pollutants and no dispersed mud of mineral origin. Sac fry, in particular, need transport water with air bubbles, i.e., released air contained in water in oversaturated condition.

Before putting the fry in the bag, the procedure of catching, counting and distributing the fry in the bags should have been thoroughly prepared to finish the operation as quickly as possible. The polyethylene sac, or sleeve with a closed bottom end, is first put in the outer transport case; if a double bag is to be used the inner bag is to have been inserted in the outer one. Then, water is poured in the bag, about 20 litres if the volume of the bag is 50 litres, and the fry are placed inside. Air is displaced from the space above water in the bag and a hose, connected to the pressure regulator of an oxygen cylinder, is introduced in the bag, the upper end of the bag being held tight around the hose by hand. Then, technical oxygen from the pressure cylinder is left to blow via the pressure regulator to the upper part of the bag. If the volume of water with fry is 20 litres, the volume of oxygen atmosphere should be 30 litres.

The supply of oxygen is stopped when the bag is filled: the hose is quickly drawn out of the bag and the upper end of the bag is twisted to prevent oxygen from leaking and to produce some overpressure by reducing the volume. If the bag if to be transported in a horizontal position, the pressure should be 0.05 to 0.06 MPa but for vertical transport the pressure should be 0.02 to 0.04 MPs. In practice, this means that after filling the bag is tight: when pressed with thumb the foil quickly returns to its original position.

During air transport the pressure in a vertically kept bag reaches -0.01 MPa, owing to the lower outside pressure. Finally the opening of the bag is closed. There are several ways of closing the bag; the simplest way is to tighten the end of the plastic foil with rubber, preferably duplicated. Rope or adhesive tape can also be used. The bag can also be closed with a metal screw cap. In hatcheries or fry rearing farms with regularly repeating mass dispatching of the fish, it is recommended to build a dispatching line.

After transport, or during control on a longer journey, the condition of the fry should be checked before release. The fry are examined for position, i.e., swimming, lying on the bottom, staying in physiological position or turning to one side, for motility, readiness of reaction to light, touch, and/or number (proportion) of dead individuals.

The fish are released only when the temperature of the water in the bag reaches the same level as that of the receiving water. For sac fry the difference in water temperature should not be greater than 1°C, for older fry 2°C in both directions. To balance the temperatures it is best to put the closed bag on the surface of the receiving water. When the temperature difference is reduced to 2-3°C at the maximum, the bags are opened step by step and the receiving water is slowly added to the transport water. Releasing can start when about 50% of the receiving water has been added to the bags. The behaviour of the fry should be constantly examined.

If the bags are handled with maximum care, if they are closed in the most careful manner and transported in suitable outer cases, they can be used repeatedly. However, this is not a general recommendation because damage to the bags, however tiny it may seem, can never be avoided during fish release. As Kruzhalina, Averina and Vol'nova assert, it is also possible to use bags - tanks, made of 4-12 layers of polyethylene foil ("sleeve" 80 cm in width), having a total volume of 300 litres. However, these types of bags are hard to handle and are used only for individual transports of large and broad fish.

Containers similar to polyethylene bags may be sealed. Generally made of cured plastics they can do the same job as bags and do not require as much care during handling, despite repeated use. However, their unit price is much higher.

Fry Densities in Plastic Bags

Calculation formulae were worked out for the theoretical determination of fish densities in plastic bags; they take into account factors such as changing environment, transport time, volume of water and coefficient of free space. Nevertheless, for practical purposes, it is simpler to use the guide data published by some authors, either individually or as fish-transport tables.

The standards of fish fry transport published in the instructions by Orlov et al., for Soviet conditions can also be considered as practically verified. The data apply to fish densities in bags, volume 40 litres, including 20 litres of water and 20 litres of oxygen, from the point of view of the possible total weight and number of fish transported; the standards are indicated for cyprinids, salmonids, for fish of the perch family, and for Soviet sturgeons. Similar details concerning the transport of fish fry in polyethylene bags are given in the monograph by Kozlov et al., on the acclimatisation of aquatic organisms in which fish transport forms an inseparable part of the acclimatisation processes.

The transport distances were up to 2 500 km. The fry were kept in polyethylene bags containing 7.57 litres of water with a supply of oxygen, and the bags were protected in insulated polystyrene containers. The transport density of the fry was 3 000 per litre. To ensure that the fry would be ready to begin feeding when they were released into rearing ponds, they were shipped at 1, 2 or 3 days of age, depending on the distance of their destination. Shipments were made by commercial airline or bus, but automobiles were also successfully used.

Open Systems of Fish Transport

The open systems have many technical variants, ranging from small transport fish-cans, containers for fish transport within the territory of a fish farm, up to special fish transport trucks and tank wagons.

In all cases of fish transport in open systems, it should be borne in mind that even a short-time transport of 10-30 m in open plastic or metal tanks should be done under the conditions of constant air or oxygen supply. This is very important to the welfare of fish even if dissolved oxygen content of water seems to be satisfactorily high in the tank. Transport longer than half an hour should be in completely filled and closed tanks to prevent splashing and injuries to young fish bumping into each other in the well of the tank.

The weight of fish that can be safely transported in a tank depends on the efficiency of the aeration system, duration of the transport, water temperature, fish size and fish species. If environmental conditions are constant, the carrying capacity of a transport unit depends upon fish size. It has been suggested that the maximum permissible weight of trout in a given tank is directly proportional to their length. Thus, if a tank can safely hold 50 kg of 5 cm trout, it could hold 100 kg of 10 cm trout, and 150 kg of 15 cm trout.

Reported loading rates for fish vary widely among farms, and maximum carrying capacities of different types of transport units have not been determined. Some calculations of loading rates for various fish species are presented by Piper et al.. Under ideal conditions, the maximum load of 20-28 cm rainbow trout is 3-3.1 kg/litre of water for 8 to 10 h. Similar loading rates are appropriate for brook, brown, and lake trout of the same size. Channel catfish can be safely transported at loadings presented in Table 2. If the trip exceeds 16 h, it is recommended that a complete water change be made during transport.

Table 2. Weight (in kg) of channel catfish that can be transported per litre of 18°C water.

Number of fish (per kg)	Transit period (in h)		
	8	12	16
2	0.75	0.66	0.57
4	0.71	0.57	0.41
9	0.60	0.49	0.35
110	0.41	0.30	0.24
276	0.35	0.26	0.21
552	0.26	0.21	0.18
1 100	0.21	0.20	0.15
2 200	0.15	0.12	0.08
000	0.02	0.02	0.02

The following guidelines may be of value for transporting channel catfish:

- 0.5 kg of 40 cm channel catfish can be transported per litre of water at 18°C;
- loading rates can be increased by 25% for each 5°C decrease in water temperature, and reduced proportionately for an increase in temperature;
- as fish length increases, the weight of fish per litre of water can be increased proportionally for an increase in temperature. For example, a tank holding 120 g of 10

cm catfish will safely hold 250 g of 20 cm or 500 g of 40 cm fish per litre of water;

— if the transport time exceeds 12 h, the loading rate should be decreased by 25 percent;

— if the transport time exceeds 16 h, loading rates should be decreased by 50 percent or a complete water change should be arranged;

— during the winter, transporting temperature of 7-10°C are preferred, whereas 15-21°C are preferable during summer months.

Table 3 suggests loading rates that have proved successful for northern pike and walleye.

Table 3. Weight (in kg) of northern pike and walleye that can be carried per litre of water at temperatures between 13–18°C.

Size of fish (cm)	kg of fish per litre	Transit period (h)
7.6	0.15	8.0
5.1	0.08	8.0
2.5	0.07	8.0

From the technical point of view, most tanks constructed in recent years are insulated, usually with styrofoam, fiberglass or urethane. Styrofoam and urethane are preferred materials because of their superior insulating qualities and the minimal effect that moisture has on them. A well-insulated tank minimizes the need for elaborate temperature-control systems and small amounts of ice can be used to control the limited heat rises.

Circulation is needed to maintain well-aerated water in all parts of the tank. Transport success is related to tank shape, water circulation pattern, aerator type and other design criteria. Warmwater transport tanks may be compartmented. Compartments facilitate fish stocking at several different sites on a single trip, permit separation of species, and act as baffles to prevent water surges.

Tanks in current use have 1 000-2 700 litre capacities, averaging about 1 700 litres. However, 4 500 litre tanks occasionally are used in the USA to transport catchable size catfish, trout and bass. Although most tanks presently in use are rectangular, the trend in recent years has been towards elliptical tanks, such as those used to transport milk. This shape has several advantages: V-shaped, elliptical or partially round tanks promote better mixing and recirculation of water as the size of the tank increases. This shape also conforms to a truck chassis and holds the centre of gravity towards the area of greatest strength.

Water circulation systems are of various sizes and designs. Suction lines to the pumps lie on the bottom of the tank and are covered by perforated screens. Water is carried to the pumps and then forced through overhead spray heads mounted above the waterline.

In most systems, oxygen is introduced in one of the suction lines just ahead of the pump. This usually is controlled by a medical gas-flow meter; because of the danger involved in handling and transporting bottled oxygen, care must be taken to follow all prescribed safety procedures. Self-priming pumps powered by gasoline engines are used to circulate water in many transport units.

Pumps may be close-coupled or flexibly coupled. Although the former type is more compact, it tends to transfer heat to the water. Depending upon ambient air temperature, close-coupled pumps may increase the temperature of 1 500 litres of water by about 4°C an hour, whereas flexible coupling will reduce heat transfer to approximately 1.7°C per hour.

A method of circulating water with 12-volt mechanical aerators uses carbon rods and micropore tubing for dispensing oxygen. Aerators alone may not be sufficient to provide the oxygen needed to transport large loads of fish, but a supplemental oxygenation system can increase the carrying capacity of the transport tank. Some advantages of aerator systems over gasoline-driven water pump systems are:

— Temperature increases from aerators are less than 0.5°C per hour, compared with 1.3°C with pumps;
— aerators and the oxygen injection system can operate independently. There are advantages to carrying small sizes of certain species of fish on oxygen alone. Oxygen also can be used as a temporary backup system if aerators fail;
— usually, aerators have fewer maintenance problems;
— costs of recirculating equipment and aerators strongly favour aerators;
— use of aerators eliminates the space required between the tank and truck cab for pumps and plumbing.

The most efficient tanks have the highest water circulation rates, but circulation rates must be balanced with water capacity. Pumping or aerating systems should be able to circulate at least 40 percent of the tank water per minute when 20-22 cm salmonids are transported, though lesser rates are appropriate for smaller fish.

Technical Designs of Open System

The survey of the technical designs of the open systems of fish transport can be started from a small fish can (Figure. 4), described by Gilev and Krivodanova. Its volume is 39 litres, transport time without replacement of the oxygen cylinder 30 hours, oxygen cylinder capacity 2 litres, full can weight 53.5 kg. The oxygen is conducted from the cylinder into porous distributor installed in can bottom to oxygenate the water with the fish.

The small transport container for fish fry or for a small number of trout is similar to the can. Its volume is from 50 to 150 litres, oxygen is conducted from the cylinder into the porous distributor in container bottom.

Aeration grates connected with separate sources of air, e.g., compressors or oxygen are usually installed in the bottoms of the larger containers. The transport tanks for internal transports inside the fish farm are supplied without the top closure. Their volume is from 200 to 1 000 litres. A removable gutter is used for releasing the fish through the sluice.

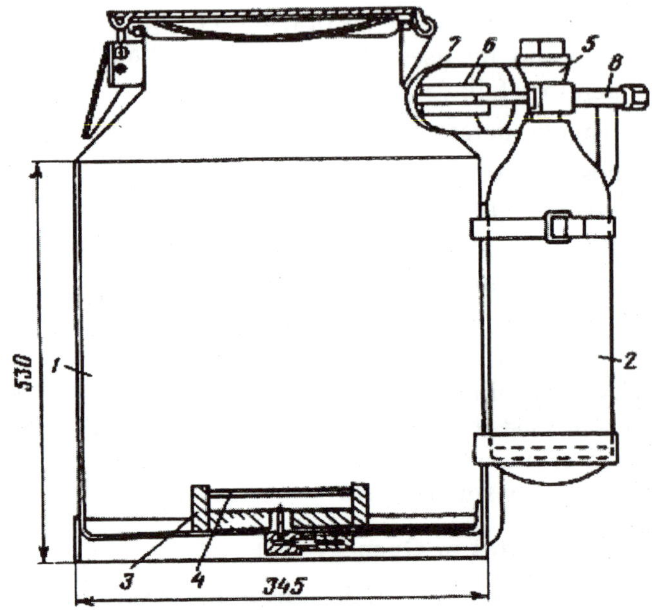

Figure 4. Fish fry transport can.

Tanks for internal transports, commercially produced by the Ewos Company. Small transport tanks, usually of glass-reinforced plastic, which can be transported in a passenger car are used with success for the transport of small amounts of fish. The commercial product of Tess Aquaculture Ltd., is an example of such a tank. The tank has a separate pump, managed from the electrical system in car, with a capacity of 1 800 litres of water/hour; it keeps good oxygen conditions for the fish.

Small amounts of fish can also be transported by passenger-car trailers on which the fish tank is divided into two compartments. The trailer also has a compressed oxygen cylinder. It may also be equipped with a non-traditional tank of plastic foil, suspended on a tubular frame. The commercial product - a passenger-car trailer for fish transport - of Grice and Young Ltd.

Single-purpose transport trucks

Special single-purpose trucks are also built for fish transport. For instance, Leitritz and Lewis, 1976, Californian fish farmers, use vehicles with four sizes of tanks - 11 400, 5 400, 2 700 and 1 800 litres - for fish distribution. All tanks are insulated so that temperatures can be held more constant. The three larger tanks have refrigerating units; ice is used for temperature control in the smallest unit. The newer tank trucks are equipped with a generator so that the refrigerators and water circulating pumps can be run by electricity.

The pumps and refrigerators are driven by separate gasoline engines on other models. The aeration system is generally designed with the water drawn from the bottom of the tank by pumps. It passes through a venturi to inject air into the water and is then sprayed back into the tank over refrigeration coils. The 1 800-litre tanks have small electric pumps at each end of the tank which operate from a heavy-duty truck battery. The water is picked up at the bottom of the tank and sprayed back. This type of tank holds the temperature very constant without refrigeration because the water does not pass through a venturi on the outside of the tank and warm air is drawn from the atmosphere into the water. Some tanks are also supplied with bubbles of oxygen through a carborundum stone from a bottle of compressed oxygen. The fish planting equipment, particularly the larger tank trucks, are complicated and expensive. There should be an operating manual with each piece of equipment.

Soviet special vehicles for fish transport are also differentiated as to capacity, the container volume being usually between 2 400 and 4 000 litres. Their detailed descriptions and operation conditions are given by Mackevich and Shiyanov, Pavlov, Kozlov et al., and Dyagilev. The water in the tank is aerated by means of an own compressor; truck engine is used for supplying the air in some types of trucks, or water is oxygenated with gaseous oxygen from pressure bottles. In large-volume tanks partitions are installed to damp water movements during transport. Bigger trucks (volume above 4 000 litres) are also equipped with an aggregate for water cooling; a thermoregulator is used to control this device.

A special truck with a 13 000-litre tank is used in the USSR for fish shipment, mainly for transporting brood fish to longer distances. The truck has a powerful ejector device for water aeration, keeping the orientation of the fish during transport. The transport tank is thermally insulated, the space for the fish has the dimensions of 4.2 × 1.4 × 1.6 m. The minimum flow rate of water through the tank for orientating the fish is 0.2 m.s-1.

References

Dupree, H.K. ad J.V. Huner, *Transportation of Live Fish*, Pages 165-176 *in* H.K Dupree and J.V. Huner, editors., Third Report to Fish Farmers. U.S. Fish and Wildlife Service, Washington, D.C, 1984.

Piper, R.G., *et al.*, *Fish Hatchery Management*, U.S. Fish and Wildlife Service, Washington, D.C. 517pp, 1982.

Johnson, S.K., *Transport of Fish and Crustaceans in Sealed Containers., Inland Aquaculture, Handbook*, Texas Aquaculture Association, College Station, TX. A1504-A1509, 1988.

5

Transportation of Milk

Milk is picked up at the farm every two days by an insulated transport tanker. The driver is responsible for determining whether a producer's milk is fit to be loaded into the tanker after checking its temperature, appearance and smell. He then takes a sample of the milk to determine the protein, lactose and butterfat content. He may also take a second sample for quality control testing in laboratories.

The capacity of the regular tankers varies between 10,000 and 35,000 litres. The pick-up routes have been designed to avoid overlaps. The transport tanker is insulated to prevent the milk from getting hot in the summer or freezing in the winter. The reflecting surface of the trucks also provides protection against infrared rays and reduces the degree of heat on the tank. Likewise, insulated silos at the plants keep the milk below 4°C.

The type of liquid milk distributed, the packaging system, the number and location of retail centres, the distance between the retail centres and the plant or depots, and the type of vehicles are major factors affecting the techno-economics of transport. In some areas milk is sold only in the morning, in some twice a day and in some others—particularly where refrigeration is available or UHT or sterilized milk are popular-throughout the day. These purchasing habits of the consumers have also to be considered when assessing transport requirements.

In order to work out a comparative analysis of the techno-economics of transport of different types and quantities of liquid milk, simplified distribution models had to be designed. The analysis is made under these model conditions. It is assumed that a daily production of 10000 to 100000 litres will be distributed within a square 10 km × 10 km and for 2500001/day the area to be served will be a square 20 km × 20 km.

Focal points around which 10001/day are sold are marked with a cross. They do not necessarily indicate the locations of retail shops, but rather represent the topographical designation of centres of milk sales areas. This implies the assumption that the additional distance which the milk delivery vans have to cover around the focal point in order to reach the actual retail shops is negligible as compared to the distance between focal points and the plant. The analysis of delivery vehicles routeing has been done separately for each capacity and each milk packaging system.

The routeing indicated for the transport is not necessarily the shortest. In a real area access to roads, density of traffic, local regulations, etc. will affect the selection of routes and will certainly deviate from the theoretically shortest. In the model presented, routeings have been selected following a common pattern thus permitting comparisons between different systems and capacities. It was found that the quantity of milk distributed has little influence on specific distance expressed in km/1000 litres. For practical calculations the specific distance may be considered as constants for each of the distribution systems.

Transport costs of UHT milk are affected by the fact that the expense of UHT treatment and aseptic packaging can only be justified for markets which require a shelf-life of the product of at least 2 months. Such markets include those where distribution involves very long distances or times, i.e. where the processing plant is at a long distance from the retailer. Transportation costs from the plant to a depot in the consumption centre could not be included in the calculations presented since no relative model conditions could be drafted.

The type and capacity of milk distribution vehicles cannot be standardized beyond certain limits, since requirements are different for different systems. A prime-mover with a chassis of 5 carrying capacity was selected as standard. On this standard chassis three types of body may be placed according to requirements:

- a closed uninsulated chamber for UHT and sterilised milk;
- a closed insulated chamber for all pasteurised milks, except for delivery to vending machines;
- an insulated milk tank for deliveries of pasteurised milk to vending machines.

The milk-carrying capacity of the chassis was calculated excluding the weight of the appropriate body. It was also assumed that the required platform area may be chosen without affecting the costs of the chassis. Standard timings of milk delivery to retail centres have been adopted as follows:

- Pasteurised milk to vending machines, UHT milk and sterilised milk are delivered during two 8-hour shifts, since the products can be kept safely in the retail centre.
- Pasteurised milk is delivered to retail centres within one 8-hour shift. Empty bottles and cans are collected during the second 8-hour shift.
- Empty sterilised milk bottles and crates and the crates for pasteurised milk in single-service containers are collected during delivery trips.

Simultaneous distribution of milk and collection of empties for pasteurised milk in bottles and cans is generally considered as impractical in conditions prevailing in developing countries as the lack of refrigeration necessitates sales during a short time and whole-day storage of uncollected empties at the retail centre is undesirable. In order to arrive at comparative costs for the various packaging systems studied it is necessary first to identify a number of basic factors and to evaluate these for the model transport systems outlined above. These factors can be considered in groups.

Group 1-Factors associated with the packaging system and the topography of the area,

g_1 - weight of containers (kg) per 1-ton load

g_2 - weight of crates (kg) per 1-ton load

g_3 - quantity of milk (litres) per 1-ton load

g_4 - quantity of milk (litres per 5-ton load

s_1 - number of filled crates or trays in one stack on vehicle

s_2 - number of empty crates or trays in one stack on vehicle

k_1- specific distance for milk distribution (km/1 000 litres)

k_2- specific distance for collection of empties (km/1 000 litres)

K - total specific distance (km/1 000 litres) (K = k1 + k2)

Group 2 - Factors associated with operation timing

n_1- number of nominal 8-hour shifts per day for distribution

n_2- number of nominal 8-hour shifts per day for empties collection

t_1- specific time for loading packaged milk at plant (hours/1 000 1)

t_2- specific time for unloading at retail centres (hours/1 000 1)

t_3- specific time for loading empties at retail centre and unloading at plant (hours/1 000 1)

t_4- time for washing vehicles (hours per shift)

t_5- workers' rest time (hours per shift)

c - average speed of vehicles on road (km/h)

m - average number of workers in one vehicle crew

Group 3 - Other factors

The following factors may be considered constant for all systems. The numerical values given below are based on practical experience.

F - Coefficient for vehicles under repair and stand-by F = 1.25

K_L - average mileage of one vehicle during its lifetimeKL 250000km

B - rate of annual interest on capital input B = 10%

E - rate of annual expenditure on insurance and taxes E = 3%

G - rate of maintenance costs during lifetime of vehicle G = 300%

H - fuel consumption H = 4 km/litre oil

PROBLEM OF TRANSPORTATION MILK IN HOT CONDITION

Since glass-lined tanks mounted on railroad cars and automobile trucks have come into use for the transportation of milk, the question has again been raised as to whether milk could not be heated and kept hot during transportation and bacterial growth checked by heat rather than by refrigeration. This is a logical question for an engineer to ask, for he is not expected to have any knowledge of the thermophilic types of bacteria.

But the bacteriologist will at once think of these bacteria and will question the practicability of shipping the milk hot. However, even though we admit there are thermophiles in milk, we can not tell in advance what their action will be or how quickly they will act, without actual data on the subject.

As early as 1867 Muller (4) while studying the influence of temperature on milk souring found that milk held at 50°C. (122°F.) became sour and appeared greenish-yellow, the same as at 35°C. (98°F.). He came to the conclusion, however, that at 50°C. (122°F.) the souring appeared to be due to a different kind of fermentation from that at lower temperature, and that it should be investigated.

Leichmann in 1894 found that milk coagulated after twelve to fifteen hours when held at 50°C. (122°F.) and that a fine coagulum appeared. He pointed out that this fermentation was not due to the ordinary milk-souring organism.

These fermentations were undoubtedly due to thermophiles, which under favourable conditions may develop and play an important rSle in the changes that take place in the milk and dairy products. Jensen has recognised this fact and recommended that skimmed milk be cooled after pasteurisation at the creamery, instead of being returned hot to the producer, because changes were produced in it by the growth of tiler-mophiles.

Bernstein in 1893 advanced the idea that instead of refrigerating milk it could be heated to about 70°C. (158°F.)

and kept at that temperature during transportation. His general plan, which may be of interest, was as follows:

At suitable stations along the railroad he planned collecting stations. There milk was to be tested and heated to the desired temperature for transportation. For transport, differently constructed railroad cars were to be used according to the distance of shipment. For long distances, tank cars were to be used, consisting of long cylindrical tanks surrounded by a hot-water jacket.

The temperature was to be kept constant by a hot-air oven and the milk kept in motion by an electric motor which was to receive its current from a storage battery. For short distances, heating could be omitted because of the large volume of heated milk, surrounded by insulation, which would change temperature only slowly. Upon arrival at its destination, the milk was to be cooled rapidly to a very low temperature and then supplied directly to distributors in closed vessels.

Bernstein made one experimental run from Hamburg to Berlin, a ten-hour trip, with a small experimental apparatus, and says the milk was found to be excellent upon its arrival. Probably ditficulties were encountered, as one might expect, for the method has not been used commercially so far as is known. It is true, however, that the heating of milk in an evaporated form has been resorted to in some instances in this country for short shipments when refrigeration has not been easily available.

Henry Ayers, S., et al., have made number of experiments in which fresh milk was heated and held at various temperatures and examined at frequent intervals up to twenty four hours. One liter of milk was used in each experiment which was flashed to the desired temperature, then placed in a sterilised glass museum jar of 1.5 liters capacity.

This jar was covered with a heavy brass top which fitted on to the ground-glass top of the jar so that evaporation was practically eliminated propeller shaft extended through the brass top into the milk and this propeller was rotated at a speed just sufficient to prevent the melted butter fat from rising to the surface. The jar of milk was held in a water bath and the temperature kept constant at the desired point.

In a preliminary experiment with milk held at 60°C. (140°F.) it was found that after twenty-four hours the acidity had increased and the milk was coagulated to a very fine curd. This indicated that thermophilic bacteria were present, and therefore in most of the experiments bacteria counts were made at two temperatures.

Milk can not be held at any temperature from 50°C. (19.2°F.) to 60°C. (140°F.) for twenty four hours without undergoing changes produced by bacteria growth. When held at 50°C. (122°F.) a rennet curd is likely to develop with some acidity as well. When the milk was not coagulated and appeared normal, it had a strong bitter taste, clearly indicating proteolysis with peptone formation.

At 60°C. (140°F.) the fermentation was more strictly of the acid type. Even though the acidity did not develop to a point which might be expected to be required to coagulate milk, coagulation usually occurred after twenty-four hours holding. However, it must not be forgotten in this connection that the effect of acid is increased by the long heating at high temperatures.

The other type consisted of weak acid-producing bacilli resembling Lactobacillus thermophilus. These organisms grew more rapidly at temperatures from 50°C. (122°F.) to 60°C. (140°F.), which probably explained the difference in the type of fermentation observed in milk held at 50°C. (122°F.) and 60°C. (140°F.). From these results it is evident that milk can not be held at high temperatures for a period of twenty-four hours without undergoing changes which would make it valueless for commercial purposes. Therefore, for this holding period heat can not replace refrigeration.

It is possible to conceive conditions where the use of heat in place of cold might be practicable for short shipment distances, provided the period of holding is less than twenty-four hours. As an example of such a condition, the collection of milk in tanks on automobile trucks where it can be heated to and held at a desired temperature by hot exhaust gases from the engine may be mentioned. Here the holding period during transportation would only be a few hours.

Whether or not such a plan is feasible will depend upon a number of things: First, the growth of thermo-philie bacteria during holding periods shorter than twenty-four hours; second, the physical and chemical changes produced, and third, the use which will be made of the milk. We do not have complete data on these points, but that which is available may be of interest.

Apparently the thermophilic bacteria had not developed to any great extent during these holding periods, although in one experiment where milk was held for eight hours at 60°C. (140°F.) the thermophiles increased to 75,000 per cubic centimetre.

Milk to be used for manufacturing purposes such as burrer making could perhaps be shipped hot if the transportation period did not exceed six hours. In suggesting this possibility we are considering only the bacteria changes. It remains to be determined whether or not the effect of long heating would show an effect on the butter made from it.

While the experiments were only a few in number they indicate what the probable effect of long heating will be. Heating for six hours at temperatures of 50°C. (122°F.) and 55°C. (131°F.) apparently had no effect on the cream volume. After twenty-four hours at 50°C. (122°F.) the cream volume was not affected in one experiment, although in the other it was reduced nearly 50 per cent.

When milk was held at 60°C. (140°F.) variable results were obtained with short holding periods, and some reduction was observed after three hours heating. No measurements could be obtained after twenty-four hours holding, since the milk was always coagulated.

When the milk was heated to 62.8°C. (145°F.) and held for one hour the cream volume was not changed, although it was reduced after two hours holding. The effect of long heating on the cream volume causes another complication in the transportation of hot milk which is to be consumed in the fluid state.

References

Bailey, J.C. & Brace, A.W., "Experience with aluminium milk cans", *Journal of the Society of Dairy Technology* 9 (4) 155, 1956.

Ball, S., "The design of complete aseptic processing systems", *Journal of the Society of Dairy Technology* 30 (3) 143, 1977.

Ellis, J.G., "Aseptic processing and packaging of milk", *Journal of the Society of Dairy Technology* 30 (3) 148, 1977.

Gill, C.O. & Phillips, D.M., The efficiency of storage during distant continental transportation of beef sides and quarters, *Food Res. Int., 26 (4):* 239-245, 1993.

Hall, H.S., "Retail packaging of liquid milk", *Journal of the Society of Dairy Technology* 26 (2) 94, 1973.

Kader, A. et al., *Post-harvest technology of horticultural crops,* Cooperative extension, University of California, 1985.

Leonard, M.H., "Progress and development of UHT milk and milk products in the UK Dairy Industry", *Journal of the Society of Dairy Technology* 30 (3) 160, 1977.

Lopez Camelo, A.F. , *Manual for the preparation and sale of fruits and vegetables,* FAO Agricultural Services Bulletin No. 151, Rome, 2004.

Maryland Office of International Trade, Department of Economic and Employment Development. Maryland Exporters' Guide. Baltimore, MD, January 1988.

McGregor, Brian M. Tropical Products Transport Handbook. HBK-668. USDA, AMS, September 1989.

Morris, C.G., *What should be the price of milk,* Olsen Publishing Company USA., 1940.

Nicholas, C. J. Export Handbook for U.S. Agricultural Products. HBK-593. USDA, AMS, March 1985.

Olson, N.F., *Cheese manufacturing in the year 2000,* Dairy Industries International 42 (1) 16, 1977.

Poulsen, P, Ronkilde, *Selecting packaging systems,* International Dairy Federation Annual Bulletin Document No. 92, 1976.

Regez, W., "The future of UHT milk and milk products in Europe", *Journal of the Society of Dairy Technology* 30 (3) 164, 1977.

Roberts, A.W., "Quality assurance of UHT products", Journal of the Society of Dairy Technology 30 (3) 157.

Sargent, M.J., *Economics in horticulture,* Macmillan Press, 1973.

Sea-Land Service, Inc. "An International Shipment." Unpublished paper, February 1982.

Shepherd, A.W., *Understanding and using market information,* FAO Marketing Extension Guide No. 2, Rome, 2000.

Weber, G. & Reuter, H., *Flachenbestimmung fur Milchwirtschaftliche Produktionsbetriebe' Kieler Milchwirtschaftliche Forschungsberichte* 27 (2), 1975.

6

Maintaining Product Quality in Food Cargoes

Biodegradation of perishable foods takes place naturally unless some stratagem is adopted to prevent or delay this process, Perishable foods can, for example, be frozen, chilled, dried or placed in ambient—or controlled-atmosphere storage. According to international agreements, frozen products should be held at temperatures lower than -12°C, at which significant biodegradation cannot take place, When product temperature rises above the -12°C threshold for carriage the risk of biodeterioration becomes greater, and at about -10°C actual biodeterioration can begin, with eventual detectable effects.

Many products are carried chilled, The respiration of fruits and vegetables generates heat, uses oxygen and creates carbon dioxide and water vapour, and ethylene gas may be produced which accelerates ripening, Chilling slows these processes, The aim is to reduce the product's temperature and maintain it at the lowest possible value without causing damage. Controlled-atmosphere carriage is used with respiring fruits, such as bananas, where both the temperature and the gas composition in contact with the product must be held very precisely to ensure that ripening does not occur in an uncontrolled way, Both chilling and atmosphere control are delicate procedures demanding fine control.

Dried products can remain stable, without significant biological activity, but they do deteriorate if they lack appropriate packaging to prevent them from absorbing or releasing water vapour, If bulk products, such as grain, that cannot be packaged readily are loaded at high ambient temperature, the water content should be reduced more than is necessary at lower temperatures to maintain product stability. The stability of other products when stored under ambient conditions is largely determined by their prior processing and packaging, Sterile packaged products, such as canned foods, are stable over a wide temperature range.

Packaging and Transportation

Some products, such as grains, may be transported dry in bulk, while others, for instance, fish, may be conveyed wet in bulk in the deep holds of sea-going vessels. Tuna frozen at sea may be stacked up fish on fish in the refrigerated hold of a mother vessel, unprotected from handling, the surrounding fish or the handlers. Other perishable cargoes are packaged in units in cartons, bags, boxes or polyethylene or may be palletised before loading.

Many such cartoned products are then dispatched in 20 - or 40-foot containers. To protect the food, packaging has to be suitable for the purpose, the duration and the complexity of the storage and journey. Suitable packaging is more likely if the selling and buying parties make a contract before the product is transported. Much produce, however, is sold after manufacture and packaging to buyers who do not specify how it is to be protected en route to destination. This oversight can result in disputes when the product arrives.

A 20 - or 40-foot container provides considerable advantages over bulk transportation since the control over the conditions for perishable products is potentially greater, raising the total product security. A refrigerated or controlled-atmosphere container can carry cargo under pre-set conditions, and if loss of control occurs it may be limited to one unit, However, one container load is not as valuable as a hold full of material, so insurers may have less incentive to investigate damage claims for a single unit.

The duration of journeys can vary tremendously from a few days to a period of months (Figures 1 and 2).

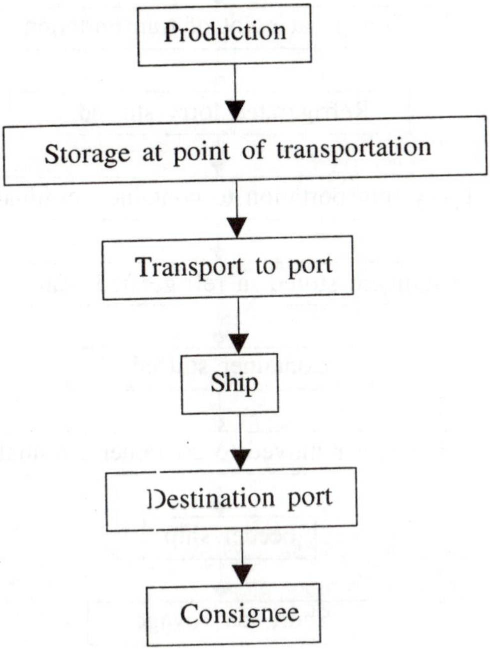

Figure 1. Stages in a simple journey - Diverses etapes d'un trajet simple - Etapas de un viaje en un solo sentido

A perishable commodity may spend time at container terminals or in warehouses which may be owned and managed by different companies, each following instructions for carriage and passing the product to the next carrier or storage facility, Contractual and legal relationships determine the levels and limitations of responsibility for the commodity at any one time.

Quality of Product

The overall quality of a product is judged by a number of parameters, Perishable products can be defined by their stable

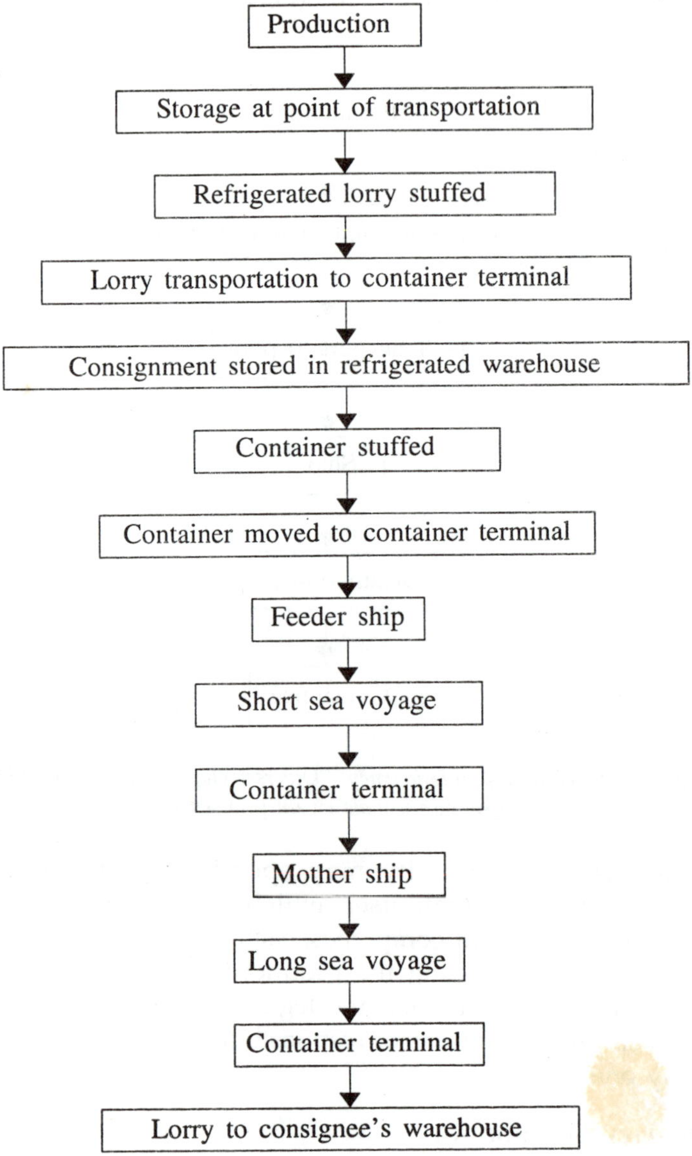

Figure 2. *Stages in a complex journey - Diverses étapes d'un trajet complexe - Etapas de un viaje de ida y vuelta*

quality features and by those that change. For instance, for fruit the parameters are size, ripeness and fullness. For salmon fillets, visible features such as the pinkness of the flesh, the absence of blood spots, the texture and the absence of gapping in the flesh are important, Other parameters can be considered; for example, the surface dryness of soft fruits can influence the probability of mould growth.

Defining information such as the weight of the unit and the number, size and grade of the items is stamped on the outer packing, and these features do not change. If the date of production is included on the packaging it implies that the goods are perishable and that some of the quality features change with time. Good quality is judged by freshness, expected appearance, smell and texture. Since these features change with time, the maintenance of good quality depends on retarding this natural progression as much as possible.

The range of changes varies among products: in fats unacceptable flavour changes occur because of oxidation; in fruits ripening causes changes in colour, texture and sweetness; in head-on, shell-on prawns blackening can occur; in meat the slow activity of enzymes causes texture changes; in produce held at temperatures above -10°C microorganisms can begin to grow and cause change and quality loss; in grains and other dry products absorbed moisture can allow mould to grow. Microorganisms affect many products and may cause soft rots. Fresh vegetables naturally dehydrate (wilt), and the loss of crispness is a loss of quality,

Quality loss is judged in terms of demonstrable and inferred defects. Some faults are indisputable even to the untutored eye, By sorting, the proportion of food damaged can be assessed and the defective product may still be acceptable to a section of the market.

Quality loss is also judged by interpretation of signs that indicate that the product was handled less than optimally, If the temperature recorder of the container of cargo shows deviations from the requested temperature it is inferred that the product is damaged, and the cargo is examined for visible defects. Physical changes may indicate how the product was handled en route. For example, frozen products may show ice formation which indicates that temperature fluctuations in refrigerated storage have occurred, causing water to sublime from the product and then to recondense inside the packet, This leads to dehydration of the product, known as freezer burn, Severe temperature abuse may be evident through signs of thawing and refreezing, seen when, for example, individually quick-frozen items stick together.

To avoid poor practices and give guidance for improvement, FAO and the World Health Organisation (WHO) have developed a series of guidelines and codes of practice both to protect the quality of products and to ensure that temperature control can be maintained and appropriately monitored, The Codex Alimentarius Commission and the European Economic Community (EEC) (now the European Community (EC)) have published examples of the controls required and recommended sampling methods.

Any perishable product has a finite life span under given conditions which is divisible into two stages, During the period of apparent quality stability, from X to A, the quality is in fact reduced to a point (A) where there are noticeable changes in one or more of the quality parameters. During the second stage, from A to B, the changes continue, eventually rendering the product unacceptable at B.

Problems may arise under three circumstances:

- when the product is transported very near the end of period X-A;
- when the rate of quality loss is accelerated, that is the slope of X-A (which is primarily temperature dependent) is steepened and the product moves more rapidly from period X-A into period A-B;
- when a product is already in period A-B when the journey begins.

While quality loss occurs naturally, the time it takes for a perishable product to become unacceptable depends on handling, storage and temperature experience, Ideally a product should arrive and be distributed completely within period X-A, Even under optimal conditions, time is not on the side of perishable products, and they are more likely to arrive in an acceptable condition if only a short time within this period has elapsed prior to dispatch.

In some countries the export quality of certain goods is controlled, particularly if the country wishes to emphasize an image of quality in selling, For some goods an accompanying health certificate or phytosanitary certificate may be required to control the transmission of disease to human beings, animals or crops. Some countries have instituted systems of quality management in particular sectors of the food industry, generally drawing on internationally recognised standards of good management practice such as ISO 9002, Such cross-industry systems are intended to raise and ensure the quality of the products.

Suppliers can often use quality control and quality assurance methods, such as those developed for seafoods by FAO, to ensure that goods meet a definable standard, The factory should be able to certify the quality of each consignment; however, the terms may be limited, covering only certain parameters and omitting those that are perceived as crucial at the time of receipt. Certainly the standards for all principal foods described in the Codex Alimentarius provide a fundamental basis for mutually understood product descriptions. The standards define limits for composition and contaminants and in some cases list the tolerances for defects.

When the sellers and buyers are known and the goods travel familiar routes, the opaqueness of quality definition on paper may seem unimportant. However, with goods travelling greater distances and being bought by large, powerful, possibly multinational interests, the nature of trade is changing, The personal element may be diminishing, and the formal description of goods is becoming more essential. Many goods are sold through markets, and at the time of production the buyer may be unknown. Where the goods to be purchased are of the highest quality and command the highest price, the seller and the buyer may work together.

In fact, good manufacturing practice (GMP) would demand the development of a manual for use between them which would provide details of many features and which might use photographic data to define some parameters. However, if a declared definition of the product's quality is lacking, situations arise when the receiver's perception of tolerable quality loss differs from that of the sender. Between the seller and the buyer is the carrier. Worldwide, the costs and availability of transportation as well as levels of assurance of quality maintenance vary (Gill and Phillips, 1993), Some but not all transporters develop considerable expertise in the carriage of products. If product quality loss occurs in consignments, determination of when loss has occurred is crucial in dispute settlement. Thus, expertise and good management practices at all stages are vital.

Dispute Settlement

The companies that produce the perishable commodities are most familiar with them and are best able to define their qualities, The quality definition should be a confidential matter between the seller and the buyer; the properties need not be declared unless a dispute arises, The carriers should not need to know the condition of individual cargoes because the shipper should declare that the goods are fit for transportation under specific carriage conditions of certain limited duration. The willingness of a producer/shipper to declare fitness for carriage should be a strong indication of the level of confidence in the product and its quality, temperature and durability.

If a declaration of fitness for carriage is received, the carrier only needs to know whether the packaging is intact and appropriate for the anticipated handling and whether the product is received within previously agreed temperature tolerances. The carrier should discern whether the conditions requested are adequately described; if not, a risk is involved in the decision to accept the cargo. The carrier should know whether it can provide the conditions requested. Finally, the receiver should be able to demonstrate that the quality received does or does not match expectations.

If a dispute about quality arises, the shipper should be able to demonstrate the validity of the claim of fitness for carriage; the carrier should be able to demonstrate adequately that it has provided the requested conditions of carriage; and the consignee should be able to demonstrate that the product has moved outside its acceptable quality range in relation to contractual description between shipper and consignee. The settlement of responsibility for quality loss should depend on the documented evidence of quality control at all stages between production, transportation and receipt of goods.

Successful implementation of TQM systems requires effective training of key personnel within food and carrier companies and of quality standards enforcement officers, Furthermore, to ensure that products leave the hands of the producer in defined condition and pass to the carrier in the same defined condition also requires independent assessment by surveyors holding internationally recognised qualifications, conversant in quality management techniques and capable of assessing the risk to products involved in individual operations, This observation is in line with the 1991 recommendations that FAO continue to develop procedures for inspection and sampling and help developing countries to improve import/export controls. Independent assessors would verify the quantity, the condition and integrity of the packaging, the presence of any visible defects, the temperature conditions under which the product was loaded and the temperatures of the cargo itself.

Post-shipment surveys are commonplace, but pre-shipment surveys are less common, not least because of the cost. However, from the viewpoint of cargo interests and carriers' insurance interests, pre-shipment surveys under the conditions described would lead to greater levels of certainty that perishable commodities could be successfully carried, and would contribute greatly to the attribution of responsibility should disputes arise. There is a need for specialist knowledge in the hands of independent assessors, who could also be surveyors, to pursue on behalf of insurers the validity of producers' records leading to the declaration of fitness for carriage, A successful assessment would require detailed specialist knowledge of the nature of food commodities and the hazards to which they are subject, and could lead to a new breed of independent professionals capable of investigating and protecting the interests of producers, carriers or consignees.

Globally, trade in foods takes place in the framework of broad national, trading block and international agreements such as the General Agreement on Tariffs and Trade (GATT). However, the national food safety laws of importing countries, which primarily have the role of protecting the safety of consumers, can act as non-tariff barriers to trade, This has long been recognised by the Codex Alimentarius Commission, which has been the main world body working for the technical harmonisation of international trade agreements to ensure that their use is equitable and non-discr-iminatory. There is still much to be done in the area of avoidance or satisfactory settlement of disputes regarding quality of imported foods, The interested parties—the producer, the carrier and the receiver (consignee)—need to agree on the limits of their responsibility, yet each should be able to demonstrate due diligence in its execution.

The implementation at points of production of systems of quality management compatible with the standards of the ISO 9000 series could be appropriate and should include control of product identification, product traceability and non-conforming products, The well-accepted Hazard Analysis and Critical Control Point (HACCP) system for food production is among the available tools. The ideas contained in this system could be extended to anticipated or imputed hazards in the chain of transportation of perishable foods.

References

Gill, C.O. & Phillips, D.M., The efficiency of storage during distant continental transportation of beef sides and quarters, *Food Res. Int.*, *26* (4): 239-245, 1993.

7

Basics of Agricultural Marketing

Marketing is an ongoing process of planning and executing of the marketing mix (Product, Price, Place, Promotion) of products, services or ideas to create exchange between individuals and organisations.

Marketing systems are dynamic. They are competitive and involve continuous change and improvement. Suppliers who have lower costs, are more efficient and can deliver quality products are those who survive and prosper. Those who have high costs, do not adapt to changes in market demand and provide poorer quality are often forced out of business.

Role of Marketing

Rural Marketing Businesses

Those who carry out marketing have a strong incentive to increase the value of rural trade, because increased sales should lead to higher profits. Rural businesses include suppliers of inputs, buyers of produce, transporters, storage companies, processors and wholesalers. They can range in size from individual entrepreneurs to large-scale agribusinesses, but whatever their size, all stand to gain from improvements in the marketing process. Businesses are often said to be exploiting farmers and making unfair profits. They certainly try to maximize their profits, but without such businesses farmers would not be linked to markets and would not be able to sell all their produce.

Traders and other rural businesses can help farmers find new markets and lower their costs. All of this leads to improved production opportunities and higher incomes for farmers. Rural marketing businesses are often small, have limited resources and are traditional in outlook. Identifying new markets, advising on technologies and improving understanding of markets are all ways in which extension workers can help traders and farmers to increase sales.

Governments can help farmers in many ways, without actually working with them directly. Promotion of competition, provision of market information and improvement of market infrastructure are powerful ways to ensure good returns for farmers.

Marketing and Consumers

Consumers want to pay low prices. Farmers want to receive high prices and to be paid as much of the consumer price as possible. The best way of achieving a balance between these two conflicting aims is through an efficient and low-cost marketing chain. This generally involves using larger scale transport (achieving economies of scale), reducing losses, and reducing other costs. An example of how costs can be reduced is the promotion of competition between buyers. Consumer preferences for food products are constantly changing and developing, particularly in the case of horticultural products.

Consumers need a production-marketing chain that can respond to their changing tastes. The marketing system needs to deliver the volumes, quality and variety of safe and nutritious food products that consumers require. It needs to be sufficiently dynamic so that it can continue to provide consumers with choice by developing and delivering new products.

Factors Affecting Profitability

In the past, ministries of agriculture and even NGOs worked mainly on improving agricultural production and yields. This involved carrying out field trials, testing varieties and developing improved production techniques. The extension officer's primary role was to advise and encourage farmers to use improved production technologies. Although farmers do, of course, benefit from improved yields, their primary concern must be to make a reasonable living from their farm. They need to generate sufficient profit from their sales to be able to cover their living costs. The key issue for them is how to do this. The main role of the extension officers should therefore be to help farmers farm more profitably. To do this they must have a basic understanding of the factors that influence profits. These are farm gate or market prices, volumes sold and costs.

Base Situation

— Summarises costs and returns of a grower who produces 10 tonnes (10 000 kgs) of a product. Although 10 tonnes are produced, only 80% is sold. Sale price is $5 per kg. Production costs include cultivation, seed, fertiliser, any sprays and labour costs and are $10 000. Marketing costs are $2 per kg sold. The farmer's total sales are $40 000, the costs are $26 000, leaving a margin of $14 000 to cover any fixed costs (rent, bank charges, salaries) and profit. In the cases that follow (2 to 7) a single variable (in bold) has been altered, thus affecting the gross margin of each case

— Additional production inputs result in the yield being improved by 10%. Production costs are increased by $1 000 and marketing costs by $1 600 as additional production is marketed. Margin increases by $1 400 or 10%.

— Only half the production is sold (e.g. because of oversupply, a lack of buyers, poor demand). Margin falls dramatically to $5 000, or about a third of the typical profit in the Base Situation (down by 64%).

— Shows impact on profits when prices are 10% down. This will happen when there is low demand or oversupply. Profit margin falls by about a third (29%) to $10 000.

— Sets out the situation where prices are increased by 10%. This could happen when demand is high and/or supply is low. Profit increases by 29%, or by $4 000.
— All production is sold. This might be because the market linkages have been improved, because the farmer works harder at marketing or because of strong market demand. Profits improve by $6 000, or over 40%.
— Reflects the situation where 10% savings are made on marketing costs. Margin increases by 11%, or $1 600.

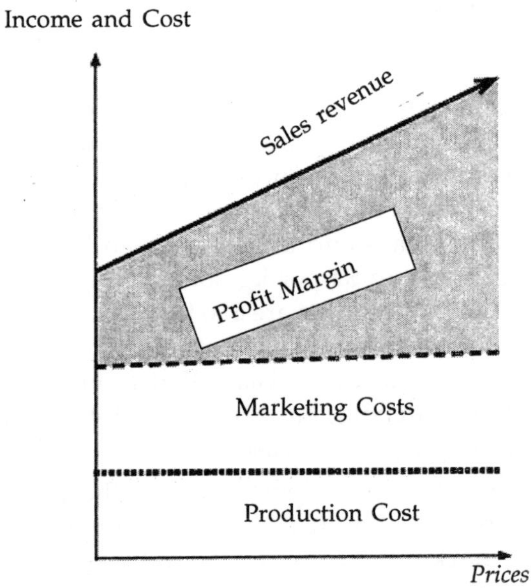

Figure 1 The relationship between prices and farmer profit

Profits and Prices

Balancing Risk and Profit

High profits are closely linked to high risks. In agriculture, the enterprises that offer the possibility of the highest profit are usually the most risky. For example, if there is only a small demand for some products, such as flowers or some fruits, they can easily be oversupplied, leading to dramatic falls in price. Some products may be technically difficult to produce or susceptible to pests and diseases. Farmers, and particularly poorer farmers, need to consider the importance of balancing production of potentially more profitable, but riskier, crops with those that provide a lower, but more stable and reliable income. Enterprises that usually provide reliable incomes include staple crops and contract production for agricultural processors.

Farmer Prices

The prices that farmers receive are mostly influenced by supply and demand. Other important factors affecting the price a farmer receives include:

- How much competition there is between buyers. When there is only one buyer, he or she will possibly offer a low "take it or leave it" price. Prices are likely to be higher and more profitable when there are many buyers competing with each other.
- The amount of information the farmer has. A farmer who is poorly informed of market prices and demand will be less able to negotiate with traders.
- The quality of the produce. Buyers will sometimes, but not always, offer higher prices to producers with better quality products. If most farmers produce low quality produce it is difficult for a trader to market high-quality produce separately.
- The transport costs. Lower prices are generally offered to producers whose product is costly to transport.

Production-Marketing Chain

As produce moves along the production-marketing chain, prices increase. Unit prices are lowest when farmers sell a standing crop. An example of this is when fruit growers sell their fruit on the tree to fruit contractors, who then harvest and pack it. This is common in Near East and South Asian countries. Harvested produce sold at the farm gate to rural buyers obtains a lower price than produce sold at a local assembly market which, in turn, is sold at a lower price than produce sold at a wholesale market. Retail sales achieve the highest price.

The price the farmer gets depends on the point in the marketing chain at which he or she decides to sell. Although prices are higher, selling further along the marketing chain involves additional costs for transport, market fees, meals and accommodation. There are also costs in terms of farmers' time. Farmers who take produce to market and sell directly to consumers will usually get the highest price but they do need to decide whether this is the best use of their time, as it may be more usefully spent managing the farm.

New Products and New Markets

Products sold in larger volumes, such as grains, may make low prices, but these prices are usually more stable. Such crops offer greater security but lower potential profits. Products with an increasing demand offer good opportunities. The market is less likely to be oversupplied. Such products provide the opportunity for producers to expand their business as the market grows. The market for food in developing countries very often follows the same patterns of growth as have been experienced by developed countries.

New products and new markets provide opportunities for more rapid growth and more profitable production. For example, processors and supermarkets sometimes like to secure supply of crops by contracting farmers or intermediaries to supply them. These changes in the market for food lead to the development of new marketing channels, new buyers and a move away from more traditional assembly and wholesale markets.

Farmers Marketing Costs

Marketing costs can be reduced, especially by achieving economies of scale. The larger the volume of product marketed, the greater the scope for lowering unit costs, for example through using larger vehicles or bulk-buying of packaging. Sometimes, traders operating on a commission basic will accept lower percentage commissions for large quantities. Small farmers working on their own are naturally at a disadvantage. Cost savings have sometimes been achieved by farmers working as a group to jointly purchase inputs and hire transport.

Traders also have costs. Because these are not always visible, traders are often accused of making unreasonable profits. Although traders can sometimes exploit a situation and make exceptional profits, there are also occasions when they are unable to sell products that they have purchased and therefore make losses. High profits on some occasions compensate for risks of losing money on others.

Losses of Products

Losses of products will inevitably occur during marketing and are one example of a marketing cost that is often invisible. Types of loss are:

— *Loss of weight*: Produce can lose weight, mainly through water loss in storage, transport and marketing. A trader may buy a tonne of products, but as a result of water loss may only sell 975 kilos.

— *Loss of value over time*: The fresher the product, the higher the price. Fresh produce will last longer, will probably taste better and may be more nutritious. Over time, bruises and pest damage become more apparent and water loss leads to many products starting to shrivel, all leading to losses in quality and in price. The most obvious loss occurs when produce has to be thrown away.

— *Physical losses*: Fresh produce losses in developing countries can be exceptionally high. Losses of ten to thirty percent are often quoted. In practice, only on rare occasions is this volume of produce thrown away. These figures more accurately reflect the loss in value that occurs from the combination of moisture loss, damage, disease and loss of freshness, as well as the proportion of the harvest that is thrown away.

For a trader, minimising losses is very important. Part of the difference between the consumer price and the price paid to the farmer is because the trader needs to make a large margin, to cover wasted or damaged produce. By only looking at the selling price it is easy to think that the trader is making an unfair profit. However, when losses are taken into account the picture changes.

Impact of Supply and Demand

The quantity of produce that consumers want to purchase is affected by many factors, the most important being:

- — price of the goods;
- — tastes and preferences of the consumers;
- — number of consumers;
- — incomes of consumers;
- — prices of competing produce;
- — range of products available to consumers.

The quantity that producers supply is also affected by a number of factors, the most important being:

- — price of the goods/products on the market;
- — price of inputs/costs of production;
- — technological factors;
- — climate;
- — storage possibilities.

The price of a product is mainly determined by supply and demand. Basically, a balance is achieved between what people are prepared to supply at a price and what people are willing to pay for the product. As the price rises the quantity that will be supplied also rises and the quantity demanded falls, and vice versa.

While supply is influenced by production it is not always the same as production. For less perishable crops, farmers or traders may decide to store them in the hope that prices will rise, rather than sell them immediately. When prices do rise they may take the products out of store to sell. At this time supply is equal to production harvested for immediate sale plus products taken out of store. However, it should be stressed that demand is not how much people would like to buy, nor what they should buy for a healthy lifestyle. It is what they are prepared to buy at the prevailing price.

Short-term Price Changes

Unlike the prices of staple foods such as maize or rice, horticultural product prices fluctuate enormously. They can fluctuate from day to day and during the day, depending on supply and demand.

The main causes of short-term price changes of fresh produce are:

— The amount of produce on sale in the market on a particular day and the quantities sold in the previous few days.

— Short-term demand changes.

— The effect on demand of prices of competing products.

To take advantage of opportunities when prices are high a supplier needs to be in close communication with the markets and able to transport produce rapidly. In many countries farmers are increasingly able to deliver products, such as leafy vegetables, to markets when prices are high, using mobile telephones to contact buyers.

Seasonal Price Changes

In countries with pronounced seasons, supplies are low at the start of the harvest season, so prices are high. Prices are at their lowest when the crop reaches maturity in the main production areas. At the end of the season prices normally increase again as supply diminishes. Prices are generally highest during the off-season, when only a small percentage of farmers are able to grow the crop.

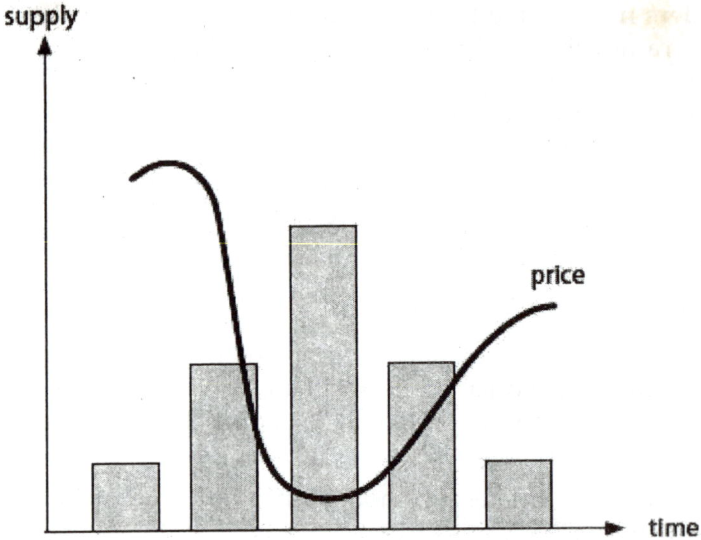

Figure 2 Supply and price changes over a season

Farmers who are located in areas where early or late-season crop production is possible or who can use production methods, such as plastic tunnels or greenhouses, that bring forward the harvesting date, are best placed to take advantage of high early or late-season prices.

Long-term Price Changes

Figure 3 shows how production and prices can fluctuate from year to year. The graph shows how a season of high prices and low supply is often followed by a season of low prices and high volumes. This is because many farmers individually make the same decision to expand production in response to high prices in one year. Wiser farmers often deliberately decide to do the opposite to what their neighbours are doing.

Figure 4 shows that the lower the price, the greater will be the demand. However, as the price goes down less will eventually be supplied (because farmers will produce less). Conversely, the higher the price, the more will be supplied. The relationship between what people are prepared to buy and what farmers are prepared to grow at different prices should eventually lead to a balance between supply and demand.

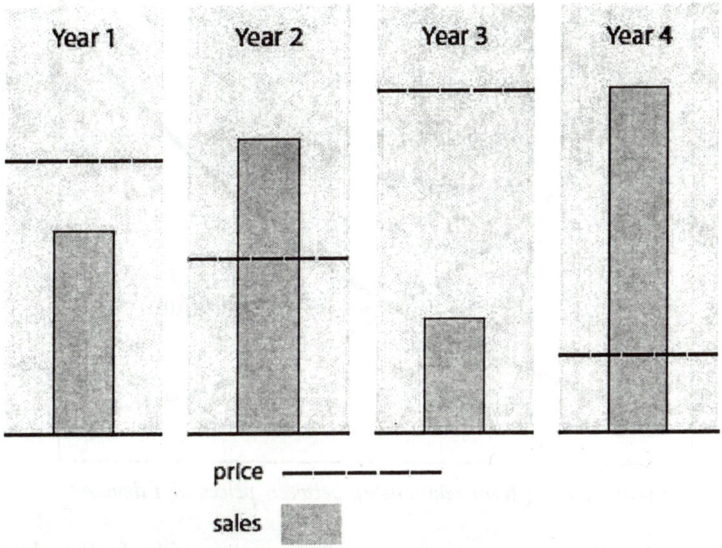

Figure 3 Fluctuations in price and production over several years

The theoretical point at which supply and demand are in balance is referred to by economists as "equilibrium". At this price there is enough incentive for farmers to produce the quantity that consumers will buy at that price.

In practice, although the marketing chain tries to achieve this balance it is rarely done because there are so many factors affecting both supply and demand and because farmers lack adequate information about demand.

Understanding of Markets

The way horticultural markets operate is complex. Markets are not very rational. Very often they appear to panic or overreact. If traders believe that there is a shortage of a product, prices will rise. Often, the increase is out of all proportion to any shortfall in supply. The converse is also true.

If the market expects even a small oversupply, then prices fall rapidly.

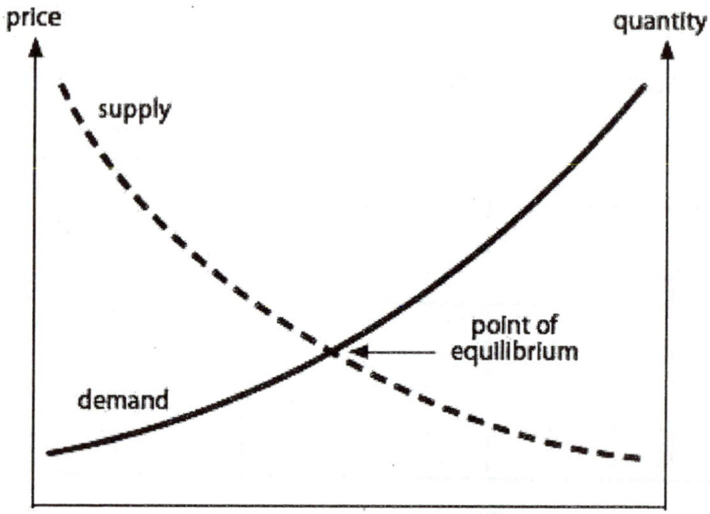

Figure 4 Long-term relationship between prices and demand

High prices have a large effect on farmers' profits. In the short term a farmer's response to high prices will be to try to increase the quantity of produce marketed. For example, tomato farmers may harvest green, unripe tomatoes. In the longer term the farmer will consider expanding the crop area and look for ways to increase production. In response to high prices farmers usually increase their production in the next season. As many of them make the same decision, there is a large increase in supply and oversupply occurs. Prices fall and farmers reduce production in the following season.

When prices fall consumers increase their purchases. They buy less when prices rise. However, the response to price changes depends on the type of product. For example, increases in the price of staple foods eaten daily, such as maize, rice, roots and tubers or green bananas, have a relatively small effect on volumes of sales, as people still need to eat. Similarly, falls in price will not lead to major consumption increases. This is not the case with luxury or nonessential food items such as oranges and apples. Small falls in price can cause a disproportionately large increase in sales, while small price increases can lead to a big fall in sales.

Condiments, spices and other products that are used in small quantities are relatively insensitive to changes in price. Low prices do little to increase sales as people do not change their recipes to use more spices when prices are low. This means that when products like garlic are in oversupply, prices fall dramatically, as consumers do not respond to price changes by buying more.

Consumer demand and tastes change constantly. Short-term changes can be caused by the weather. In northwest Europe, sunny days increase the demand for salad crops (tomatoes, lettuce, cucumbers) but when the weather becomes cooler vegetables for cooking are in stronger demand. This leads to short-term fluctuations in the prices of these commodities. Longer-term changes in demand are caused by changes in taste, attitude and society.

In Europe there has been a fall in the sale of fresh vegetables that need to be peeled and cooked (carrots, potatoes, etc.) and an increase in demand for semi-processed, cleaned, easier-to-prepare products such as frozen peas and carrots and frozen potato chips. This is because people are now reluctant to spend as much time cooking as they used to. Richer European consumers are often described as "cash rich-time poor". While prices of oranges have fallen, those of easy-peeling types of citrus have increased because consumers prefer the convenience of mandarins and clementines.

Food consumption patterns change as the amount of money that consumers have to spend increases.

- — Consumption of cereals barely increases as incomes improve.
- — Sales of milk products and beverages increase rapidly as incomes increase and, at higher income levels, these become the first and third most important expenditure categories.

Fruit sales increase most rapidly with increased income. Information such as this helps to indicate the relative importance of specific products and identifies which products are likely to increase in sales as economies develop. Farmers in countries with growing economies need to be aware of these opportunities and extension workers need to have the knowledge to help them take advantage of the changes that are taking place.

References

ITC, *Manual on the packaging of fresh fruits and vegetables*, International Trade Centre, UNCTAD/GATT, Geneva, 1988.

Kader, A. et al., *Post-harvest technology of horticultural crops*, Cooperative extension, University of California, 1985.

Lopez Camelo, A.F. , *Manual for the preparation and sale of fruits and vegetables*, FAO Agricultural Services Bulletin No. 151, Rome, 2004.

Sargent, M.J., *Economics in horticulture*, Macmillan Press, 1973.

Shepherd, A.W., *Understanding and using market information*, FAO Marketing Extension Guide No. 2, Rome, 2000.

8

Agriculture and Food Marketing Systems

In many countries, and virtually every less developed country (LDC), agriculture is the biggest single industry. Agriculture typically employs over fifty percent of the labour force in LDCs with industry and commerce dependent upon it as a source of raw materials and as a market for manufactured goods. Hence many argue that the development of agriculture and the marketing systems which impinge upon it are at the heart of the economic growth process in LDCs.

In LDCs the consumer frequently spends in excess of fifty percent of the household's income on basic foodstuffs—much of which is inadequate both in quality and nutritional content. By contrast Americans spend approximately twelve percent of their total disposable income on food. In Western Europe the figure ranges from about sixteen to nineteen percent of disposable income.

Furthermore, whereas in developed countries the poor are relatively few in number, and therefore it is economically possible to establish special food distribution programmes to meet their needs, the scale of poverty in most LDCs is such that the commercial marketing system must be relied upon to perform the task of food distribution to poor and not-so-poor alike. This being so, it is imperative that the marketing system performs efficiently.

Economic development itself provides the impulse towards more sophisticated and more efficient marketing systems. Dixie suggests that as countries experience economic growth, their rate of urbanisation tends to increase substantially. Whereas the rate of population growth, in developing countries, averages around three percent per annum, their cities and towns are increasing their populations at about four percent per annum. In essence, this means that the number of people, in urban areas, needing to be fed by rural people, will double within sixteen years. This has clear implications for agricultural production and the marketing systems that direct that production and distribute the output to the points of its consumption.

Subsistence farming is likely to diminish in importance as farmers respond to the increased opportunities that development and urbanisation create; farms are likely to decrease in number whilst increasing in size; and agriculture will probably become less labour intensive and more capital intensive. Dixie also highlights the potential contribution of agricultural and food marketing, towards attempts to improve rural incomes in developing countries.

The inequality of incomes between the rural and urban areas draws people away from agricultural production and places great stress upon the infrastructure and social services of a country's towns and cities. Nowhere was this more dramatically demonstrated than in Nigeria when petroleum oil was discovered and then exploited in the 1970s. A large number of jobs were created in the urban areas and people abandoned agricultural production in large numbers. Nigeria became a net importer of many agricultural products of which it had formerly been a net exporter.

For as long as the world price for petroleum remained high the economy thrived and could well afford the food import bill. However, as soon as the world price for oil fell, the food import bill became a serious burden. Nigeria would only have avoided this scenario if it had been able to motivate people to continue in agriculture and this would only have been possible if the disparity between urban and rural incomes had been reduced.

Rurally based enterprises, including smallholdings, can greatly improve their earning potential by adopting a market orientation. They can be encouraged to add value to commodities by adding to their utility. Value added products normally carry a higher margin than raw commodities. Another development which has in recent times increased interest in marketing practies is the trend, in many developing countries, towards market liberalisation as part of economic structural adjustment programmes (ESAPs).

The view that direct and indirect government participation in production and distribution had brought about structural distortions in economies has become widely accepted. Measures intended to correct these distortions include a return to market prices for all products and resources, the encouragement of a competitive private sector and the commercialisation, and sometimes privatisation, of all or some of the functions of marketing parastatals.

All of this requires a better understanding of marketing practices and processes within the country implementing ESAPs, in general, and within the agricultural marketing parastatals affected, in particular. So far this discussion has been set in the context of commercial marketing but social marketing should also be acknowledged. Social marketing identifies human needs in noncompetitive economies and/or sectors of society and defines the means of delivering products and services to meet these needs.

The marketing mix of social marketing strategies is evaluated using quite different criteria from those employed in assessing purely commercial marketing strategies. Criteria such as the percentage of the target population reached with the technology, products, processes or services, quantities produced and distributed and uptake of the product, service or technology are more often employed. Benefits are measured in terms of development goals, such as improved nutritional status or increased rural incomes.

The use of economic criteria is usually limited to the latter and to selecting the least-cost strategy to achieve a quantitative goal. However, the criteria used to evaluate commercial marketing strategies should not automatically be eliminated, because these improve the efficiency of some aspects of social marketing strategy without preventing the attainment of social objectives.

Marketing Concept and Systems

Marketing is not simply an extension of the production process but its only purpose as Adam Smith emphasised when, in his text The Wealth of Nations, he said that:

> "Consumption is the sole end purpose of all production: and the interest of the producer ought to be attended to only so far as it may be necessary for promoting that of the consumer."

Dixie relates what he describes as a definition of marketing which is:

> "The series of services involved in moving a product from the point of production to the point of consumption."

This is a definition which many organisations, and governments, would recognise as describing their own activities in commodity marketing. Indeed in many developing countries it aptly describes, or in some cases, did in the past describe, the functions carried out by marketing parastatals with respect to staple foods. However, as Dixie himself points out, the definition omits two key elements of any definition of marketing production to effuse the marketing concept, i.e. a customer orientation and inbuilt sustainability. Gaedeke and Tootelian offer an alternative definition which overcomes the problems caused by these two omissions:

> "...a management orientation focusing all the activities of the organisation on satisfying customer needs and wants, thereby helping achieve the organisation's long-range objectives."

This definition promotes a customer orientation and since the organisation's long-term objectives will include it's own continued existence it takes account of the need for sustainability. Moreover, this definition of the marketing concept does not preclude non-profit making organisations. Marketing is just as relevant to development projects, aid agencies, extension service organisations, and the like, as it is to commercial enterprises. Thus the marketing concept is that an organisation achieves its goals through the provision of customer satisfaction.

Put another way, marketing is the integrative force that matches production to customer needs and satisfaction. Marketing is not an activity to which an organisation turns its attention at the end of the production phase of operations. Rather marketing needs to be directing production in accordance with clear signals from the marketplace as what is needed by customers. The marketing concept must be adopted throughout not only the entire organisation, but the entire marketing system.

A system is a complex of interrelated component parts or subsystems which have a defined common goal. Thus, an agricultural and food marketing system comprises all of the functions, and agencies who perform those activities, that are necessary in order to profitably exploit opportunities in the marketplace. Each of the components, or subsystems, are independent of one another but a change in any one of them impacts on the others as well as upon the system as a whole. There is a danger that the marketing concept will be adopted by some parts of the system but not others. Thus, for example, a food manufacturer may be trying hard to implement the marketing concept and offer products that meet the precise needs of a target market.

If, however, the manufacturer has to rely upon a farming community that is still very much production oriented, for raw material supplies, then the overall marketing objectives may be frustrated. In the same way, if only some functions are performed according to the marketing concept then the system as a whole may not achieve a market orientation. For instance, the marketing department may set out to serve the market for a high quality fruits and vegetables, for which it can obtain premium prices, but if transportation is performed using the same open-topped bulk carrying wagons used to ship grain and other aggregates then it is unlikely that the enterprise will deliver the product in the right condition for the target market.

The lesson from all of this is quite simple. If the decision has been made to adopt the marketing concept, then consideration has to be given to the implications for each of the participants and the functions performed within the marketing system. Where one or more elements of the system are found to be other than market orientated, then either a change towards the marketing philosophy has to be introduced in those elements or a change in the configuration of the marketing system has to be implemented.

Food Marketing Subsystems

Rosson conceives of agricultural and food marketing systems as consisting of 4 main subsystems; production, distribution, consumption and regulatory.

The key players in the chain of activities that connect food and agriculture are the farmer, intermediaries, the food processors, and the consumer. In practice they each see the agricultural/food marketing system from a perspective of self-interest and these interests are sometimes in conflict. Illustrative examples of some of the conflicts which typically arise are given in table 1.

Table 1. Conflict of interest in agricultural/food marketing systems

Key Players	Interests
Farmers	Maximum price, unlimited quantities
Manufacturers	Low purchase price, high quality
Traders and retailers	Low purchase price, high quality
Consumers	Low purchase price, high quality

The farmer's interest is focused on getting the best return from his produce, which usually equates to maximum price for unlimited quantities. Manufacturers want least cost, best quality produce from the farmer so that he can sell it at competitive, but profitable, prices. Traders and retailers want high quality and reliable supplies from the manufacturer or farmer, at the most competitive prices. Consumers are interested in obtaining high quality products at low prices. Clearly, there are conflicting interests here. In an ideal world there should be some form of strategic partnership between these key players. It is obvious that, in the long run, any one of the four groups would find it difficult to survive if the others do not.

However, in real life, attitudes are not those of the ideal world or of the longer term. It is focused more on the shorter term and in preserving the interests of each group. Only by allowing each group to take care of its interests, can a balanced longer term relationship evolve. This must be borne in mind when considering what the food industry expects from agriculture. Moreover, those expectations will vary according to the level of sophistication of the markets the food industry itself is attempting to serve.

Functions of Marketing System

A little earlier it was said that a marketing system has two distinct dimensions. One of those dimensions is the institutions, organisations and enterprises which participate in a market and the second is the functions that those participants perform. Kohls and Uhl have classified the functions involved in agricultural and food marketing processes as under three sets of functions of a marketing system. Each of these functions add value to the product and they require inputs, so they incur costs. As long as the value added to the product is positive, most firms or entrepreneurs will find it profitable to compete to supply the service.

Exchange Functions

Buying

The marketing concept holds that the needs of the customer are of paramount importance. A producer can be said to have adopted a market orientation when production is purposely planned to meet specific demands or market opportunities.

Thus a contract farmer who wishes to meet the needs of a food processor manufacturing sorghum-based malted drinks will only purchase improved sorghum seed. He/she will avoid any inputs likely to adversely affect the storage and/or processing properties of the sorghum and will continually seek new and better inputs which will add further value to his/her product in the eyes of the customer.

In making his/her buying decisions his underlaying consideration will be the effect upon the attractiveness of his/her output to the markets he/she is seeking to serve. The buyer's motive is the opportunity to maintain or even increase profits and not necessarily to provide, for example, the best quality. Improving quality inevitably increases the associated costs.

In some cases the market is insensitive to improvements in quality, beyond some threshold level, does not earn a premium price. Under such circumstances, the grower who perseveres and produces a 'better product', is not market oriented since he/she is ignoring the real needs of the consumer. The most successful agribusiness is the one which yields the largest difference between prices obtained and costs incurred.

Selling

Of the nine functions listed, this is probably the one which people find least difficulty in associating with marketing. Indeed to many the terms marketing and selling are synonymous. Kotler suggests that:

> "Most firms practice the selling concept when they have over capacity. Their immediate aim is to sell what they can make rather than to make what they can sell."

There is no denying that 'high pressure selling' is practiced, where the interests of the consumer are far from foremost in the mind of the seller. This is not marketing. Enterprises adopt the marketing philosophy as a result of becoming aware that their own long term objectives can only be realised by consistently providing customer satisfaction.

Whereas selling might create a consumer, marketing is about creating a customer. The difference is that marketing is about establishing and maintaining long term relationships with customers. Selling is part of marketing in the same way that promotion, advertising and merchandising are components, or sub-components of the marketing mix. These all directed towards persuasion and are collectively known as marketing communications; one of the four elements of the marketing mix.

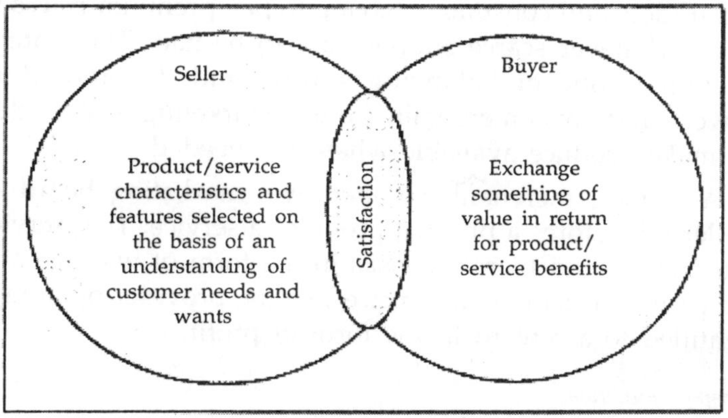

Figure 1. The exchange function

Physical Functions

Storage

An inherent characteristic of agricultural production is that it is seasonal whilst demand is generally continous throughout the year. Hence the need for storage to allow a smooth, and as far as possible, uninterrupted flow of product into the market. Because he is dealing with a biological product the grower does not enjoy the same flexibility as his manufacturing counterpart in being able to adjust the timing of supply to match demand.

It would be an exaggeration to suggest that a manufacturer can turn production on and off to meet demand—they too have their constraints- but they have more alternatives than does the agricultural producer. A manufacturer can, for example, work overtime, subcontract work, and over a longer time horizon, the manufacturer can increase or decrease productive capacity to match the strength of demand. In agriculture, and especially in LDCs, supply often exceeds demand in the immediate post-harvest period.

The glut reduces producer prices and wastage rates can be extremely high. For much of the reminder of the period before the next harvest, the product can be in short supply with traders and consumers having to pay premium prices to secure whatever scarce supplies are to be had. The storage function is one of balancing supply and demand. Both growers and consumers gain from a marketing system that can make produce available when it is needed.

A farmer, merchant, co-operative, marketing board or retailer who stores a product provides a service. That service costs money and there are risks in the form of wastage and slumps in market demand, prices, so the provider of storage is entitled to a reward in the form of profit.

Transport Function

The transport function is chiefly one of making the product available where it is needed, without adding unreasonably to the overall cost of the produce. Adequate performance of this function requires consideration of alternative routes and types of transportation, with a view to achieving timeliness, maintaining produce quality and minimising shipping costs.

Effective transport management is critical to efficient marketing. Whether operating a single vehicle or a fleet of vehicles, transportation has to be carefully managed, including cost monitoring—operations on different road types, fuel and lubrication consumption and scheduled and remedial maintenance and repair.

Skillful management of all aspects of vehicle operations can also make a substantial contribution to efficient marketing especially with respect to optimum routing, scheduling and loading and off-loading; maximisation of shift hours available, maintaining the vehicle fleet at an optimum size, taking account of time constraints on delivery, and collection times and judicious management of vehicle replacement and depreciation. Transport managers also have to weigh the advantages and disadvantages of owning, hiring or leasing transport.

Processing Function

Most agricultural produce is not in a form suitable for direct delivery to the consumer when it is first harvested. Rather it needs to be changed in some way before it can be used. Kohls and Uhl observe that:

> "The processing function is sometimes not included in a list of marketing functions because it is essentially a form changing activity."

However, it is for this very reason that processing ought to be included as a marketing function. The form changing activity is one of that adds value to the product. Changing green coffee beans into roasted beans, cassava into gari or livestock feed, full fruit bunches into palm oil or sugarcane into gur increases the value of the product because the converted product has greater utility to the buyer. How the form of produce is to be changed and the method to be used in bringing about such changes are marketing decisions.

At that point, tests were undertaken in which the product was compared with others already on the market. The results were encouraging. However, in the course of the marketing research, it was also discovered that ninety percent of the black tea consumed is blended and not the pure variety placed in tea bags by the Ethiopians. By going past the point of changing green leaf into high quality black tea, the Ethiopians were entering a nice market which is not what they intended at all.

Timely marketing research would have directed Ethiopia to stop the form changing activity short of bagging since, at that time, Ethiopia did not have the acreage of tea, nor the resources, to develop a tea blending facility of its own. In the same way, a producer of fresh fruits may have pulping and/or canning facilities but if potential buyers want the flexibility of using the fruits in a variety of ways, then these stages of processing serve to reduce utility and value, rather than increasing them.

Of course, processing is not the only way of adding value to a product. Storing products until such times as they are needed adds utility and therefore adds value. Similarly, transporting commodities to purchasing points convenient to the consumer adds value. In short, any action which increases the utility of the good or service to prospective buyers also adds value to that product or service.

Facilitating Functions

The facilitating functions include product standardisation, financing, risk bearing and market intelligence. Facilitating functions are those activities which enable the exchange process to take place. Marketing, in simple terms, is the act of supplying products to someone in exchange for something perceived to be of equal or greater value, (usually, but not always, a given sum of money). Facilitating functions are not a direct part of either the exchange of title or the physical movement of produce.

Standardisation

Standardisation is concerned with the establishment and maintenance of uniform measurements of produce quality and/or quantity. This function simplifies buying and selling as well as reducing marketing costs by enabling buyers to specify precisely what they want and suppliers to communicate what they are able and willing to supply with respect to both quantity and quality of product.

In the absence of standard weights and measures trade either becomes more expensive to conduct or impossible altogether. In Nepal such was the diversity of weights and measures used with respect to grain within the country, that it was easier for some districts to conduct trade with neighbouring states in India than it was to do business with other districts within Nepal. Among the most notable advantages of uniform standards, are:

- — price quotations are more meaningful
- — the sale of commodities by sample or description becomes possible
- — small lots of commodities, produced by a large number of small producers, can be assembled into economic loads if these supplies are similar in grade or quality
- — faced with a range of graded produce the buyer is able to choose the quality of product he/she is able and willing to purchase.

Quality differences in agricultural products arises for several reasons. Quality differences may be due to production methods and/or because of the quality of inputs used. Technological innovation can also give rise to quality differences. In addition, a buyer's assessment of a product's quality is often an expression of personal preference.

Thus, for example, in some markets a small banana is judged to be in some sense 'better' than a large banana; white sugar is considered 'superior' to yellow sugar; long stemmed carnations are of 'higher quality' than short stemmed carnations; and white maize is 'easier to digest' than yellow maize. It matters not whether the criteria used in making such assessments are objective or subjective since they have the same effect in the marketplace. What does matter in marketing is to understand how the buyer assesses 'quality'.

Financing

In almost any production system there are inevitable lags between investing in the necessary raw materials and receiving the payment for the sale of produce. During these lag periods some individual or institution must finance the investment. The question of where the funding of the investment is to come from, at all points between production and consumption, is one that marketing must address.

Consider the problem of a food manufacturer who wishes to launch a range of chilled products in a developing country where few retail outlets have the necessary refrigeration equipment. This is a marketing problem. It might be solved by the food manufacturer buying refrigerators and leading these to retailers. A common marketing problem, in developing countries, is the low level of incomes leading to low levels of effective demand for many products. The challenge to marketing is to somehow channel what income is available into effective demand.

In the case of agricultural equipment marketing this might involve offering hire-purchase schemes where the prospective buyer makes payment in regular installments. During this time he/she is deemed to have hired the machine. If payments are not forthcoming, the machine can be recovered since its ownership remains with the seller up until the final payment is made, at which point the farmer is considered to have purchased the machine. Alternatively, the seller might set up leasing, rather than purchasing schemes where again the farmer is making regular payments but never takes title to the machine.

Where a food item is being marketed, to a low income market, the seller can consider reducing the until price of the product by making the pack or lot size smaller. Another tactic is to make the product more affordable by using cheaper ingredients and/or packaging. Instant coffee can be sold at lower prices by substituting some of the coffee with chicory; the price of meat products is reduced by increasing the percentage of cereals in these products and including less meat and/or making use of less expensive parts of the animal such as entrails, offal, feet and head.

Marketing is also concerned with the financing of the enterprise itself. Here again some creative solutions can be developed. Where internal financing is insufficient for the purposes in view, an enterprise in a developing country can look to several alternatives including:

— development banks

— commercial banks

— shares issues
— credit co-operatives and/or credit unions

Where these sources of finance are considered inappropriate, or are simply not available to a particular enterprise, a strategic alliance in the form of a joint venture could be the answer. These are partnerships formed to exploit market opportunities more effectively and/or efficiently than either party can on its own. An enterprise, in a developing country, may engage in a joint venture with either an indigenous partner and/or with a foreign partner. The agreement between parties to a joint venture normally specifies their respective contributions of resources, share of management control, profit and risk.

Whatever the source of finance under consideration marketing has a role to play in evaluating the appropriateness of that source as well as identifying it in the first place. A common requirement is that marketing proposals include a forecast of the payback period. Those responsible for developing these proposals are best placed to evaluate the compatibility between the market opportunity under consideration and the alternative modes of financing it. Of specific interest is the prospect of the investment payback period matching the repayment schedule. Enterprises which finance long term investments through short term sources of finance are either badly misinformed or have adopted a high risk strategy.

Risk Bearing

In both the production and marketing of produce the possibility of incurring losses is always present. Physical risks include the distruction or deterioration of the produce through fire, excessive heat or cold, pests, floods, earthquakes etc. Market risks are those of adverse changes in the value of the produce between the processes of production and consumption. A change in consumer tastes can reduce the attractiveness of the produce and is, therefore, also a risk. All of these risks are borne by those organisations, companies and individuals.

Risk bearing is often a little understood aspect of marketing. For example, when making judgements as to whether a particular price is a 'fair price' the usual reference point is the producer or supplier's costs. However the risks borne are rarely taken into account by those passing judgement and yet, almost inevitably, there will be occasions when the risk taker incurs losses. Stocks will spoil, markets will fall, cheaper imports will enter the country, consumer tastes will change, and so on. These losses can only be observed if adequate surpluses were generated in previous periods. Risk bearing must be acknowledged as a cost since what is uncertain is not whether they will occur, but when they will occur.

Market Intelligence

As for as is possible marketing decisions should be based on sound information. The process of collecting, interpreting, and disseminating information relevant to marketing decisions is known as market intelligence. The role of market intelligence is to reduce the level of risk in decision making. Through market intelligence the seller finds out what the customer needs and wants. The alternative is to find out through sales, or the lack of them.

Marketing research helps establish what products are right for the market, which channels of distribution are most appropriate, how best to promote products and what prices are acceptable to the market. As with other marketing functions, intelligence gathering can be carried out by the seller or another party such as a government agency, the ministry of agriculture and food, or some other specialist organisation. What is important is that it is carried out.

Agriculture and the Food Industry

The link between agriculture and food continually evolves. In primitive societies, the farmer and consumer were either the same family or close neighbours who bartered their products, but as societies develop other linkages are added. Commodity traders, processors, manufacturers who convert produce into food items and retailers, among others, are interposed between the producer and consumer. A more recently introduced link into the chain is the scientist.

Scientists as breeders, plant biologists, nutritionists and chemists have made an immeasurable contribution to the development of agricultural production and food manufacture over the past 50 years. It would appear that we have passed through the age of machines in agriculture, and the age of chemicals, on to the age of biotechnology in agriculture. Biotechnology has great potential for the developing countries since it is likely to be less capital intensive and more research and know-how intensive.

Thus its benefits can flow faster into the poorer countries who do not have the capital. Therefore its impact could be faster, more widespread and more significant. As the link between food and agriculture continues to evolve, we see the emergence of an agribusiness i.e. where agriculture and food become a continuum. Multinational companies like Cargill, Brooke Bond Liebig, and Del Monte are examples of vertically integrated organisations with links all the way through from agricultural production to retailing.

There is a line of argument which says that it makes sense that those who are closest should the consumer should assess his/her needs and interpret them back to the primary producer. As disposable incomes increase, the food industry will increase the quality and diversity of the products it produces. Food manufacturers will have particular expectations of agriculture as a supplier of their raw materials, including:

Quality

To build a profitable business, food manufacturers seek to establish a preference for their products by differentiating those products in some way which is meaningful to consumers. Then, in order to enable consumers to recognise the differentiated product, manufacturers brand that product. Manufacturers can then work on building consumer loyalty to these brands. Brand loyalty is normally only established by delivering high quality consistently.

As disposable incomes rise, the market tends to develop more sophisticated needs and the quality of the raw material becomes even more critical. Where agriculture is seeking to serve a food industry, that itself is seeking to meet these more sophisticated needs and wants, it can expect to face increasing emphasis on quality. Equally well, agriculture can expect to share in the better return for innovative improvements in quality.

Cost

Next to quality will come cost. With an increased capability to search the world for raw materials, the food industry is able to find the lowest cost source for any given level of quality. For the food manufacturer, the country in which he/she manufactures, or markets, need no longer be the source of agricultural produce. Improved transportation and communications mean that the world is becoming his/her source of supply. This is a significant change in the competitive environment of agriculture which the farming community has to realise, because they have, hitherto, been largely concooned in their respective domestic markets.

Non-seasonality

Agricultural products were traditionally seasonal in their production and supply. Modern technology and husbandry practices mean that food manufacturers need not have their production schedules dictated by the seasons. Indeed, the capital intensive food industry cannot afford to incur the high costs of under utilising its capacity. This means that farmers will have to complete in terms of reducing seasonality or fitting into a pattern of social competitiveness.

Reliability

A manufacturer who has invested heavily in building up his brand will be very keen to get reliable supplies in terms of quality, timing and cost. Producers of agricultural produce will be increasingly judged on their reliability in all of these respects.

Processing

Ease of processing will become an increasingly important expectation of the food industry. Like all industries, reductions in the costs of capital equipment, wages and inventories are important objectives. For example, farmers who can deliver on the 'just-in-time' principle will contribute towards reducing a manufacturer's working capital and space requirements. Farmers who can do part of the secondary processing and/or performing functions such as the post harvest treatment of the crop or transporting will be adding another advantage. Crops that are specially bred or designed to facilitate processing are another type of advantage that the food industry could expect from agriculture. In short, the competitive advantage will rest with those able to add most value and can differentiate what they are offering from that of other suppliers.

Product Differentiation

In competitive brand marketing, the food industry has to innovate continuously to create new products that are different from and superior to existing ones of their own or competitors. The scope of innovation has traditionally been at the processing stage. Whilst this will continue to be an important area for innovation, manufacturers will increasingly tend to look for innovative changes in the agricultural produce itself. This may be in terms of novel tastes, improved texture, more attractive shapes, etc.

Health Aspects

We have already said that in the more sophisticated food markets, healthy eating can become a priority among consumers. Therefore, farmers will have to consider the health connotations of what they choose to grow. There are two aspects of health to be taken into account. First, consumers may be interested in the food itself i.e. low fat, low/no sugar or low/no salt. It would be a mistake to think that health issues are confined to the more sophisticated food markets or to the wealthier segments of the community.

Nutrition is important in all segments of the market. Even where the poor receive adequate amounts of food to fend off starvation, they are often malnourished. Thus farmers have to be concerned about the nutritional value of the produce they grow. Second, the consumer may be more, or equally, concerned about the food production methods i.e. the avoidance of chemicals like herbicides, pesticides etc. This may mean a change to the farmer's husbandry practices with implications for the costs of production. The consumer and the food industry will expect the farmer to produce without potentially dangerous chemicals, but at no extra cost to them. This will be another challenge for agriculture.

Agricultural and Food Marketing Enterprises

The principal component of any marketing system are the institutions and enterprises of which it is comprised. Three of the principal forms of enterprise to be found in developing countries are discussed in this section. These are: private companies, marketing boards and co-operatives.

Private Enterprise

Private enterprise has much to commend it, including a much higher level of financial independence from government than public enterprises. Moreover, private enterprise is able to adapt, rapidly, to changing circumstances and opportunities and is usually able to provide what consumers want at a lower cost than public enterprises.

Marketing Boards

Marketing boards are, in most instances a government agency and/or statutory organisation having the function of intervening in the marketing process, with a view to serving the cause of efficient and orderly marketing. Less frequently they are voluntary organisations established by farmers/ producers. Put another way, marketing boards tend to be born out of government policy rather than by consensus among commercial parties. This is especially true of Marketing boards in the tropics where their chief object is to improve the income of the smallholder, grower, and/or livestock farmer.

Marketing boards do not normally provide marketing services to large estates or plantations. Prior to the adoption of structural adjustment and market liberalisation in nearly all Marketing boards served as 'price stabilising boards'. Another characteristic of marketing boards is their focus on durable products. Marketing boards are normally given authority for 'controlled' or 'scheduled crops'.

In many countries fewer than 5 crops are controlled. These tend to be traditional crops like millet, sorghum, rice, maize, groundnuts and palm oil and 'colonial' crops such as cocoa, cotton, coffee, tea, tobacco and rubber. Some governments have opted for boards that control more than one crop. In some cases, the marketing board performs all of the marketing functions itself but in others it cooperates with private enterprise by, for example, hiring storage facilities or appointing local buying agents.

The effectiveness of a particular marketing board is often viewed in terms of three factors:-

- Its contribution to orderly and efficient marketing
- The reduction in the capacity of intermediaries to manipulate margins at the expense of producers and consumers
- The generation of producer-oriented monopoly power

In many cases the establishment of a marketing board was a reaction to situations where middlemen and/or foreign buyers were perceived to hold monopsonistic power over producers. Hence the role of the marketing boards is frequently articulated as being one of organising producers into monopolistic agencies with real countervailing power; to reduce inefficiencies due to unwarranted competition, and duplication of effort between intermediaries.

In theory at least, the marketing board contributes to orderly marketing by acting as an agent for improving marketing practices, as a market regulator and as a provider of facilitating services. The role of marketing boards in bringing about more efficient marketing is most often framed by policy makers in terms of modifying the market structure. That is, trying to make what is perceived to be an imperfect market structure more advantageous to producers.

Of course, in doing so, account ought to be taken of the effect on both consumers and other players within the marketing system. This is not always done and the question is begged whether a market structure which is organised to the principal benefit of one particular set of players is anything other than imperfect to the others. However, the argument in favour of giving producers real countervailing powers is strongest in situations in which the marketing system is characterised by a myriad of largely powerless producers and a relatively small number of powerful intermediaries.

In these circumstances, the price-makers are the middlemen and both producers and consumers are price-takers. One particular way that a marketing board may act to modify an existing market structure is to rationalise the system in an attempt to reduce inefficiencies seen to be caused by unwarranted competition and duplication of effort between intermediaries. For example, there may be duplication of transport, storage and processing facilities to the extent that capacity utilisation cannot rise to economic levels without extremely high charges to compensate. Marketing boards may try to rationalise the system through, for example, a system of licenses.

Buying Operations

Marketing boards would normally buy at fixed prices. Each season or year, the government sets the price for scheduled crops. In the case of tree crops, this price is announced before harvest and before planting or sowing in the case of annual crops. It is subsequently kept at the same level for a period of time: typically about 6 months. These procedures give some security to producers. Buying takes place at official buying points where there are either appropriate storage facilities for the produce, or transportation so that it can be moved before any significant deterioration in quality occurs. Clearly farmers are concerned that buying points should be conveniently located. However, maintaining an extensive network of buying points adds substantially to a marketing board's operating costs and so the interests of the two parties often conflict. One compromise is for the marketing board to operate mobile buying teams to supplement permanent buying points.

In some countries the buying points are staffed by board employees, but the costs of running the buying points and the associated transportation costs can become too high and some governments seek alternative solutions such as transferring buying points to local co-operatives, and/or by appointing licensed buying agents (LBAs). It is common in anglophone West Africa to have co-operatives operating as LBAs, in competition with private traders who are also LBAs.

The use of buying agents promises some degree of competition, which in view of the fixed prices, expresses itself in the secondary conditions, in particular better service. Selling operations of marketing boards: Some marketing boards, like grain boards, are concerned entirely with domestic consumer markets. These tend to be handling staple crops such as maize, millet and rice. Other boards are dealing exclusively with export markets and, therefore, industrial buyers. The two types of markets are quite different from one another and so therefore are the operations of the boards serving them.

A distinction is sometimes drawn between these two types of board by referring to Food Marketing Boards (FMBs) and Export Marketing Boards (EMBs). Among the major differences is the position of governments with regard to them. First, governments have no control over demand in export markets whereas they can, and do, exert control over demand within the domestic market. Second, since governments have to take account of the interests of domestic consumers of staple crops, they sometimes instruct FMBs to adjust their marketing strategies to meet social and/or political rather than commercial objectives. The interests of consumers in export markets are of no direct concern to the government of the exporting nation.

Selling Operations of EMBs

Some export markets are governed by commodity agreements such as the Sugar, Cocoa and International Coffee Agreement, but in the majority of cases they must operate within free or open markets where vigorous competition exists. EMBs tend to favour early sales. That is, they try to minimise the time period between buying and exports. This is sometimes termed a 'rapid evacuation' policy. It keeps storage and capital investment requirements to a minimum, since the burden of holding and financing stocks is carried by the recipient of the produce.

Most EMBs practice 'forward selling' which as the term itself suggests, means signing sales contracts well in advance of delivery. Sometimes it means selling the crops well in advance of their being harvested, or sometimes even before they are planted. The practice of 'export parity pricing' is prevalent among EMBs. This means that the producer price is calculated as a residual of the export price minus marketing costs. There is no particular motivation to minimise those marketing costs in such a system, since a major source of uncertainty for EMBs has always been the instability of prices in the open world markets. As EMBs cannot influence these prices, they tend to take the defensive approach of lobbying for low producer prices. In this way they hope to avoid a trading deficit when world prices fall.

Selling Operations of FMBs

In many developing countries the FMB's selling price is set by government. Concern for the welfare of consumers often encourages governments to set low prices. This means the gross trading margin of an FMB is often small. The margin is invariably a source of conflict between FMBs and the government. In its desire to please both consumers and farmers, government will often suppress the profit margin and insist upon the FMB reducing its outgoings. The government usually has the upperhand but since it has to bear any deficit it is a hollow victory. Consumers needs determine the timing of the release of stocks. Staple crops, usually have a fairly constant demand throughout the year, and FMBs have to bridge the usual, and considerable, interval between buying after harvest and staggered selling over the year. Stockholding is an important but expensive function of FMBs especially immediately after harvest when there is often insufficient storage space for the incoming produce.

Conversely, as the stocks are slowly released FMB stores are under capacity for much of the year. A common objective of FMBs is basic 'food security' in times of shortage. This policy makes a lot of political sense but commercially it presents difficulties. Working capital is required for a longer period, and, if after all there is no shortage, the FMB is left with decaying stocks. Nearly everywhere there is a 'dual marketing system', with a parallel market which allows farmers, traders and consumers to bypass the FMB.

In some countries the parallel market is permitted by the government. Where FMBs have been given a monopoly, parallel markets become black markets, suppression of which has proved impossible. Indeed whether the parallel market is permitted or forbidden, the FMBs have to reckon with its competition. Some boards do not fit easily into the two categories discussed so far. Produce such as groundnuts, sunflower seed oil and palm oil, have both domestic and export markets.

Marketing boards handling these products have been mainly been established in countries where a surplus for export exists. These boards are normally classified as export boards. However, there is always the possibility that domestic demand will increase to the point where it absorbs the export surplus, at which point the board becomes a domestic marketing board. On the whole the picture of marketing boards in the literature is a depressing one. They are largely portrayed as weak organisations which have achieved little success. There are however some outstanding success stories like the Zimbabwean Cotton Marketing Board (CMB) part of which is related belowa.

When setting out to evaluate the economic performance of marketing boards, it is all too easy to neglect to acknowledge that to a very great extent they are charged with achieving political as opposed to purely commercial objectives. Indeed policy makers often refer to them as 'instruments'. Those who readily identify the "mistakes" of marketing boards more often than not neglect to distinguish between those errors which could be rightly attributed to the boards' management, and therefore can be corrected by that management, and those lying outside the board itself. Some criticisms would best be addressed to those governing the activities of the board. For example marketing boards are frequently used, by governments, as instruments of national policy, including:

— the promotion of agricultural and rural development with social goals overriding commercial objectives

— as instruments of fiscal policy

— as a mechanism for containing urban wages through price restraint on staple foods

— as a device to encourage farmers to grow and sell more food and export crops, by pushing higher producer prices

— as a means of consolidating power by placing political appointees on to the Board.

Thus, many of the decisions and activities undertaken by marketing boards which adversely affect profits and cash flow are not the product of poor commercial judgement on the part of management but are attributable to individuals, outside of the boards themselves, who have goals that are entirely divorced from the efficient and effective operation of those boards.

Co-operative Enterprise in Agriculture and Food Sectors

The co-operative enterprise has its origins in the 19th century and has become one of the most ubiquitous examples forms of business/economic enterprise. Co-operatives exist in all countries of the world and operate under diverse political systems: from communism to capitalism. The majority of these co-operatives are, through their national apex organisations, ultimately in membership of the International Co-operative Alliance (ICA), the representative world body of co-operatives of all types.

The motivation to form co-operatives has three particular aspects:

- — the need for protection against exploitation by economic forces too strong for the individual to withstand alone
- — the impulse for self-improvement by making the best use of often scarce resources
- — the concern to secure the best possible return from whatever from of economic activity within which the individual engages whether as a producer, intermediary or consumer.

It is the belief that each of these aspirations can most advantageously be pursued and secured in concert with like-minded people that provides the stimulus to co-operative action. The underpinning principles with are those of self-help, voluntary participation, equity, democracy, and a common bond of common need and purpose. The cohesion of the group is maintained by ensuring that individual members cannot secure power or gain advantages at the expense of the others.

Co-operatives reward participation in the co-operative venture rather than rewarding capital Self-interest is a primary motivator in co-operative enterprises, with economic gain being the primary objective. In these respects, co-operatives differ little from capitalistic enterprises; self-interest is simply pursued in a different way from the capitalist enterprise. Thus, the rate of interest paid on share capital is fixed and limited, and not subject to variation according to the amount of profit made. Secondly the use and distribution of surplus is restricted to one or more of the following purposes:

- — allocation to reserves, where it becomes collectively-owned capital and is thereafter non-distributable
- — for use on, or donation to, common-good, community project
- — distribution to members in proportion to the trade each member has done with the co-operative. In other words, the distribution is made not in relation to capital held, but by declaring a bonus or dividend per cash unit of trade done

Structure and Organisation of Co-operatives

There are two principal forms of co-operative organisations: primary co-operatives and secondary co-operatives. The basic unit in the co-operative systems is the primary co-operative. A primary co-operative is one in which the shareholder are individuals; each of them having an equal share in its control.

Primary Co-operatives

The General Meeting of Members makes policy and through this meeting members exercise control. In most countries there is a legal requirement to hold an Annual General Meeting which has the particular responsibilities of receiving and deciding upon an audited statement of account, deciding how any surplus shall be used and distributed, and of electing a committee.

The General Meeting of Members delegates the operational control of the co-operative to a management committee, which controls the works of the co-operative on behalf of the members. One member of this committee is elected chairman or president. A manager is appointed by the management committee as the chief administrative officer of the co-operative. He/she is responsible to the committee for the day-to-day control of the business. In small co-operatives he/she may be a member elected to do the work without pay.

Secondary Co-operatives

Secondary co-operatives (also variously described as "union" or "federal" co-operatives) can be organised for many different purposes. It is quite possible, and quite common, for a primary co-operative to be a member of several secondary co-operatives, depending on its needs and the local co-operative structure.

Through the device of federation, co-operatives are able to organise very large-scale business operations at the national—or even international—level without detriment to the democratic control of the primary co-operatives by their own members. The secondary co-operative can, because of its larger volume of business or its wider representational base, undertake functions, provide services, and make representations, which would be beyond the capacity of all but the very largest primary co-operatives.

Secondary co-operatives are a from of vertical integration providing the opportunity for economies of scale, scope for development and improved administration. Secondary co-operatives can in turn form other secondary co-operatives—sometimes called tertiary co-operatives. In many countries there is one apex federation representative of all other co-operatives in the country and providing, at the national level, representative, advisory and professional services to the co-operative movement as a whole. These national co-operatives can then be affiliated to international organisations such as the International Co-operative Alliance.

Control and Management of Co-operatives

The control and management of secondary co-operatives is similar in form to that of primary co-operatives. The share holding members—the primary co-operatives—exercise policy control through the General Meeting and elect a management committee to act on their behalf. The management committee in turn appoints a chief officer to manage the operation under its direction. The bye-laws of secondary co-operatives, as with the primaries, set down the organisational rules and procedures and are subject to the approval of the responsible local authority.

The operating surplus of a secondary is also used and distributed following the same principles as a primary co-operative. The federal co-operative can tend to become the masters of their member co-operatives rather than their servants. This situation can arise two reasons. Secondary co-operatives engaged in manufacture and trade can usually only operate efficiently given a high level of integration between their operations and those of their members.

This requires a commensurate high level of discipline or some from of contractual compulsion. Secondly, the operational size and volume of trade of secondaries can be such, compared to individual primaries, that there is a strong tendency for them to behave as the dominant partner in the relationship. It is a tendency that has to be monitored and, where necessary, checked. The secondary co-operative has as its chief obligation, the provision of services to member co-operatives.

The potential of co-operatives is immense. Co-operatives appear well suited to the economic, social and institutional needs of development in the rural economy. Co-operatives can provide the mechanism to organise and mobilise people for self-help action in providing the services they require as a farming and rural community. As self-administered rural institutions, co-operatives have the capacity to reflect, and to respond to the needs of their members; and, at the same time, to help foster attitudes of self-reliance and self-confidence within a framework of mutual aspirations and mutual action.

In the delivery of services to their farmer-members they can provide an essential support to the development objectives of both the farmers themselves, and of national development policy. As business organisations co-operatives also have the capacity to act directly as development agencies. In their steady accumulation of business assets, the expanding range of their services, the acquisition and use of management skills, the employment of staff, they are involved in a positive and measurable development function.

Moreover, the flexibility of cò-operative organisation, for example through the potential of secondary co-operatives, offers opportunities for collective action in the development of agro-industrial enterprise to help support and strengthen local initiatives, and to give a further boost to rural development. There are few countries where co-operatives are not recognised as potentially important agencies of development.

Weakness of Co-operatives

Unfortunately, the potential of co-operatives, and the extent of their development, has, in many cases, fallen for short of expectations. Low standards of performance, bad management, financial failure, corruption and misuse of funds, use of co-operatives for political ends, have been common features of co-operative enterprise in many countries.

As a consequence, a great deal of understandable criticism has been levelled at the co-operative system, and many, including some members, have become cynical as to its ability to play an effective role in the development process. There are a number of problems which inhibit co-operative development and adversely affect performance, the more important of which are discussed below.

Realism of Objectives

Commitment and purpose are two important ingredients in motivation. Achievement of purpose is equally important. Objectives are expressions of purpose and expectation. To serve as motivators and guides to action they have to be attainable. The resources available have to be adequate to achievement of the objectives, and aspirations must be matched to ability. Neither members nor others should expect too much of co-operatives, including expecting them to expand too quickly.

Most agricultural co-operatives in developing countries operate in commercial circumstances which any form of business enterprise would find difficult. Like their farmer-members, co-operatives have to operate in very marginal conditions. Their members are usually poor, often subsistence, farmers. High operating costs, low margins, relatively low turnovers, narrow stock inventories, seasonal trading patterns, exposure to the consequences of crop failure, high credit risk, fluctuating demand, are all familiar aspects of trading in such circumstances.

Indeed, were it not so, it could be expected that private enterprise would have moved in to exploit a profitable market. It is not uncommon for co-operatives to be introduced to provide essential services because other agencies have either failed, or refused, to do so. Expecting too much of co-operatives is one fault, expecting too much too quickly is another. The mistake is frequently made that once a co-operative appears to be reasonably well established, injection of loan capital from some external source will permit it to rapidly expand its services.

Such hasty injection of loan capital can strain management resources, encourage unwise risk-taking, weaken financial judgement, lead to overstocked inventories and promote loss-making enterprise. Co-operatives ought to be allowed to develop at a pace commensurate with the ability of members to manage, control and finance the development. They should be permitted to expand steadily like any other successful business enterprise, finding the resources to do so largely from surpluses made in their own trading operations. Business capacity should not be strained, for example, to meet the objectives of a government development policy. Revolution rather than evolution, will only prove detrimental to both the viability of the co-operative and to the attainment of the policy objectives.

Co-operative Purposes

Economic success is basic to the achievement of co-operative purpose for, in the long run, unprofitable enterprises cannot be sustained. However, co-operatives are constrained in the extent to which they can mimic the objectives and practices of capitalist enterprise without abandoning the fundamental values of the co-operative movement. For example, in the pursuit of business growth there can be a strong temptation to weaken member control and concede greater control to professional management, to make the creation of profit a paramount consideration, and to ignore the concepts of equity and fair dealing.

The creation of collectively-owned capital by reinvestment of profits is a highly important and desirable practice, but has its disadvantages in that if the element of members' share capital as a proportion of the total capital structure becomes so insignificant that professional management can afford to ignore it and so ignore member control in making policy decisions. The outcome is an enterprise largely indistinguishable, except in name, from a capitalist enterprise. Misuse of co-operatives to pursue political objectives: Attempts to divert the purpose and resources of co-operatives to the support of particular political objectives adversely affects the co-operative movement.

Factional dissension among the group distracts it from the achievement of its economic objectives. Members' meetings can become political forums devoted to the advocacy of opposing views. In these circumstances many members can become disenchanted and lose interest, making it easy for a minority group to take control and to attempt to run the co-operative to serve its own ends. Co-operative principles require that membership should not be assumed to imply either political commitment or obligation.

Co-operative systems organised and tightly controlled by governments as instruments of state economic policy are rarely conducive to the development of democratically-controlled, member-owned co-operatives. They are created to serve the objectives of politicians and planners; objectives which may or may not coincide with those of the members who have little effective control of the enterprise.

Management Skills

There has been a tendency to argue that a major cause of co-operative failure is the constraint imposed on the exercise of management skills and authority by the democratic nature of the enterprise. That being so, it is suggested that the authority of the General Meeting ought to be curtailed, leaving committees and managers to get on with the job of management. However, to do so would deny the purpose of the enterprise that being to enable people to run their own business. The solution lies in increasing and improving the level of member participation, not restricting it.

Moreover, the standard of management within co-operatives is often inherently poor. As has already been said, co-operatives often come into being in markets and geographical areas considered as marginal in terms of profit potential by most other forms of commercial business enterprise. This being the case, the salaries, working conditions and work location that they are able to offer fail to attract top quality managers.

Selling Arrangements

A principal policy question in co-operatives is the procedure to be used in selling members' produce. The alternatives are: outright purchase from members, or sale on commission.

Outright Purchase from Members

In this case members are paid for their produce, at prices fixed by the co-operative, at the time of delivery, and the co-operative takes title to the produce. The co-operative then resells the produce at the most advantageous terms it can secure. Profits made on the transaction will be used first to meet the operating expenses, any surplus balance being used or distributed by decision of the General Meeting. This approach requires the co-operative to have high levels of funds available.

Since, in the case of seasonal crops, a lot of produce is being offered within the immediate post harvest period, a serious adverse cash flow situation can arise. This can be alleviated by a two-stage payment system whereby members are paid part of the sale price at the time of delivery, and the balance after the co-operative has resold the produce. The main objection to outright purchase is that the co-operative carries all of the post harvest risks including: fall-off in demand, price fluctuation, reduction of produce value due to down-grading, deterioration giving rise to loss of quality and so value, failure of transport arrangements, spoilage, fire and theft. Some of these can be covered by insurance but most cannot.

Generally, this method is only acceptable where the risks incurred are limited and can be reasonably well assessed. For example, where forward contracts have been negotiated. These risks being taken into account, outright purchase has the advantage of permitting the co-operative to add value to the crop and thereby add to the profits of its members. There are three principal ways in which a co-operative might add value to the commodity.

— Produce can be stored for sale at a later date when prices have improved

— Value can be added through primary processing of the crop. Cotton ginning is a good example of relatively simple and inexpensive process which is best done close to the fields. The value of baled ginned cotton, is normally considerably more than the sum of the value of the raw cotton plus the cost of ginning. And there is the additional value of the cotton seed

— Opportunity for adding value exists in the packing and presentation of the crop, or in the case of livestock, improvement in condition or quality before sale. Graded, washed and well packed fruits and vegetables can attract wider markets and premium prices.

There is a caveat which ought to be added. Whilst price advantages gained by adding value are of direct benefit both to the co-operative as a whole and to individual members, the additional investment needed to capture the additional return, can be prohibitive. Apart from the risks incurred, outright purchase, storage, packing, processing, transportation, marketing etc., require substantial financing. Moreover, these more complicated operations call for a high level of management skill and judgement, which is frequently a scarce resource.

Sale on Commission

This far simpler, virtually risk-free, operation leaves the co-operative as the producers' agent with no legal title to the goods. All attendant risks therefore remain with the individual producers. The co-operative collects produce from members and sells in the most advantageous markets. It then deducts a commission at a previously agreed rate from the sale price. The co-operative meets the cost of its expenses from its commission income. With the sale-on-commission system the co-operative avoids the need to finance crop buying and it minimises its risks.

In addition, much simpler operating procedures are required and expenditure can be more accurately matched to anticipated income. The main disadvantage of sale-on-commission is that neither the member nor the co-operative is able to exploit possible price improvement. Another is the possible delays in the producer receiving cash for his crop. No payment will be made by a co-operative until it has been paid by the customer. Apart from the time taken in an 'open market' for crops to be sold, it is by no means unknown for parastatal agencies to be dilatory in paying-out for produce received from co-operatives.

References

Bird, E. R., G.L. Bultena, and J.C. Gardner (Eds.)., *Planting The Future: Developing an Agriculture that Sustains Land and Community*, Walthill, Nebraska: Center for Rural Affairs, 1995.

Feenstra, G., "Local food systems and sustainable communities," *American Journal of Alternative Agriculture* (12)1: 28-36, 1997.

Koc, M. and K. Dahlberg., "The restructuring of food systems: trends, research, and policy issues," *Agriculture and Human Values* 16(2): 109-116, 1999.

Maretzki, A. and C. Anderson (project co-directors)., *The Northeast Network: Food, Agriculture, and Health Policy Education*, Ithaca, New York: Cornell University, 1991.

9

Agricultural Production and Market Needs

Most farmers are naturally conservative and will be reluctant to go into new enterprises, because they involve risk. New crops or the introduction of new technologies or production techniques should, therefore, initially be undertaken on a small-scale trial basis.

Pre-production Issues

Growers need advice on which crops to grow and what market opportunities they can target. While the final decision must always be that of the farmers, you should be able to help them plan their production. Although production issues, such as labour availability and crop rotations, have to be taken into account, the key factor affecting production decisions is that production must be market-oriented. This means producing products for which there is a demand and which farmers can grow profitably.

Crop Selection

Crop selection should be based on the likely net returns of the major alternative agricultural enterprises. These calculations will establish which products are likely to be the most profitable. They can be discussed with farmers. Market research should have shown which local products are likely to be most successful in terms of cost, quality or seasonality, compared with products from other areas. The research should also have shown which varieties are favoured and the best time to supply them. These findings need to be converted into practical recommendations for farmers, covering such issues as:

- — varieties favoured by the market;
- — sowing dates. Whether to avoid times of oversupply;
- — other techniques to extend production into high-priced periods, such as using late or early varieties, transplanting, or using polythene tunnels or irrigation;
- — techniques to improve quality, such as optimum fertilisation, crop protection, pruning, irrigation, and weather protection.

Table 1 sets out a summary of the comparative costs and returns of three different crops. Although Crop C returns the highest sales, its profitability is less than for

Crops A and B. Farmers should be aware of the difference between gross returns (i.e. the value of sales) and net returns (i.e. the value of sales after deduction of costs). They must consider likely net returns when planning what to produce.

Table 1. Selecting crops to grow

	Crop		
	A	B	C
Expected sales from 1 ha	3 000	2 000	4 000
Costs			
Production	1 000	500	2 000
Marketing	1 000	500	1 500
Net return	1 000	1 000	500
Select crop	Yes	Yes	No

Selection of Crops

It is advisable for farmers to achieve a balance between growing a wide range of crops and concentrating on those products where they have the most advantage. Producing a range of crops reduces the impact of a possible production or market failure for one crop. For example, if farmers grow only potatoes and their crops are affected by Potato Blight, they will earn nothing. However, if they grow two or three other crops and have successful harvests they will be less affected by the potato disease.

Growing many different crops can cause problems. This is because the farmer is unlikely to have the necessary expertise in all the crops and the smaller volumes of each produced makes marketing more difficult. Very often, growers will have preferences for crops that they feel comfortable growing and/or that grow well on their land. As agriculture becomes more developed, farming become more specialised.

Individual farmers, such as those supplying supermarkets or agroprocessors, generally have to concentrate on relatively few crops. Although growers may become more skilled, they can rarely be experts in more than three or four crops. The most profitable crops are often the most risky. It is useful to have a cropping system in which risky crops are balanced against crops that can be relied upon.

An example might be to grow one or two large-volume vegetable crops, such as potatoes and onions, together with higher priced products such as capsicum and leafy vegetables or salads. Small farms often have more labour available per hectare than do large farms and they can take advantage of this by concentrating on growing labour-intensive crops. These are crops that cannot be harvested mechanically and may also require transplanting, pruning, hand weeding and harvesting on several occasions.

Farm Investments

Farmers are often tempted to make investments that are expensive but do not improve significantly the financial viability of their farm. This needs to be avoided. Decisions should have as priorities investments that can: assure an income, through reducing risk; increase incomes by improving prices; improve incomes by increasing yields; reduce production costs; or generate additional income.

Investments that can improve yield stability and hence reduce risks include:

— those that protect against pests and diseases, such as sprays and a sprayer;

— irrigation and other technology that reduces the adverse effects of the weather.

Such investments are particularly important in horticulture because when yields are low as a result of poor weather or pests, prices rise significantly. The grower whose yields are least affected makes the most profit.

Investments that improve prices include:

— technology for 'off-season' production, such as polythene tunnels and improved transplant technology;

— investments made directly in improving marketing, such as grading facilities, on-farm storage, pick-up trucks to transport produce and telephones to improve market communication;

— investments that improve the quality of produce, (e.g. irrigation, crop protection or high-quality planting material).

Investments that increase yields are:

— irrigation equipment;

— scientific fertiliser usage;

— high quality planting material.

Investments that save on production costs include:

— herbicides and mechanical hoes, which can cut down on labour for weeding.

Investments that can create additional income are:

— processing equipment to add value to products;

— transport, to take products to new markets.

Supply of Input

The supply of inputs can have a direct effect on profitability.

Planting material is particularly important. Consumers can have strong preferences for particular varieties, colours and tastes. For example, in much of the Middle and Near East there is a preference for plum tomatoes. Product colour can also be important, e.g. red apples are sometimes preferred to green or golden varieties.

Growers' returns can be improved by ensuring the supply of the correct planting material, and part of your role can be to discuss with nurseries and seed suppliers the varieties they should stock. Pest and disease damage will seriously reduce a crop's price and its potential shelf life. Sometimes these problems can be solved by the correct crop protection practices. In India, spray programmes were introduced to control scab disease on apples in Kashmir. A crucial step in the successful introduction of this programme was ensuring that agricultural chemical shops had the recommended materials available.

Critical Production Constraints

Critical production constraints are often shortage of working capital and funds for investment purposes. Potential sources of funds, apart from the farmer's own resources, can be divided into two: formal and informal.

Formal Sources

These are mainly banks and other types of financial institutions such as credit unions, savings and credit cooperatives and various types of microfinance organisations. They offer different types of loan products and normally apply market-based interest rates. In the case of banks, they require specific types of collateral in order to grant loans and credits, which, together with often lengthy loan procedures, tend to seriously limit most farmers' access.

Providing banks with cost-of-production budgets, detailed information on likely returns and other relevant information about the activity at the time of the loan request will enable them to assess more accurately the risk involved and may shorten the procedures. Credit unions and similar types of member-owned financial institutions are, by their nature, more open to farmers requiring smaller production-oriented loans. But, similar to microfinance institutions, they often face problems in providing large numbers of loans, due to limited funds.

Financial institutions have different rules as to what loan purposes they can cover. Some will only provide input loans whilst others may also offer loans to meet labour costs. In rare cases banks offer marketing loans to farmers. Such loans are needed to cover the cost of harvesting, transport, packaging and even storage of crops. The advantage of such loans is that growers are not restricted in who they sell to, which is the case when they borrow from traders.

Where growers are under contract to supply produce to an agribusiness, production loans based on the hypothetical value of the crop can be made. These are called hypothecated loans. Under a loan hypothecation scheme the bank, or the processor, advances a proportion of the expected income as production credit, without seeking any additional security. Loan recovery can be made by the agribusiness, which deducts the outstanding debt from the grower's income.

Unfortunately, such arrangements sometimes break down when the farmer decides to sell the crop to someone else who offers a higher price, thus not honouring the initial agreement. In such situations you should discuss with farmers the benefits of long-term reliable outlets for their products, and point out that such benefits may be lost if they seek short-term price advantages in this way.

Informal Credit

In many countries the availability of formal funds from financial institutions is very limited and farmers often have to depend on informal sources. Sources of informal credit include moneylenders, family members, friends, traders and input suppliers. Informal loans are often made on the basis of close family links or mutual trust and are free of time-consuming bureaucracy.

In some countries, the most important source of informal credit is often the trader. The role of traders as sources of loans is much misunderstood. Traders provide credit to farmers to secure future supply and, therefore, income. The true costs of such credit to farmers are difficult to determine. Common criticisms are that high interest rates are charged and that growers who have borrowed money are forced into selling their produce at low prices.

In some cases this is no doubt true and, in the case of poor prices, farmers cannot switch to another trader or wholesaler. However, the opposite can also apply as farmers, knowing the trader has to buy from them, pay less attention to produce quality. Traders do not normally lend money to farmers in order to exploit them. They lend money in order to ensure that farmers will produce enough of a crop to meet the demand. Loans by traders are recovered simply by deducting the money advanced from value of the sales.

Transport

Without adequate access to transport, farmers are at a disadvantage. They are dependent on visiting buyers. With transport, growers have control over what market the product is transported to and are therefore potentially in a far stronger marketing position. Improved efficiency in transport, e.g. larger loads, quicker turnaround times and better utilisation of capacities, are all proven methods of lowering costs and opening new market opportunities. You can have an important role in helping growers to gain access to transport. This could involve introducing farmers to transporters, planning a collection route and helping organise the initial services.

Growers who do not sell to visiting traders usually have to transport produce to market in hired lorries or pick-ups. The grower generally has to either pay a fixed price for the hire of the truck, no matter how little is transported, or is charged by the box or sack. Both systems can be inefficient. If the lorry is not fully loaded the costs per unit (e.g. box, bag) go up. Cost savings can be achieved by encouraging farmers to share transport. You could help them to assemble produce on a particular day of the week at specified collection points.

When transport is charged by the unit, transporters will generally overload lorries in order to maximise their income. By assembling produce at one point so as to guarantee full loads, a fixed price for the lorry can be negotiated and the growers can themselves ensure that the transport is not overloaded, and their produce is not damaged. It is difficult to resist the temptation to try to squeeze extra containers into a vehicle and this is often done by traders, as well as by farmers. However, the benefits in terms of reduced transport costs are usually outweighed by losses in terms of damaged produce.

Generally, the larger the individual load the cheaper the unit cost of transport. For example, in Pakistan, an 8-tonne lorry travelling from northern Punjab to Karachi used to cost 4 000 rupees while a 20-tonne articulated lorry cost 7 000 rupees for the same trip.

Farmers who are able to make investments in transport mainly buy small pick-up trucks. The unit costs of transport are therefore higher than when hiring space in a larger lorry, but such pick-up trucks do offer farmers the possibility to:

- transport produce to the market immediately after harvest;
- supply transport services to neighbouring growers;
- take produce for sale to farmers' markets;
- make direct sales to retailers and caterers.

Production Possibilities

Production possibilities are often underdeveloped because buyers and sellers are unaware of each other's existence. A buyer may be unaware of the products produced by farmers of a particular area or of the products they could produce if a market were available. A group of farmers may sell produce individually to a small-scale local buyer, unaware that a wholesaler is prepared to pay better prices if sufficient volume can be supplied. As noted earlier, you should draw up a list of the buyers, the agribusinesses and the transporters in your area.

This list would need to provide contact names and addresses and explain the products they buy or services they provide. It is important that negotiations are carried on directly between the farmers and the buyers. You can help farmers by providing them with some information in advance, such as terms of business of traders, likely range of prices and other companies worth contacting, but you should not be involved in reaching agreements on their behalf. Box 6 sets out ways that you can help with business introductions and in supporting farmers to overcome problems and set up new trading relationships.

Harvest and Post-harvest Practices

The main emphasis here is on the commercial implications of different harvest and post-harvest practices. The key issues are:

- — maintaining quality;
- — maximising shelf life;
- — supplying produce when and as the market demands it.

The main way that you can help improve post-harvest handling is by training farmers, both through practical training and by presentations. In the following pages the main ways in which post-harvest techniques can increase farmers' profits are set out.

Conditions of Harvesting

The timing, techniques and conditions of harvesting can significantly affect prices.

Harvesting and Prices

Harvesting early in the season can be carried out to take

advantage of opportunities for high prices, e.g. cabbage harvested as spring greens, young carrots sold in bunches, green plums and new potatoes. Taking advantage of these short-term market opportunities requires close links with the market.

Harvesting and Crop Maturity

The shelf life of the crop and its suitability for long-term storage is affected by the maturity of the crop at harvest. The optimum harvesting stage for most crops depends not only on the climate and distance to the market but also on the variety and the growing conditions. When distant markets are being investigated, experiments should be carried out to find the best maturity to harvest fruits. Send samples at different degrees of ripeness and assess which gives the best results. It may be necessary to call in expert assistance to identify whether long-term crop storage could significantly improve farmer incomes.

Harvesting and Quality

Growers often do not understand the effect of their harvesting and handling on the quality of the produce when it reaches the market. Once a fruit is plucked from a plant, or a root or leaf vegetable is harvested, it is cut off from its source of food and, particularly, water. The effects of poor treatment normally show themselves some days later, when the produce is being presented for sale or is in storage. This can often result in disputes, because farmers have sent to market what they consider to be good quality products but by the time these arrive at the market the trader sees produce that has deteriorated badly. An example of this comes from Tonga, in the South Pacific, which used to export capsicum (green pepper) to New Zealand.

When the fruit left Tonga they appeared to be in excellent condition but after four days in a ship they arrived in very poor condition. The problem was traced to the use of dirty knives for harvesting. Poor post-harvest handling leading to low quality produce has two effects; firstly the price is reduced and, secondly, the reputation of the production area is, over time, diminished. Improved harvesting and handling of produce will result in a product with better appearance and shelf life and thus better prices.

Harvesting Time

Ideally, harvesting should take place when the crop and the climate are coolest and the plant has the highest moisture content. This is in the early morning but other issues have to be taken into account. For example, labour and transport may not be available early in the morning. If transport is a problem the harvest should be rescheduled to avoid produce being left standing in the field for too long. Specific crops often have ideal harvest times. For example, citrus should not be picked until the dew is dry. The best time for harvesting mangoes is mid-morning, when the latex flow is at a minimum.

Containers

Bags or baskets attached to the waist of the picker enable both hands to remain free. The crop damage associated with moving sacks of produce through the field is thus reduced. When using bags it is preferable to be able to release the bottom so that the produce can be let out gently, rather than upending the bag. Containers must be emptied carefully to minimise drop heights and fruit-to-fruit damage.

Containers should be cleaned as often as possible. Using baskets or boxes with sharp or rough edges should either be avoided or the containers should be lined with paper or leaves. Damage is often caused by transferring produce from one container to another. If possible, produce should be harvested directly into the container in which it will be stored and/or transported.

Drying

Drying is used mainly on bulbs in order to extend shelf and storage life. Crops such as onions and garlic can be dried in the field over about six days, by being spread in a single layer. Alternatively, drying can take place under cover in stacked, shallow trays. The aim is to harden the outer scales and remove moisture from the neck of the bulb, in order to extend storage and marketing life. Most root crops respond to warm, moist conditions after harvest by thickening and hardening their skins. This provides protection against dehydration and infection. Wound healing occurs. This is called curing and it significantly improves storage life of products like potatoes and carrots.

Grading

Grading is carried out so that:

- — disease-free and blemish-free produce can be selected for long-term storage;
- — top-quality produce can be selected for transport to distant markets;
- — produce can be separated according to quality, ripeness, colour and size. Separated produce is packed into different containers to facilitate marketing to consumers with differing quality requirements.

Grading is sometimes carried out on the ground under the shade of a tree. This is both unhygienic and inefficient. Specialist grading areas or sheds are generally open-sided with tin or, preferably, thatched roofs to provide shade. Standing or sitting at tables enables people to grade quickly. Tables covered with polythene sheeting are easy to clean and the sheeting can be replaced cheaply. Lighting should be good. Tin roofs can be painted white to reflect heat, while water trickling down the outside of a shed helps reduce the heat inside the building.

Packaging Design

Good packaging design enhances the attractiveness of produce, enables it to be handled and marketed in convenient units, and helps to prevent mechanical damage.

Types of Mechanical Damage

The four main types of mechanical damage are cuts, compression bruises, impact damage and vibration rubbing.

— *Cuts*: Care in harvesting and handling will help eliminate cuts and wounds. Lining of packaging with paper or leaves can also prevent damage to the contents.

— *Compression bruises*: These can be reduced by using containers that are strong enough to withstand multiple stacking. The packaging materials need to be particularly strong at the vertical corners. The packaging should also be shallow enough to prevent the bottom layers of produce from being damaged by the weight of produce above. Cartons must not be overfilled or damage will be caused by the full weight of the pile of produce pushing down on the top layer of fruit or vegetables, causing the weight to be transmitted to the lower layers.

— *Impact damage*: Shocks in transport or dropping of containers can result in this kind of damage. Dropping may occur either because a package is small enough to be thrown or because it is too big to be easily handled. A packing unit should not exceed 50 kg as this is the maximum weight that can be easily handled. Package size specifications usually depend on the customers' requirements, although in many countries the supply of good packaging materials is limited and buyers may have to accept what is available.

— *Vibration rubbing*: This kind of damage generally occurs during transport. It can be significantly reduced by preventing the produce from moving within the packaging while, at the same time, ensuring that fruits or vegetables are not forced together. Fruits can be prevented from rubbing against one another by the use of cellular trays, individual wraps or cushioning pads. An example is the use of paper and straw to separate layers of apples. An alternative approach is for the container to be gently shaken, in order to settle the produce, with the space created then being filled.

Packaging

Packaging can be the single most expensive cost, as the calculation in Table 6 showed, particularly with nonreturnable containers made of wood or cardboard. The benefits of packaging must clearly justify the investment. Traders usually aim to minimise costs and are reluctant to invest in packaging unless the financial benefits are clear.

Five types of packaging materials are listed below.

— *Locally available natural materials* (e.g. wooden boxes or trays, baskets woven from bamboo or willow or cartons made from thin strips of wood or rushes). While use of local materials is normally recommended, overuse can have negative consequences for the environment. In northern India, for example, there have been problems of deforestation because of the use of trees for wooden boxes for apples.

— *Fibreboard/corrugated cardboard* are increasingly being used, particularly in developed countries.

— *Plastic crates* are expensive and generally have to be imported. They have the advantage of being reusable but a system needs to be in place for the containers to be returned to the farms to be refilled.

— *Bags and nets* are cheap but provide no protection from damage. They are used to package onions, garlic, cabbages and potatoes.

— *Plastic and paper* are often used as lining or wrapping for produce.

Packaging presentation: Attractive printing and brand names can add value to fresh produce but only in markets where consumers are wealthy and appreciate aesthetics and image. In the produce markets of the Arabian Gulf and Southeast Asia multicoloured printing is common because it helps to sell the produce and lift prices.

Storage

Produce can be stored for both short-term and long-term purposes. Short-term storage is mainly used to provide flexibility in marketing, or because buyers are not immediately available. Most horticultural crops are perishable and can only be stored for a few days. Only rarely is it worthwhile storing perishable crops to await higher prices, as storage will reduce quality and shelf life whilst adding to costs.

Storage is costly and, in most instances, when the produce is withdrawn from storage it has to compete in the market against much fresher produce. A few crops are adapted for long-term storage. These can be held in store well beyond the normal harvesting period. When they are eventually sold higher prices can usually be obtained and, by extending the marketing season, a larger volume of produce can be marketed. Often, the most successful stores are located in urban areas because:

- produce can be released rapidly onto the market when prices increase;
- refrigerated facilities in urban areas can also be used for a variety of products.

Refrigerated storage is expensive and can only be justified if it can be run profitably. This requires an adequate demand for storage, good management and a reliable supply of electricity. Shelf life can, however, be extended without investment in expensive storage equipment. The first priorities should be selecting high-quality produce, maintaining a high humidity and keeping produce in the shade. In the right conditions, with good management, ventilated stores can be extremely cost-effective, especially for potatoes and onions. Ideally they require cool temperatures at night.

Improving Handling, Grading and Packaging

Emphasis has been given here to improved handling, grading and packaging. Improved prices can result from the quality of an individual consignment. In the longer term, groups of farmers can obtain premium prices by establishing an identity and a reputation as consistently high-quality suppliers by:

— applying minimum grading specifications for a top-quality product;
— grading to this standard;
— agreeing on a name, symbol or 'brand' image, which can be printed on the packaging;
— agreeing that they will only send high-quality produce under the brand name;
— requiring all growers to mark branded packages with their own identification marks so that any produce which is below specification can be traced back to the culprit.

There are many examples of production areas that obtain premium prices because of their reputation for supplying quality produce, but it is important to remember that a reputation that takes years to establish can be quickly destroyed by one or two poor consignments.

References

Brklacich, Michael and others., "Forum: review and appraisal of concept of sustainable food production systems," *Environmental Management* 15(1) : 1-14. New York: Springer-Verlag, 14 p.

Doolittle, William E., "Agricultural change as an incremental process," *Annals of the Association of American Geographers* 74(1), 1984: 124-137, 13 p.

Engelman, Robert and Pamela LeRoy, *Conserving land : population and sustainable food production*, Washington, D.C.: Population Action International, 1995, 48 p.

Feath, Paul., "Evaluating agricultural policy and the sustainability of production systems: an economic framework," *Journal of Soil and Water* (March/April, 1993): 94-99, 1993.

Kaiser, Harry M. and Thomas E. Drennen., *Agricultural dimensions of global climate change*, Delray Beach, FL: St. Lucie Press, 1993. 311 p.

10

Product Management

Many enterprises take too myopic a view of what their product actually comprises and, therefore, their view of how it can be marketed is similarly myopic. We should think of a given product on three levels: the core product, the tangible product and the augmented product. The base level is the core benefit which, in essence, is what the customer really buys. It is productive to think of a product as merely the mechanism by which the benefit the customer is demanding is delivered. Thus, people do not buy toothpaste (the product), they buy confidence that their breath is inoffensive to others (the benefit); the farmer doesn't buy fertilizer, he buys extra grain in the store; a mother does not buy baby food, she demonstrates the virtues of a loving and conscientious mother, and a buyer of premium priced foods is not simply satisfying his/her hunger for food but also, perhaps, a hunger for status. Hence the need to know what the customer is buying and market those benefits, not products.

Care must be taken that any benefit that is marketed is valued by the potential consumer. Manilay relates how, in the Philippines, an improved milling machine which produced a better quality end product and reduced grain losses failed in the market place because broken and discoloured rice kernels were not perceived to be a problem by consumers, who were more interested in rice varieties and aromas. This example illustrates that it is the consumer and not the engineer, scientist or marketer who decides, in the market place, what is of benefit to him/her.

The core benefit has to be converted into a tangible product to become the carrier of the benefit. Corn oil, cotton shirts, poultry feeds, seed planters and meat pies are all tangible products. According to Kotler tangible products have as many as five characteristics: a quality level, features, styling, a brand name and packaging. These too can be marketed to potential customers if they differentiate the product from that of competitors, so long as this differentiation is both meaningful and valued by consumers.

Additional services and benefits might need to be offered to differentiate a product from that of competitors to give it a competitive edge. That is, an augmented product is offered. The cotton available to international buyers from the Zimbabwe Cotton Marketing Board is also available from other countries and suppliers. However, Zimbabwe's CMB have augmented their product with an advisory service to merchants and spinners which helps them choose the right cotton for a specific application.

Similarly, the agrochemical manufacturer who builds in a metering device into his product's packaging is augmenting his product; the tractor manufacturer/dealer who gives an extended warranty or performs a pre-delivery inspection is augmenting his product, and the food manufacturer who offers wholesalers/retailers a sale-or-return deal on products which they carry is augmenting the product offered.

Caterpillar's oil-analysis service is an interesting example of product augmentation. Owners of Caterpillar machines are encouraged to take periodic samples of oil from the machine's engine and to send this off to Caterpillar. The oil is subjected to chemical analysis and the incidence of certain elements, such as metal content, is plotted on a graph. Over successive samples, a picture of the condition of the engine can be built up. Engine breakdowns are invariably preceded by an upward step in the graph as the metal content of the oil increases substantially.

Customers are thus able to anticipate potentially serious engine damage and can respond by commissioning remedial maintenance before a vastly more expensive major engine overhaul becomes necessary. Caterpillar machines are expensive to purchase but the durability of the machine combined with the early-warning oil-analysis service serves to convince customers that the product will prove economic over the longer term. Thus we see that products can be marketed on several levels. If it is found that the product is perceived, by potential customers, to be similar to those of competitors at one level then the offensive differentiation can take place at another level. The key questions are whether the basis of our product differentiation is meaningful and valued by our prospective customers.

Product Mix

Single product organisations are, in practice, fairly rare. We have already encountered the product life cycle concept and this alone should warn of the dangers of relying upon a single product. One reason for the rarity of single product firms is the inherent seasonality of agricultural products be they inputs or outputs. Another major reason for offering a complementary range of products is to gain entry to the channels of distribution.

Most distributors will want to handle a product range rather than a single item. This is because the distributor's customers expect to be able to satisfy a number of their needs on the occasion of a single visit to the sales outlet. If the distributor does not carry a full product line, not only is a potential sale lost but the credibility of that distributor, as a source of knowledge on that product category and its applications, is called into question. Credibility as a source of information is particularly important where products are augmented by technical advice, as in the case of agricultural equipment, agrochemicals and other agricultural inputs. Hence, the more successful agribusinesses have a reasonably broad product portfolio.

A product mix is an assortment of types of products and product lines. A product line is a series of related products. For example, a dairy company might offer a product line of full fat milk, semi-skimmed milk and skimmed milk. The same dairy company might have a second, and distinct product line of yoghurts, plain yoghurt, vanilla flavoured yoghurt and yoghurt with nuts. Figure 1 illustrates the difference between a product line and a product mix.

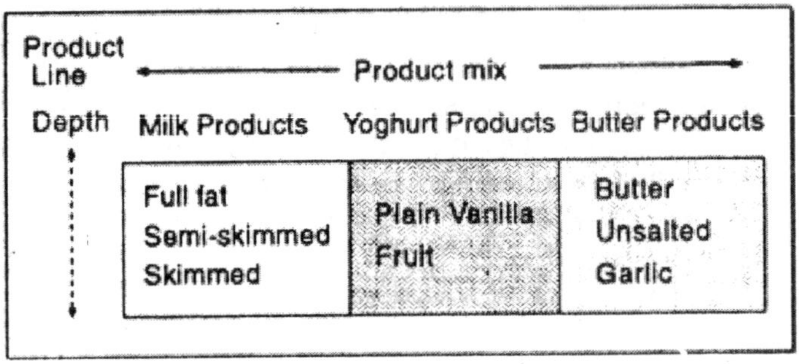

Figure 1. The product line and the product mix

The width of a product mix refers to how many different product lines an organisation carries (in this illustration there are three product lines). Product line depth indicates the number of product variations within a particular product line (here we have three product lines and three product variations within each).

Extending the Product Line

The decision as to whether a given product line should be extended is a strategic issue. There are several reasons why firms would consider adding to the number of product lines (breadth) and/or to the number of variants (depth) within a product mix. By extending the range of products offered, a company might gain entry to as new segment of the market. It may be necessary to attract distributors who are interested in offering a full product line, or the business may have spare productive capacity and wish to increase the contribution to fixed costs by increasing the level of capacity utilisation.

Alternatively, they may need to bring in products to support other product lines, or as part of their competitive strategy they want to fill gaps in the market which otherwise might give others a foothold in their market. Whatever the motivation for extending the product line or mix, it has to be recognised that supplying more products (or product variations) carries costs as well as opportunities. The organisation's inventories, and those of its distributors, will increase; there is added complexity in production scheduling and the costs of production/manufacturing, with larger stocks of raw materials and work-in-progress.

Rather than expanding its markets, the product additions merely cannabilise the sales of its own existing product lines. Moreover, rather than offering the consumer greater choice, a plethora of similar products could have the negative effect of causing customer confusion. Clearly, the product mix must be managed carefully. At any point, the product or marketing manager must know the sales (in volume and value terms) and profit for each product line and item. He/she must also be aware of the percentage of both sales and profits which each product contributes. Using techniques such as Lorenz curves, often reveals that a relatively small number of products, within the total product range, accounts for the larger proportion of both sales and profits.

Product Line Deletions

Adding new products to a company's portfolio is a positive and creative course of action and most marketing managers find this easier to do than deleting products from their range. There are many reasons for this, but perhaps foremost among them is the reluctance to prune products from the line whilst they make some, even if modest, level of profit/contribution. In the end, however, 'sick dogs' and 'problem children' will sap and organisation's resources. Quelch and Kenny cite the following costs of product line proliferation:

- — Fragmentation of the overall marketing effort and dilution of the brand image
- — Increased production complexity resulting from shorter production runs and more frequent line change overs
- — More errors in forecasting demand and increased logistics complexity, resulting in increased remnants and larger buffer inventories to avoid stockouts

— Increased supplier costs due to rush orders and the inability to buy the most economic quantities of raw materials and

— Distraction of the research and development group from new product development.

Where items within a product line no longer have a clear role, it is in the long term interests of the organisation to either harvest or divest themselves of these items. Techniques such as Lorenz curves and the Boston Matrixa can help identify products that ought to be removed from the product line.

Branding Products

According to the American Marketing Association a brandis "a name, term, sign, symbol or design, or a combination of them intended to encourage prospective customers to differentiate a producer's product(s) from those of competitors."

Murphy defines a brand as:

> "A trademark which ...comes into the mind of the consumer to embrace a particular and appealing set of values and attributes, both tangible and intangible. It is therefore much more than the product itself; it is much more than merely a label. To the consumer it represents a whole host of attributes and a credible guarantee of quality and origin. To the brand owner it is in effect an annuity, a guarantee of future cash flows."

Murphy views branding as the output of a commitment by management to invest in the development of an asset. In some parts of the world, established brands are appearing as assets on balance sheets and are being assessed for their profit earning capability. Branding can add value to a product and is, therefore, an important aspect of product management. For example, most farmers would perceive Monsanto's herbicide brand Roundup as a quality product from a reliable company; but the same chemical formulation in an unmarked drum is unlikely to gain the same level of farmer confidence. Branding can also provide the basis for non-price competition.

The initial decision is whether to brand or not. Historically, most unprocessed agricultural outputs have been sold as generic products i.e. unbranded. Agricultural product is frequently marketed as a commodity where within particular grade bands a product from one source is considered identical to that from another source. This is true, for instance, of black tea and green coffee beans. Blue Mountain Arabica from Kenya is a perfect substitute for Blue Mountain from Colombia, and vice versa. Similarly, the same grade of B.O.P. (Broken Orange Pekoe) from Sri Lanka and from India are ready substitutes for one another. Until relatively recently, most fruit and vegetables were largely unbranded.

The exceptions have been fruit and vegetables marketed by multinational companies like United Fruits with the Chiquita brand and Geest. Some country exporters such as South Africa (Cape brand) and Israel (Jaffa and Carmel brands) broke from tradition at an early stage and adopted a strategy. Recently there has been a remarkable increase in the interest in branding amongst other exporting countries. A few years ago, Algeria decided to brand their dates so that consumers could identify both the variety and the country of origin. Previously most of their date exports went to France where they were mixed with dates from other regions and branded by the French.

Advantages and Disadvantages of Branding

All of this raises several questions about the need to brand, the benefits of branding and the steps involved in branding a product. The truly marketing orientated organisation will be especially concerned with the question of how branding serves the consumer. Branding can help consumers in a number of ways.

Brand names tell the consumer something about the product's characteristics and assure them that if they buy the same brand they will get the same product characteristics each time. As the number of competing products increases branding can increase the shoppers' efficiency by helping them to differentiate between products and identify that which best meets their needs.

Brand names also help draw consumers' attention to new products which might meet, or better meet, their needs. Producers and suppliers can also benefit from branding their products. Branding makes it easier for a producer or seller to match his/her products to the customers' needs. For instance, if a food manufacturer produces three blends of instant coffee (1) 70% robusta, 30% arabica, (2) 80% robusta, 20% arabica, and (3) 85% robusta, 15% chicory, if each has a distinctive brand name it is easier for the buyer to indicate the nature of the product he/she wants.

The ultimate objective is to establish a measure of loyalty among consumers towards the brand. After all, a product will only prove profitable if a sizeable proportion of the market can be persuaded to repeatedly purchase it. A distinctive seller's brand name and trademark make it possible to legally protect unique product features. Branding also provides a basis for non-price competition by removing a product from the commodity category. Lastly, market segmentation and target marketing are made more effective because branding enables the producer to serve separate markets with separate products.

There are also potential disadvantages attached to branding, for both producers and consumers. In the case of the consumer, there are at least two possible disadvantages. These are:

— *Higher prices*: In most cases branded products carry higher retail prices than their generic equivalents. In part, the higher price is explained by the additional production costs and marketing expenditures incurred by the supplier in developing and supporting the brand. The higher price sometimes also carries a premium for the unique benefits and/or features of the brand. Whether or not these higher prices can be justified depends on the customer's perception of the added value he/she receives in return for the price premium.

— *Brand proliferation*: Whilst consumers generally like to have a degree of choice when buying products, does encourage a proliferation of products. There is a real danger that so many brands are on offer that the consumer becomes confused thus negating some of the benefits of branding mentioned previously, especially shopping efficiency aiding to product differentiation. The dangers of brand proliferation are only realised when the differences between brands are either marginal or are not meaningful to the consumer and yet, the supplier continues to support the brand rather than let market forces dictate that it ought to be deleted from the organisation's product portfolio.

The possible disadvantages of branding for manufacturers, producers or suppliers include;

— *Higher costs*: Branded products tend to require heavy promotional support and more stringent quality control to ensure the consistency of the brand. Moreover, both production and marketing costs are higher where several brands of a product type are offered rather than a single product. However, if the brand is truly distinctive and offers potential buyers benefits and/or features which they value, then additional costs can usually be recovered through premium pricing.

— *Adverse publicity*: The relationship between the product and the enterprise which produces and/or markets it is all the more apparent when that product is branded. Brands which fail in the market place can place a stigma on an organisation which makes distributors and consumers cautious about handling or purchasing new products/brands which that organisation subsequently launches. It is for this reason that pre-market testing must be all the more rigorous in the case of branded products.

Brand Management

There are some basic product characteristics which will help determine whether branding is feasible. First, it must be possible to identify at least one unique dimension in the product. This can be in the core benefit, the product features and/or in the augmented product. Moreover, these unique selling propositions must be meaningful to the target market. There is little point in seeking to brand a maize seed if the only distinguishing feature is that it is dyed blue, unless the market displays a penchant for blue maize seed. Second, it must be possible to consistently replicate the distinguishing characteristics of the brand.

For instance, if a cheese brand is sold on the basis of its sharp taste, due to the high acidity of the cheese, but the manufacturer's production processes cannot guarantee that exact same level of acidity in every batch, then the reputation of the brand will quickly suffer. The decisions to be made in brand management are many. The main ones having made the initial decision to brand the product there are then several other related decisions to make, the most important of which are:

Brand ownership: There are three possibilities. The product can carry a manufacturer's brand name, that of a middleman (often termed a private brand, a distributor's brand or a dealer's brand) or the manufacturer might put some of the product under his/her own name and some under that of a middleman.

The competition between middlemen and manufacturer brands can be intense. Middlemen usually work on the premise of contracting manufacturers with excess production capacity to supply own-label products, at relatively low prices. When selling, middlemen's own-labels are normally priced below that of the labels belonging to comparable manufacturer's brands. Where they exist, large scale retailers, such as supermarket chains, are sometimes able to demand that they be supplied with own-label products since they control limited shelf space. Many manufacturers, especially those new to a market and smaller operations, experience difficulty in getting access to the market throught the distribution channel.

Branding products for middlemen may be an appropriate market entry strategy for these smaller agribusinesses. However, the smaller scale manufacturer is only likely to be successful in supplying own-labels to middlemen who want to position their private label as a premium priced private brand because the unit production costs of smaller manufacturers and processors are usually too high for them to supply brands which can be priced to undercut the manufacturer brands of larger scale businesses.

Brand quality: When developing a brand, the manufacturer has to choose a quality level that will support the brand's position in the target market. Some markets are more quality conscious than others and even within the same market some consumers will prefer premium brands and others will choose economy brands.

Brand name strategy: Producers who brand their products also have to decide what brand name strategy to pursue. The choices include:

- — Individual brand names, e.g. Coca Cola, Nescafé, Johnny Walker Black Label, Roundup, Outspan.
- — A blanket family name for all products, e.g. Heinz, Bayer, Massey-Ferguson.
- — Company branding: trade name combined with individual product names, e.g. Nestlé Gold Grain, Nestlé Rice Krispies, Nestlé Raisin Brain.

If a company has a distinctive product with actual or protential sizeable demand it is probably best to develop a separate brand identity for each such product. Using a blanket family name reduces the costs of introducing the product because there is no need to create brand recognition or preference. Moreover, if the manufacturer's name is strong the product will achieve a certain level of immediate acceptance. When a company produces a range of quite different products it is best to use family brand names for each product line. Finally, some manufacturers elect to preface all brand names with the company name to benefit from the carry-over effect of an established and trusted corporate identity.

Brand positioning and repositioning: The position of a product in the market place is multidimensional in nature. For example, a food manufacturer could develop a milk-based drink which is fortified with vitamins. The product could be positioned in one of several markets. It could be promoted as an infant food, a health food or a food for those active in sport. Whichever market is selected, the product could be priced at the top, middle or bottom end of the market and it could be formulated as a powder, fresh or UHT milk, skimmed, semiskimmed or full fat.

Brand extension opportunities: A brand extension strategy is one where an already successful brand name is used to launch new or modified products. The American confectionery company Mars have enjoyed long running success with their Mars Bar. More recently they have launched a Mars Bar flavoured milk drink and a Mars Bar flavoured ice cream.

The Jaffa brand which was originally attached solely to oranges from Israel, and then later was extended to grapefruit, has more recently been used to gain consumer acceptance of a new fruit which is a cross between an orange and a grapefruit and branded Jaffa Sweetie. Both the Outspan and Jaffa brand names have been franchised to the food giant Gerber for use on a range of fruit juices.

Multitibranding: A multibrand strategy is one where the producer develops two or more brands in the same product category. This is useful in market segments where there is a good deal of brand switching among consumers. Moreover, a multibrand strategy creates healthy competition between brand managers within the organisation and each brand can be developed to present different attributes and appeals to the market place. However, there is always the danger of cannibalising is own sales. This means that a new brand gains market share primarily at the expense of the firm's own established brand(s) rather than from competitors' brands.

However well a brand is initially positioned in the market, it may be necessary to reposition it at some time. Competitors may introduce similar products or consumer preferences change. For instance, a maize biscuit may have been positioned as a food for all the family then repositioned as a highly nutritious food for growing children. It is sometimes better to reposition exiting products before incurring the risks and expense of launching new ones. In this way, the company can build upon existing brand recognition and consumer loyalty.

Among the desirable features of a brand name are that:

— It should suggest something about the product's benefits and qualities
— It should be easy to pronounce, recognise and remember
— It should be distinctive and not easy to confuse with others
— When exporting, it should translate easily into foreign languages.

Brand names communicate denotative and/or connotative meaning. Denotative meaning is the literal and explicit meaning of a name. Connotative meaning is the imagery which the brand name conjures up in the mind of the prospective buyer. The brand name Easi-Cook Rice is both denotative and connotative. It is suggestive of a product which gives maximum performance with minimum care and effort.

Kenya's Tusker beer carries a connotative brand name which suggests that the product has some of the characteristics of the elephants, e.g. strength, nobility, imposing and on nature. It remains the case, however, that no matter how good a product's brand name, it will not compensate for inadequacies in that product, but an unimaginative or inappropriate brand name can adversely affect the prospects of a good product.

Brand Loyalty Models

At least four levels, of brand loyalty may be distinguished:

— *Brand Loyal*: purchase sequence- A-A-A-A-A-A.

— *Divided Loyalty*: purchase sequence- A-B-A-B-A-B.

— *Unstable Loyalty*: purchase sequence- A-A-A-B-B-B.

— *No Loyalty*: purchase sequence- A-B-C-D-E-F.

Suppose research reveals that for some product a family purchased brands A, B, and C, in the following sequence:

A-B-A-A-B-A-A-C-A

The question arises as to how this purchase history can be modelled and what can be deduced about the family's future purchasing behaviour. If this, or any other purchase sequence is to be described and future brand choice predicted, some starting point is necessary. This starting point is commonly referred to as a state. A state can be defined in a number of ways. For example, it might be defined as a purchase, in this case brand A. Or, it might be defined as pairs of purchases, e.g., AB. Other definitions could also be used.

A brand loyalty model also requires some mechanism to describe the relations among states at different points in time. The connecting mechanisms that are most commonly used are transitional probabilities. Assume for example, that a family has the following purchase history: A-A-A-A-A-B-A-C-A-A. Given this past behaviour, it may be stated that the probability of the family buying brands A,B, or C on the next occasion are 0.6, 0.3 and 0.1 respectively.

Different assumptions can be made concerning the characteristics of the transitional probabilities. For example, it might be assumed that brand choice at any point in time is completely independent of brand choices in the past. Or it might be assumed that only the most recent purchase influences the next brand choice. Or again, the assumption could be made that the previous 2,3, or 4 purchases affect brand choice on the next buying occasion. Some assumption must also be made about the behaviour of transitional probabilities over time. For example, it could be assumed that the probabilities are constant or stationary from one state to the next (stationarity assumption). Conversely, it could be assumed that probabilities change over time.

Finally, it is necessary to make assumptions concerning the representativeness of the transitional probabilities among consumers comprising a market segment. That is, we have to take into account the degree of homogeneity/geneity within the segment. If we assume that all consumers in the segment have the same transitional probabilities then we have the homogeneity assumption and if we assume that they vary from one consumer to another we have the heterogeneity assumption.

In designing a brand loyalty model then, decisions need to be made concerning how states are defined, as well as the determinants of the connecting mechanisms (transitional probabilities) and their behaviour over time. The brand loyalty models most frequently in use can be differentiated primarily in terms of the assumptions which are made about each of these factors.

Markov Chain Analysis

Markov chain analysis is a basic extension of probability theory developed in 1907 by the Russian mathematician A.A. Markov was attempting to understand and predict the movement of gas particles in a container. Using the location of particles at one point in time (state 1) and the probabilities that the particles would remain stationary or move at subsequent states (transitional probabilities), Markov found that he could predict the concentration of gas particles at various points in time.

A general Markov chain, then, is a way of describing a phenomenon moving from one state to another. The process begins at one of the states with a given probability according to a given probability distribution and then moves to the next state according to transitional probabilities of the next state given the present state. Marketing researchers have come to recognise the potential of this model in predicting the movement of buyers from one brand to another. Indeed this model has become one of the most commonly used to describe and predict brand loyalty.

Consider 100 consumers buying any one of three brands, A, B, and C. Assume that in period 1,50 consumers bought brand A, 25 bought brand B and 25 purchased brand C. Assume that in period 2, of the 50 buyers of brand A in period 1, 25 repurchased brand A, 5 switched to brand B and the remaining 20 bought C. Similarly, of the 25 initial buyers of brand B in period 1, 5 switched to brand A in period 2, 15 bought brand B again and 5 switched to brand C. Of the 25 consumers buying brand C in period 1, 5 switched to A, 10 switched to B, and 10 repurchased C during period 2. If the number of buyers, for each brand, in period 1 is known, and the transition probabilities are also known, the number of buyers in period 2 can be determined. The number of purchasers of brand A in period 2 is calculated as follows:

— Buyers of brand A in period 2 = $50 \times .5 + 25 \times .20 + 25 \times .20 = 35$

— Buyers of brand B in period 2 = $50 \times .10 + 25 \times .60 + 25 \times .40 = 30$

— Buyers of brand C in period 2 = $50 \times .40 + 25 \times .20 + 25 \times .40 = 35$

By the end of the third period one of the basic characteristics of stationary first-order Markov chains has become apparent i.e. the percentage of buyers in each period will change. For example, the number of purchasers of brand B changed from 25 to 30 to 35.5 over the first three periods. If these calculations were continued then the purchasing level of a brand become smaller from period to period until, eventually, a steady state of the purchasing level for each brand is reached in the long run.

Higher-order Markov Chains

As we have seen, first-order Markov models assume that transition probabilities are affected only by the immediately preceding purchase. Since there is some evidence that purchases prior to the immediately preceding purchase may affect brand loyalty, higher-order Markov chains can be used. Higher-order models define as some series of purchases rather than as a single purchase.

Market analysts are not limited to second-order models. Third-order, fourth-order to n-th order Markov chain models can be built. Until relatively recently higher-order Markov chains were considered impractical because since the transitional matrices were intolerably large. For example, a 9 brand, third-order model would have 729 states! Thus, the amount of data required to estimate transition probabilities was unmanageable.

However, the computing power available to contemporary analysts has made the use of higher-order Markov chains a feasible technique for modelling brand loyalty. Having said this, there is little evidence that practicing marketing researchers have reassessed the potential of Markov chains. Certainly there are few published studies which have incorporated higher-order Markov chains. The reasons for this apparent lack of interest in the technique are not at all clear but it is not the case that it has been rejected on the basis of empirical evidence.

Packaging

McCarthy's original classification of the marketing mix into the 4 Ps product, price, promotion and place is constantly under review. Some authorities want to expand to a fifth P to include packaging, but most continue to view it as a component of product strategy. Coles and Beharrell give emphasis to the importance of packaging when they state that:

> "It is the package that communicates more to the consumer than the actual product, at the point of purchase where the consumer decides."

Whilst this comment was made in the context of consumer food products, it also has validity with respect to agricultural inputs. When the farmer visits the agricultural merchant it is the package which conveys the features, benefits, applications and, sometimes, quality of inputs such as seeds, agrochemicals, animal feeds, dairy hygiene and animal health products. There are four levels of packaging:

— Primary packaging: i.e. that which comes into direct contact with the product
— Secondary packaging: i.e. that containing the primary packaging
— Display packaging: e.g. crates/boxes, pallet, roll container and
— Shipping packaging: e.g. container.

Functions of Packaging

Protective function of packaging

Packaging provides physical protection for the product. The typical product is handled many times between production and consumption. Perishable produce has to be protected from excessive moisture, heat or cold, ultra violet light, pathological, physiological and/or mechanical damage in transit, storage or when awaiting purchase. In the case of horticultural produce, the demands on packaging can be great.

A package may have to facilitate both the rapid cooling of the contents from high field temperatures, for example under conditions of forced air cooling, and the maintenance of low storage or transit temperatures. It must allow removal of metabolic heat during storage and transport, and may have to contain the product throughout the ripening process, if it is a climacteric or ripening fruit. For effective ripening the product requires exposure to increased temperature in a uniform manner, and to ethylene gas. Such packaging must therefore have adequate ventilation capability, for effective warming and gassing.

Some commodities are highly sensitive to ethylene gas and hence need to avoid gas build-up in transit. In these cases the packaging must allow for effective air ventilation. A package may also have to protect the produce from moisture loss. Polyethylene liners, usually with perforations to allow gaseous exchange, are used for some commodities. Other commodities have special treatments which must be taken into account when designing the package, for example sulphur dioxide treatment of grapes, and in-pack use of ethylene absorbents. Another important function some packing provides relates to pilfering.

Packages have intentionally been designed oversized to make it more difficult for shoplifters to conceal products about their person. Packaging also serves to protect the consumer. Product tampering has forced many food companies to develop tamper resistant packages, many of which warn consumers not to purchase packs which have broken seals. Resealable packaging has been developed to preserve the product and keep it in good condition whilst it is in the process of being used. For example, Tetra Pak has recently developed resealable milk and fruit juice cartons.

Packaging-distribution Interface

All participants in the supply chains for agricultural and food products are interested in any contribution packaging can make to improving profitability and the efficiency of the physical distribution function Packaging design is capable of contributing to the improved performance of the supply chain in a variety of ways. By altering the shape and dimensions of the packaging more product can be displayed on retailers' shelves. The stacking strength of outer packaging can be increased so that warehouse space is optimised and other elements of the physical distribution system, such as roll cages, pallets, and transport containers, can be better utilised.

One can argue that packaging innovations are chiefly market-led only if the definition of the "market", relates to all parties in the marketing channel which the firm seeks to serve. It is vitally important that the aesthetic appeal and functional performance of packaging proves appropriate to customer needs. At the same time, the distribution channel also has exacting demands to make on packaging. Indeed, for distributors the packaging is the product and they seek characteristics which aid the distribution process.

Not unnaturally, members of the distribution channel are concerned with maximising operational efficiency and the contribution which packaging can make in reducing costs. Packaging that helps reduce costs by making handling easier and/or reducing handling. Coles and Beharrell have highlighted the advances made by the food packaging industry. They state, for example, that:

> "During the past five years the number of products in a supermarket has doubled on the same surface area."

The same authors add:

> "Outer packaging is being minimised for direct transfer of product from lorry to shelf display. The consequent requirement for increased quality of primary packaging also serves to present innovation opportunities."

It is true that these remarks were made in the context of the European food industry but they serve to underline the fact that the technology exists and since the companies involved in packaging tend to operate internationally that same packaging technology is available throughout the world.

Product packaging is frequently viewed as wasteful and an unnecessary expense for which the consumer, ultimately, pays. In fact, packaging can serve to add value to products. Coles and Beharrell cite the case of the company, Premier Brands, who redesigned their Typhoo tea box because the original carton was undermining the brand's image as a good quality, fresh product.

Research showed that the plastic overwrap made the box difficult to open; its thin gauge card allowed the box to easily deform, making it look shoddy and unattractive, and it leaked tea dust, creating a messy appearance and calling into question the freshness of the product. The company also discovered that most caddies hold approximately 50 tea bags whilst the box held 80 bags. The bags which had to remain in the box quickly went stale.

The redesigned carton was more rigid, with no film wrap, a perforated tear strip, better quality filter papers and foil sachets containing 40 tea bags. The labels and colour combinations were redesigned to improve their visual impact.

The package must be capable of performing under all the temperature and humidity conditions that are likely to be encountered by the produce as it passes through the channels of distribution. This means that to select or design appropriate packaging for particular products/produce, the chosen distribution channel and its environmental conditions must be thoroughly described and understood.

Packaging and product differentiation

Product packaging also has a role in helping differentiate products where there are a large number of brands competing in the same market segment. Distinctive product packaging, be it in the form of shape, size, colouring, materials and/or print, can help in the positioning of a product and in its differentiation. Suppliers of fresh produce, such as fruits, find that it is difficult to effectively brand the product without packaging.

Packaging has aesthetic properties in that attractively shaped and brightly coloured packages can enhance the product's appeal. Moreover, the quality of the packaging is often used by the prospective purchaser as an indication of the quality of the contents. A good deal of market research has to go into packaging if it is to be used to best effect as a marketing tool. Colour associations will differ by culture. In some cultures, dark colours evoke a quality image and bright colours can communicate cleanliness and purity.

Another example of aggressive packaging strategies is that of the Swiss agrochemical company Ciba. Some of Ciba's products perform in a similar way to those of leading rivals such as Monsanto, Scherings, ICI and Hoechst, Instead of pursuing product advantage claims, which would be difficult to sustain, Ciba have often developed innovative packages with built-in applicators or automatic metering devices. Manufacturers are also aware of the potential of adding to a product's utility by providing reusable packaging. Plastic containers are often preferred to cardboard cartons by consumers, because these can be used to carry and/or store other liquids.

Product-packaging interface

In certain cases packaging has evolved from being merely a container to becoming an extension of the product itself. An obvious example of this is the Coca Cola bottle. With its distinctive shape the bottle is recognised the world over and is viewed as an integral part of the product. In recent years ownership of microwave ovens has encouraged food manufacturers to develop convenience foods, or ready-prepared meals, and to use crystalline polyethylene terephalate (CPET) for the packaging. This allows the product to be put straight into a microwave oven.

The sealed unit developed by Schering is a good example of a situation where the packaging has become an integral part of the product. Many other examples can be cited: pump action packs that dispense creams, sauces and other food liquids, agrochemical containers with in-built metering systems, insecticidal sprays for the treatment of parasites on farm animals, etc.

Packaging Technology

The choice of material to be used in packaging can have a tremendous impact on total costs. Du Pont conducted a study which:

> "..indicated a 100 per cent cost advantage for aseptic (laminated card) versus glass and a 30 per cent cost advantage for aseptic versus canned one litre size containers."

The total systems cost for aseptic packaging (i.e. including equipment, materials, distribution etc.) was calculated to be about half that of either glass or steel cans. At the same time, it has to be recognised that Du Pont's research takes no account of third world circumstances. In these countries the raw materials for glass making may be more readily available than paperboard and it could be that the economic arguments are completely turned around.

Moreover, even if Du Pont's claim that paperboard has cost advantages over glass and steel apply in developing nations, this might be outweighted by the fact that glass costs far less to dispose of than paperboard. Thus, it is possible, although not proven, that the cost saving accuring to manufacturer and distributors, from using paperboard, may be outweighed by the total cost to society which has to include the cost of waste management and pollution. These are important considerations, especially for a developing country where packaging materials are often imported and where the nature of physical distribution systems demands robustness of the packaging. Whilst we expect packaging to perform a number of functions in marketing, it must do so at a reasonable cost.

Recent Packaging Developments

Among the more recent packaging developments is the increased use of polyethylene terephalate (PET). PET bottles and jars have been around for a little while now and have been extensively used to package carbonated beverages and fruit drinks, but the introduction of an oxygen barrier polymer has extended its use to oxygen-sensitive products, such as beers.

Reductions in produce losses and extended shelf-life can be achieved by modifying the atmosphere. This can mean controlling temperature and/or humidity, the removal of ethylene, in the case of fresh fruit and vegetables, or as is the current trend for meat, salad and vegetable products, adopting the sous-vide vacuum packaging system.

Flexible laminates, like polypropylene and metallised polyester, are able to extend the shelf-life of products. A very recent innovation has been active packaging. 'Active packaging' seeks to go beyond simply extending the shelf-life of fresh and pre-cooked foods and conserve quality attributes e.g. colour, flavour, nutrients. Mitsubishi's 'Ageless' system, for example, is a sachet containing iron.

The sachet is a scavenger that is placed in the pack. Another form of 'active packaging' is to put a time-temperature indicator on the pack to warn consumers that when the product is in a certain condition it should not be eaten. Packaging technology continues to change and marketing managers must be aware of the opportunities for increased effectiveness and efficiency that these developments present if they are to remain competitive in the market place.

References

Abbott, J.C., *Agricultural Marketing Enterprises for the Developing World,* 1987, pp. 152-157.

Coles, R.C. and Beharrell, B., "Packaging Innovation in the Food Industry," *British Food Journal,* 92, 1992, pp. 21-32.

Kotler, P., "Marketing Management: Analysis, Planning and Control," 6th edition, (Ed) New Jersey, Prentice-Hall International Inc., 1988, p.71.

Levy, D., "A Lobster Tale: The Collective Marketing of Brazilian Seafood," In: *Successful Agribusiness Management,* Gower Publishing Company Ltd, 1985, pp. 116-121.

McCarthy, *Basic Marketing: A Managerial Approach,* 9th edition, Homewood III.: Richard D. Irwin, 1981.

11

Planning of Marketing Strategy

An organisation's corporate strategy is reflected in the statement of its overall objectives and the means by which these are to be met. Corporate strategy is usually stated in such a way as to convey the reason for its existence, i.e. its mission and the business it is in or wishes to be in. Whilst corporate strategy and marketing strategy are not one and the same. Baker argues that:

> "..the firm's selection of a marketing strategy will influence and affect everything which it does—to this extent then marketing strategy and corporate strategy are inextricably interlinked."

Effective marketing is a necessary but not sufficient condition for business success. In market driven organisations marketing will be allowed to influence other functional areas like R & D, production, finance and personnel these will each have individual, if concerted, strategies and collectively fall into the realm of corporate strategy.

Policies in Business

Policies are bodies of rules established to guide managers in their decision making. In essence, a policy prescribes the boundaries of the alternative courses of action which the organisation leaves open to him/her within a defined set of circumstances. Thus, for example, a manager whose soft fruit is losing sales in export markets because competitors are offering extended credit to importers may be constrained in his/her actions by company policy with respect to credit. That policy may be paraphrased as, "We will never be placed at a disadvantage by offering terms and conditions of sale that customers perceive to be inferior to those offered by competitors."

In other words, the manager will know that he/she has to at least match or if possible better the terms and conditions offered by competitors. How the manager does this is a matter for him/her to decide. (The manager will not necessarily follow suit and offer similar terms to those of competitors but may look instead for ways of increasing the value of doing business with his/her organisation in other ways such as greater flexibility in minimum consignment sizes, faster delivery or improved protective packaging but the option of competing on the basis of credit terms is open to).

Alternatively company policy might be embodied in a statement like, "Never to buy custom through direct financial incentives." Here the company may be taking the view that sacrificing part of the marketing margin to gain market share does not help it reach its stated goals and is incompatible with its corporate strategy. In this case, the manager knows immediately that company policy prohibits the use of financial incentives and he/she must seek to regain lost sales in some other way.

Marketing Planning System

Basically planning involves setting objectives, designing and implementing a programme to achieve the organisation's objectives and having a monitoring and control mechanism to ascertain whether the planned programme is on track or has achieved its desired objectives. Greenley differentiates between corporate planning, strategic planning and operational planning. He says that corporate planning is the organisation's overall planning system and its two principal constituent parts are strategic and operational planning.

Strategic planning begins with an assessment of an organisation's internal and external environments.

Operational planning can be further divided into short and long term planning. Short term operational planning is also known as tactical planning. Tactics and strategy differ in several important respects. Tactics relate to the following of a plan to achieve short term objectives. Thus tactics equate to the marketing plan rather than marketing strategy.

Strategic marketing would establish policies for each element of the marketing mix and would specify how resources are to be deployed. Tactics deal with marketing problems in the short term. Consider the position of a fish supplier who has the competitive advantage of owning refrigerated trucks. The supplier might adopt a marketing strategy in which the price is set high in order to: recover his/her investment in expensive technology; establish a price-quality relationship in the mind of the consumer; and ensure that the level of demand does not greatly exceed the amount he/she is able to supply.

Since this is his/her strategy, there would be no departure from the maintenance of prices which are high relative to those of other suppliers. However, there may be tactical manoeuvering in order to overcome certain marketing problems. When the supplier, or the product, is new to the market there may be need to stimulate demand by offering discounts. This would probably be done through the use of special 'money-off' coupons, or vouchers, so that the discounts could be targeted at certain customer groups and also to underline the fact that discount prices will not be the normal practice with respect to the product and are for a limited time only.

Similarly, when there is a glut of fish on the market or when the supplier wants to improve short term cash flow or release space in his/her storage facility to accommodate new product lines, the tactic of offering '20% extra free' in a bag of white-bait or kapenta fish might be employed. Once again the supplier would be careful to communicate to the market that these extra value packs would be available in the short term only. Thus, whereas marketing strategy focuses upon achieving long term organisational goals, tactics focus upon achieving annual marketing objectives. Before moving on, it should be said that corporate strategy, business policy and marketing planning have relevance to enterprises of all sizes.

In smaller organisations these management activities are likely to be carried out in a less formal and less sophisticated way than in larger corporations but they need to be done, formally or informally, explicitly or implicitly. Even the small independent grain trader will have to give thought to such matters as his/her strategy for survival in a municipal market overcrowded with grain traders, will have to be consistent whilst remaining flexible—in his/her reactions to problems and opportunities and needs to be in a position to anticipate changes in the marketing environment so that he/she can identify and exploit emerging opportunities.

Strategic Business Units (SBU)

When businesses are small and owner operated there tends to be a high degree of entrepreneurial drive. Even after the organisation begins to grow, and salaried managers are employed, there may be no appreciable fall in the level of flair, energy and commitment to achieving success, if indeed there is any at all. However, in very large organisations managers can feel divorced from the events and decisions that are shaping the business. This is particularly the case where the enterprise is highly diversified. For example, a large enterprise could have interests in say grain trading, fertilizer procurement, the design and installation of silos, financial advisory services to farmers, the hire of transportation of bulk commodities, etc.

A manager in fertiliser procurement could well feel that he/she has relatively little effect on overall performance since decisions such as budget allocations and sales and profit targets are dictated and determined by what happens in grain related activities. This is likely to suppress that manager's search for new and better ways of doing business because he/she believes to do so would have relatively little effect and would not be recognised, or rewarded, by senior management. The concept of a strategic business unit (SBU) was developed as a means of retaining the vitality of the entrepreneurial spirit by giving management a high degree of responsibility and autonomy in decision making.

The SBU becomes a separate business entity, although still belonging to a larger commercial enterprise, having its own defined business strategy and a management with direct responsibility for its profits and sales performance. SBUs can be based around individual brands but it is more common for a large corporation to break down its business according to either product categories or markets served. Aaker advises that:

> "When strategies and competitors have a high degree of commonalty across businesses, it makes sense to combine those businesses into a single SBU. When they differ in meaningful ways, however, it will probably be more useful to use separate SBUs."

The size of a business is also a consideration when deciding on how to structure the organisation. Even when an organisation's businesses have similar strategies and needs managers can feel impotent if it is a very large enterprise and it may be best to create two or more SBUs to maximise motivation and the application of initiative, and therefore corporate performance. To do so can change the way a manager thinks about his/her own mission.

For instance, the manager of the transport department within a large grain trading organisation is likely to focus his/her attention upon controlling distribution costs and maximising the efficiency with which the transport function is operated. As the manager of an independent SBU the manager may begin to see his/her task more in terms of maximising the return on investment in transportation. This requires him/her to redefine the business his/her division is in.

New opportunities may become apparent such as the hiring out of underutilised vehicles, storage capacity and equipment; offering advisory services in logistics, stock control management, fumigation procedures etc.; and so on.

The manager thus becomes less myopic in his/her view of the mission of the business. The degree of autonomy and independence of an SBU varies enormously. Much depends upon whether the SBU has its own dedicated operations such as R & D, design, production, distribution and accounting. Often, the economics of business operations dictate that SBUs share some of these facilities but this will almost undoubtedly reduce the individual manager's sense of responsibility and control.

Strategic Market Planning

Strategic planning began as a response to the inadequacy of assuming that the future will look very much like the past. It is dangerous for a business to extrapolate in economies and markets that are developing and changing. In his classic article "Marketing Myopia", Levitt gives several memorable examples of successful businesses that subsequently went into decline because their actions were based upon the implicit assumption that the status quo would be maintained. By way of example, Levitt cites the case of the dry cleaning industry which failed to see that in the future the main threat to their business would come not from continually improved chemical cleaners but from the development of stain resistant synthetic materials.

In a similar vein the American railroad companies perceived one another to be competitors but did not anticipate how transporters over road, sea and air would develop their passenger and freight handling facilities to a degree that railroads became uncompetitive. Aake explains that strategic planning encourages enterprises to abandon the notion that past extrapolations can be relied upon as a basis for future actions. Rather, they should assume that there will be discontinuities between the past and the future.

Strategic planning is also known as strategic market planning when its focus is upon the market environment within which the enterprise must operate. This reflects the fact that what an enterprise plans to do now, in order to prepare for future developments in the market, should be based upon a detailed understanding of that market and not on mechanistic projections of past and present patterns. Strategic market planning enables organisations to anticipate events rather than merely react to them. Aaker itemises the following benefits of strategic market planning:

— It focuses management's attention on external events, especially those representing threats and/or opportunities. All too often companies tend to be inward looking when, in reality, customers and competitors are external to the firm and profits are made outside not inside the organisation.

— It locks management into taking a long term perspective when the pressures are to adopt a short term focus with grave dangers of making strategic errors. The natural tendency is for managers to devote their time to dealing with the problems and opportunities of today, to the exclusion of consideration of the longer term. Strategic market management usually has a well defined time-cycle when managers have to submit short, medium and long term plans. Such cycles instill a discipline that forces managers to devote a minimum amount of time giving thought to future developments.

— It changes the basis on which resource allocation decisions are made. Resource allocations are frequently dictated by financial professionals who understand accounting conventions and terminology and this is often employed to the disadvantage of managers less well informed on these matters. In other cases, resource allocations are made according to the 'political' strength of a group, department or individual manager rather than on commercial merit. Strategic planning seeks to match resources to opportunities.

— It provides a strategic management control system. Monitoring and control are an integral part of strategic management. This enables management to deal with problems as these emerge rather than allowing problems to become crises.

— It provides a vertical and horizontal communication and coordination system. Strategic market management is a vehicle for communicating problems and proposed strategies with precision due to its vocabulary and explicit expression of expectations of the future.

— It helps enterprises operating in rapidly changing and unpredictable environments to cope.

Thus, strategic market management is proactive in that it prepares managers not merely to expect change but to anticipate it. Moreover it serves as an instrument for making management more externally orientated and less insular. Strategic market management also focuses management attention on the longer term and counters the natural tendency for management time to be totally absorbed by today's problems and opportunities.

Process of Marketing Planning

As was said earlier, planning involves setting objectives, designing and implementing a programme to achieve the objectives and developing a system for monitoring and controlling the execution of the plan. This process involves analysis, planning, implementation and control. The process of marketing planning activities can be categorised as diagnosis, planning and action. These three activities, once started within an organisation, never stop. SWOT analysis constitutes the diagnosis stage, the objectives and strategies stages are the planning activities and the action plan and monitoring, evaluation and control stages are the action part of the plan.

Plans can be categorised according to time span and complexity. Strategic marketing plans which are intended to guide management through the environment in the long term are generally complex and have a 2-3 year time horizon. Annual marketing plans which focus upon specific target marketing objectives of the marketing mix—product, price, promotion, place and people have a one year time horizon. Tactical plans which are "reaction" plans to, say, changes in a competitor's price, have a one to three month duration and are intended to bring the organisation "in tune" or to "react" to a potential disadvantage.

Depending on the agricultural organisation type, plans may vary in terms of their sophistication. A small scale farmer may leave planning to others, for example, to an extension officer who is advising him/her with respect to what and when to plant, or he may react to pre-planning price announcements. His planning may be nonexistent or very rudimentary. More sophisticated large scale farmers may have elaborate budgeting procedures, crop rotation patterns and crop production plans. Food processing organisations which deal with many suppliers, products and customers may have a whole range of tactical, annual and strategic plans. Government, which plans the economy, may enlist all types of planning devices.

Contents of the Marketing Plan

The following describes the contents of the marketing plan which includes the executive summary, corporate purpose, situation analysis (SWOT), objectives, strategies, action plan, monitoring evaluation and control and the marketing intelligence system.

Executive summary

The planning document should start with a short summary of the main goals and recommendations to be found in the main body of the plan. A summary permits management to quickly grasp the major directions of the plan.

Corporate purpose

There are two elements to the corporate purpose, one is to prepare the organisation's basic mission statement, the other specifies the basic management goals.

Basic mission

This answers the question what business is the enterprise in and what business should the enterprise be in? Periodically the basic mission of an organisation has to be reconsidered since the environment of enterprises is constantly changing. For example, in the wake of market liberalisation many marketing parastatals are being forced to revise their mission statements.

Those that formerly had exclusive rights to market staple foods such as grains, and under market liberalisation have had this exclusive function taken away from them, are wrestling with the question of what their role should be now. They may have alternative roles which they could assume such as becoming the buyer and seller of last resort, or becoming an instrument of development whereby the parastatal acts as the marketing agent of small scale farmers and with their storage and transport resources close the competitive gap between smallholders and the large farms and plantations.

Then again, the marketing parastatal may be commercialised, or even privatised, in order to increase the level of competition when new grain suppliers enter the market. Whatever role is chosen, it should be expressed within the organisation's mission statement. Another reason for reviewing an organisation's mission from time to time is that larger enterprises can find themselves gravitating away from their core business. The process can be imperceptible. Investments can be made here and there, none of which amounts to a substantial drain on corporate resources but collectively they can sap those resources and divert the organisation from its core business and core customers. This was experienced by the multinational mining company Rio Tinto.

The company's core business was the extraction of precious metals but over time it diversified its portfolio and became involved in many other types of business. Some of these were fairly closely related to mining but others had little or no connection. One sector in which Rio Tinto became involved was agricultural equipment and services. These agricultural businesses ranged from the construction and assembly of equipment to the operation of a forge and the provision of an irrigation systems design service. The management of mines and mining has little in common with the management of agricultural manufacturing businesses.

The methods of operation are quite different, the resources required are on quite different scales, as are the returns on investment, and the strategies that are applied in one sector have no relevance to the other. Eventually, Rio Tinto did what many large organisations have done before it and returned to its core business by divesting itself of these other investments. By doing so, Rio Tinto released resources which it could then channel back into the core business. It should not be concluded that only large organisations become confused over the question of what business they are in.

Some businesses never consider the question of what business they are to operate in at the outset. Foba Engineering, based in Kaduna, Nigeria, is typical of many small companies in that it makes a range of unrelated products. For instance, Foba fabricates both grain milling equipment and trunking for street lighting. It could be said that Foba's business centres around maximising the throughout of its fabrication facilities and for as long as the firm can find jobbing work, but Foba finds it difficult to develop expertise in the production of any of the items it manufactures.

More importantly, since it operates in diverse markets Foba has neither the facility to properly study the needs of each of those markets nor can they anticipate future developments since they do not have the resources to monitor trends in all of those markets. Moreover Foba, like so many enterprises, suffers from what is termed in the marketing literature as a 'technological fix'. This occurs when an enterprise defines its business in terms of its current production technology rather than according to the needs which it seeks to serve. In Foba's case they are vulnerable to competition from businesses that manufacture milling equipment by casting, machine turning and even plastic moulding.

Strategic marketing audit

By constantly monitoring and reviewing the organisation's

strengths, weaknesses, threats and opportunities (SWOT). This is an extremely important part of the Marketing Plan. The purpose of a situation analysis is to investigate the company's own strengths and weaknesses (internal analysis) and discover the threats and opportunities in the environment (external analysis) so it can avoid the threats and take advantage of the opportunities. Threats have to be analysed to see if they are "negative" or "neutral" threats. Threats may be insignificant.

Having discovered the issues with which it is faced, management must then make some decisions about objectives which will then guide the subsequent search for promotional strategies and action programmes. Objectives should be quantifiable, measurable, achievable, communicable and consistent. Objectives may be stated in economic or subjective terms. Greenley has carried out a comprehensive study of the range of objectives which organisations pursue, and drawing upon the work of such as Ansoff, Hofer, Pearce and Robinson and Thompson and Strickland has summarised these objectives and the way in which they tend to be measured.

Economic objectives have to be translated into marketing goals. For example if a company wants to earn $1.8m, profit, that is, its target profit margin is over 10 percent on sales, then it must set a goal of $18m in turnover. Further if the company sets an average price of $26, then it must sell 692,300 units. If the company only has a 7 percent market share, then it would be expecting the total industry sales to top 23 million units.

The company has to set certain targets for consumer awareness, distribution coverage and so on, if it expects to maintain or improve its 3 percent market share. Hence the overall marketing objectives might include the target of doubling consumer awareness of the brand being sold and raising the number of distribution outlets by about 10 percent over and above the other stated targets.

Strategic objective: A strategic objective is a choice and a statement of priority for the enterprise. Objectives are drawn up from an analysis of the strategic focus.

Strategic Focus

There are many ways to achieve strategic objectives and, indeed, the focus may change over time. A grower of oranges may begin by needing to achieve volume if he/she is to be able to completely fill a container and ship economic loads. Later, the organisation's focus may switch to cost reduction as the market becomes more competitive and margins are being squeezed.

There are two main ways of achieving improved performance, i.e. volume or productivity strategies. Basically the choice is to increase volume or reduce costs; ideally these should be pursued simultaneously.

For example, if the objective is to increase sales revenue by 10 percent such an objective can be achieved by either increasing the average price on all units, or by increasing the overall sales volume and/or by selling more of the higher-priced units. Each of these strategies can be achieved by increasing market growth and/or market share. In developing the strategy, the basic marketing tools can be identified: target markets, position in the market, product line, price, sales force, etc.

Customer Targets

Market segments are based on product or customer characteristics. Typical product characteristics are different sizes, prices and colours whereas customer characteristics may be age, sex, income, social class, geographical location or personality. The choice of a target market and the marketing of a product can lead to a number of product/market coverage strategies.

Core Strategy

The core strategy is a statement of what an organisation is offering to create a preference for its products and services in the marketplace. Through a careful examination of the customer and his/her needs and wants, the organisation can determine what is required to create a differential advantage.

Marketing mix

The marketing mix is a concept first introduced by McCarthy and comprises the product, price, place (distribution) and promotion decisions and is often called the "4 P's". The mix is the right combination of marketing activities to ensure customer satisfaction.

Product: The product offering can be manipulated to create different market effects at three levels: the core product, the tangible product and the augmented product. At its core, a product is not a physical entity but the benefits that it offers customers. Those benefits may be physical or psychological in nature. The consumption of imported foods, in a developing country, sometimes has as much to do with the status of being seen to buy sophisticated, and perhaps expensive, products as it has with any superior physical qualities compared to domestic equivalents.

The tangible product refers to its features, quality, styling, packaging, branding and labelling. A third level is that of the augmented product, that is, additional service elements which are attached to the product. Examples include after-sales service, extended guarantees, credit facilities, technical advice and product trials.

Price: Prices should be set in relation to specific pricing objectives. Pricing decisions include payments, terms, discounts, contract and pricing structures. Non-price competition may come through packaging, labelling and advertising. Prices have to reflect the costs of production and marketing and target profit margins. A variety of approaches may be taken to pricing including cost based, demand based, competitor based and market based.

Promotion: Promotion includes advertising, public relations, selling, exhibitions, brochures, data sheets and free gifts. Possibly the most important decision about promotion is the message to be communicated. The message(s) has to differentiate the products and/or its supplier. To this end, an organisation will seek to convey a unique selling proposition (USP), that is, to find some aspect of the product, service or organisation which others cannot, or simply do not, promote to customers and which is perceived to be important or attractive to those consumers.

Advertising is a form of communication which a sponsor pays to have transmitted via mass media such as television, radio, cinema screens, newspapers, magazines and/or direct mail. It is intended to both inform and persuade. Whereas, promotion tends to be short term in its effects, advertising tends to take time to have any effect, but then its effects, when they come, can be lasting. Whilst no one has firmly established exactly how advertising works, it is generally thought to conform to the sales-expenditure pattern depicted in figure 1.

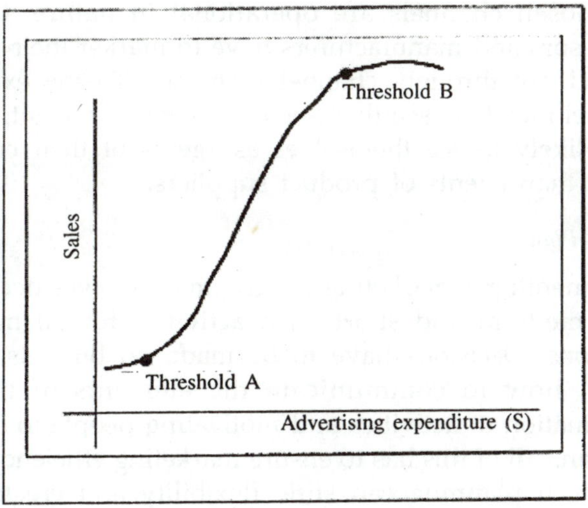

Figure 1. A theoretical advertising response curve

This S-shaped curve suggests that over a range of low level expenditures there is little response in terms of increased sales. This is perhaps because the intensity of advertising that such expenditures would buy is below a threshold where most of the target audience would become aware of the product or service. Once that threshold is crossed there is a dramatic response to increasing levels of advertising expenditure.

Eventually though, the target market is saturated and whilst advertising expenditures continue to increase the market response plateaus. Put another way, the enterprise reaches a point where for every dollar spent on advertising the sales returns are below $1.00, i.e. the law of diminishing returns applies. The challenge to strategic planners is to work out the range of advertising expenditures that will prove the above threshold A but below threshold B.

Place: Produce distribution elements include physical distribution like storage handling, transportation and warehousing, both on and off farm, and functional distribution e.g. wholesaling and retailing. The decision as to which distribution channel the organisation should seek to use falls into the realm of strategic marketing but actions within the chosen channels are operational in nature. Growers, processors and manufacturers have to market their products to, and not through, channel members. To the extent that channel members see themselves as anyone's agent, they are more likely to see themselves as agents of their customers rather than agents of product suppliers.

Action Plan

Implementing a marketing programme involves deciding on long, medium and short term activities for all marketing functions. Decisions have to be made on budgets, staffing levels, how to communicate the elements of the plan, coordination of activities and motivating people to carry out the plan. All of this has to ensure marketing efficiency. Whilst too much planning can stifle flexibility and creativity, no planning is a recipe for disaster. It leads to ill conceived product and marketing strategies, enhancing the possibility of waste and inefficiency in a vital industry: the production and marketing of food.

Evaluating and Controlling the Marketing Planning

It is the task of management to ensure that the marketing plan is carefully monitored, evaluated and controlled. Indeed authors such as Mockler see no distinction between planning and control but view them instead as steps within the same cycle. Typical controls involve setting standards of performance, evaluating actual performance against standards and, if the deviations are intolerable, taking corrective action. Marketing planning can be seen as a cycle, which begins with clear objectives that set out what the marketer intends to achieve, and ending with a feedback mechanism in order that the objectives can be evaluated, a course of corrective action can be taken and the organisation can monitor its usage of resources.

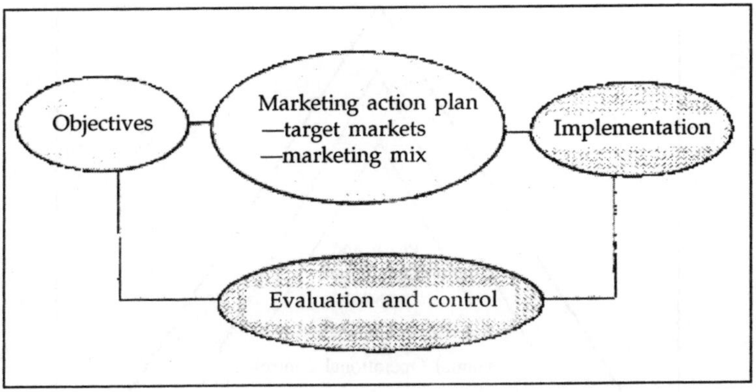

Figure 2. The planning execution and control cycle

Clearly any system of monitoring and control has to be implemented in accordance with organisational structure. That is, if there are SBUs, divisions or other business units that have a degree of autonomy and responsibility for the development of strategy and plans, then these must have their own systems of monitoring and control in place.

Marketing Controls

Marketing control involves setting a desired standard, measuring deviations from the standard and taking the appropriate action. In many cases the standard is expressed in terms of budgets and any substantial deviation from budget is investigated. Both positive as well as negative deviations can be a cause for concern. If sales are far in excess of planned levels then this can overstretch the enterprise's production, storage and distribution resources, for example. At the same time, the investigation of all deviations from budgeted levels would prove an unbearable load on managers. Instead, since not all deviations are significant, parameters are set for "allowable" deviations and only those exceeding these parameters are investigated. There are four types of marketing control: the annual plan control, profitability control, efficiency control and strategic control.

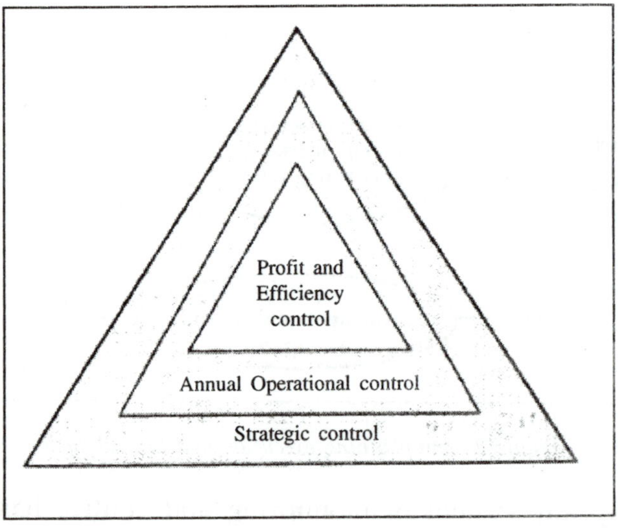

Figure 3. The different levels of marketing controls

Marketing Plan Control

The purpose of the annual plan control is to ensure that the company achieves the sales, profits and other goals established by the marketing plan. It is, therefore, an operational control plan. This type of control applies to all levels of the organisation and the process. Several measures may be taken in assessing performance in relation to the marketing plan, including sales analysis, market share analysis, marketing expenses to sales ratios, attitude tracking, profitability and efficiency. Each of these will be briefly discussed.

Sales analysis

Actual sales can be compared to sales targets and budgets and an analysis of any variance between the two would be carefully examined. Sales analysis centres interest upon the relative contribution of different factors to a gap in sales performance. Say, for example, that the managing director of the National Canning Company is told by the marketing manager that sales are up half a million units on the target and that revenues are five percent above budget, this would be cause for celebration. Or would it? Before answering this question the managing director would wished to look at these figures a little more analytically. The operating results might look those presented in table 1.

Table 1. Operating results for a canned product

Canned Produce	Planned	Actual	Variance
Sales (units)	5,000,000	5,500,000	+ 5000,000
Price per unit ($)	3.50	3.40	- 0.10
Total revenues ($)	17,500,000	18,700,000	+ 1,200,000
Total market (units)	10,000,000	12,000,000	+ 2,000,000
Share of market	50%	46%	- 4%
Variable costs @ $ 2.5 per unit	12,500,000	13,750,000	+ 1,250,000
Profit contribution ($)	5,000,000	4,950,00	- 50,000

It can readily be seen that, although sales have exceeded expectations, the planned price was not achieved and so the product made a lower contribution than expected. In this case the price mechanism would need investigating as would the estimates of market share. Whilst the Canning Company recorded an increase in sales of ten percent, the market as a whole was twenty percent above target. Seen in this light, there is more cause for concern than for celebration.

This approach to sales analysis can be extended to specific products, market segments and/or sales areas, etc. to evaluate the profit contributions of each and to identify those that were poor performers. From there consideration can be given to the underlying reason for that performance.

Market share analysis

Market share analysis shows how well the organisation is doing vis-a-vis competitors. The first step is to determine market share, either by absolute measures (overall market share) or relative to main competition (relative share), or to leading competitor (relative to market leader share). The second step is to analyse market share movements in terms of the following:

Total market share =Customer penetration (CP) ×Customer loyalty (CL) ×Customer selectivity (CS)× Price selectivity (PS)

where:

CP = Percentage of all customers who buy from the company.

CL = Purchases of this company by its customers expressed as a percentage of their total purchase from all suppliers of the same product.

CS = Size of the average customer purchases from the company expressed as a percentage of the size of the average customer purchase from an average company.

PS = Average price charged by this company expressed as a percentage of the average price charged by all companies.

Marketing expense to sales ratio

The marketing expense to sales ratio is used to ascertain whether the organisation is spending too much or too little on marketing in order to achieve its sales goals. The marketing expense to sales ratio can be made up of a number of components such as sales force size to sales, advertising to sales, sales promotion to sales, marketing research to sales and sales administration to sales.

The monitoring procedure involves determining an acceptable level (or standard) and by using a variety of charting devices (control chart or expense to sales deviation chart) look at actual to budgeted expenditure. An illustrative example may help to clarify the procedure. Suppose that management has decided that the organisation should spend around 0.01 percent of sales revenue on advertising. This equates to 1¢ in every $1.00. Over a period of time, the following pattern of advertising expenditures to sales revenues is observed.

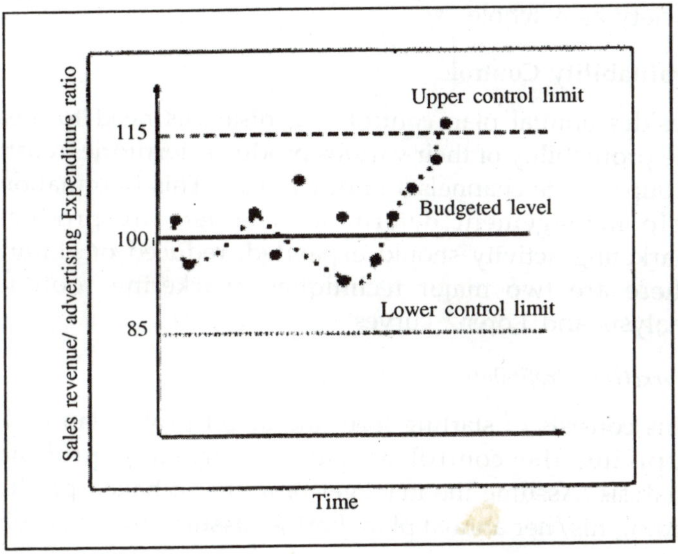

Figure 4. Marketing expense control chart

Before any decision or even interpretation, is made on the basis of these figures, management has to be clear on whether the baseline ratio was derived from some systematic evaluation of cause-and-effect or simply reflects what the organisation felt that it could afford. In the case of the latter, this chart is of doubtful value. If, on the other hand, the ratio has been arrived at after careful analysis, then when both the upper or lower boundaries are breached there is cause for concern. At the very least, management has to raise questions over the reasons why this has happened.

Customer attitude tracking

Whilst most of the control techniques described so far have been quantitative in nature, customer attitude tracking studies give qualitative information. The main customer attitude tracking measures are complaint or suggestion schemes, customer panels or customer surveys. These can be very useful in revealing what customers feel about the organisation, its products, services and behaviour towards society as a whole.

Profitability Control

Besides annual plan control, organisations need to measure the profitability of their various products, territories, customer groups, trade channels and order sizes. This information will help management determine whether any products or marketing activity should expanded, reduced or eliminated. There are two major techniques: marketing profitability analysis and Lorenz curves.

Marketing Profitability Analysis

This consists of starting from the target profit plan and then applying the control measure—marketing profitability analysis. Assume the manager of a line of baked products is setting his/her annual plan. Further assume that it is believed that:

- — demand conditions will be the same next year as this year
- — there will be no change in marketing strategy
- — the price set will reflect only changes in input costs and not competitive activity
- — the manager's interest is in making "satisfactory" not "optimal" profits.

In theory the manager should devise a plan intended to optimise the sales response function. A sales response function forecasts the likely sales volume during a specified period associated with different levels of one or more marketing mix elements. Typically he/she should assess the sales which would be generated by ever increasing amounts of marketing expenditure until the point of diminishing returns is reached.

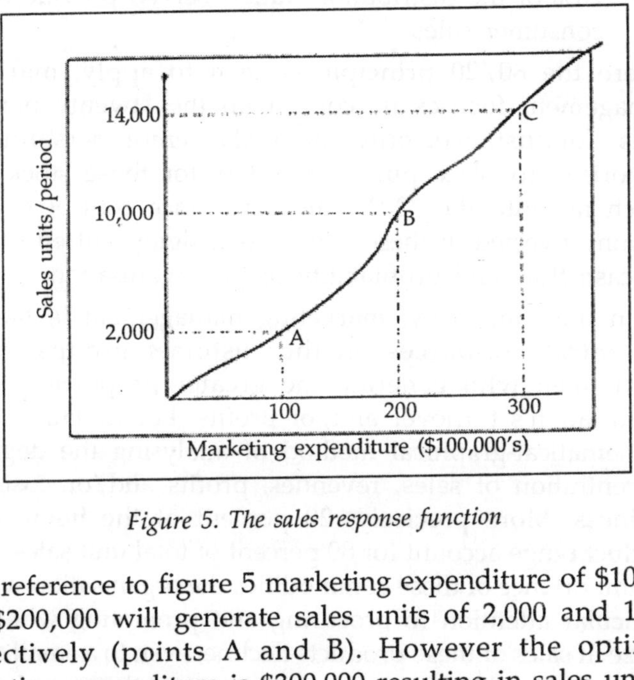

Figure 5. The sales response function

With reference to figure 5 marketing expenditure of $100,000 and $200,000 will generate sales units of 2,000 and 10,000 respectively (points A and B). However the optimum marketing expenditure is $300,000 resulting in sales units of 14,000 (point C). Any expenditure beyond this point will generate diminishing returns. In practice, estimating the optimum marketing expenditure is very difficult because of the interrelated effect of the marketing mix variables.

Lorenz Curves

The 80/20 principle enjoys wide acceptance and applicability in marketing. Typically, this principle manifests itself in statements like, "Eighty percent of an organisation's profits arise from only twenty percent of the products within the product range". Or:-

— 20% of stock items account for 80% of inventory costs, or

— 20% of customers provide 80% of sales volumes, revenues and/or profits, or

— 20% of the distribution outlets served provide 80% of consumer sales

Where the 80/20 principle is seen to apply, marketing management focuses its control on the "twenty percent". Thus, for instance, only relatively senior personnel are authorised to place purchase orders for those stock items which fall into the "20% category" since control over the amount invested in these items has a significant effect upon the cash flow and profitability of the organisation.

In the same way, marketing management is likely to concentrate resources on the customer groups and/or middlemen who generate the greater proportion of the organisation's turnover and/or profits. Lorenz curves are a mathematical-graphical method of analysing the degree of concentration of sales, revenues, profits and/or costs of a business. More precisely, 20 percent of the items in the product range account for 80 percent of total unit sales. Given the importance of these commodities the organisation will pay particular attention to procuring and promoting wheat and maize. If sales of these products decline, even to a small extent, then this would have a substantial effect on the organisation's trading position.

Of course, it rarely happens that the concentration of sales conforms precisely to the 80/20 ratio but it is surprising just how widely applicable the pattern of concentration is to business phenomena. Businesses find that a small proportion of stock items accounts for the greater part of the value of their inventory; that most of their profit arises from a relative small number of products within the total product range and that a minority of customers/distributors generates the majority of sales and/or profits.

The Lorenz curve allows the categorisation of the products marketed according to their respective contributions to sales.

In this example there appear to be three categories which have been labelled A, B and C. Category A items—which are only 30 percent of the product range—have to be managed very carefully since they add up to 75 percent of sales volume and, therefore, the performance of these items is critical to the organisation. Category B products add a further 20 percent to total sales volume and although having less impact on the overall performance of the enterprise, nonetheless should be regularly monitored. If categories A and B are combined then it is found that 50 percent of the product range is responsible for 95 percent of volume sales. Given, however, that category B products collectively yield only 5 percent of unit sales and their performance in any season will have only a modest effect upon the organisation's overall sales results these do not merit too much of management's time and effort.

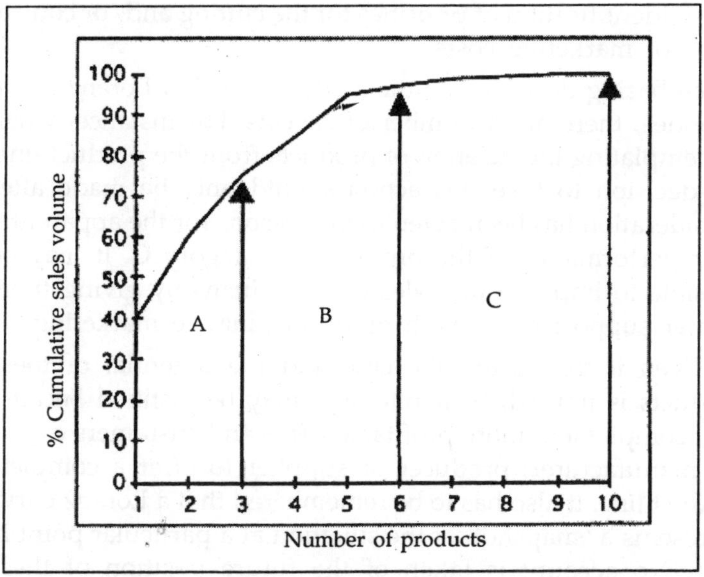

Figure 6. A Lorenz curve

An obvious response is to delete products in category C from the company portfolio on the grounds that these items contribute relatively little to the company's sales volumes. The pattern of sales volume concentration might also have implications for the structure of marketing management within the enterprise. Each of the products in category A might justify the assignment of an individual product or brand manager whereas items in categories B and C could be managed collectively as a product range and possibly by less senior personnel. Other marketing decisions which could be influenced by the degree of sales volume concentration revealed by the Lorenz curve include:

- — How the promotional budget should be allocated
- — Where sales personnel should focus their time
- — Determination of inventory and reorder levels for products
- — Production scheduling
- — Identification of priorities for the cutting and/or control of marketing costs.

When basing decisions on the analysis which a Lorenz curve provides, there are a number of caveats. For instance, when contemplating the deletion of products from the product line, the decision to take this action should only be made after consideration has been given to the reasons for the apparently poor performance of the products in category C. It may be possible to improve the sales of these items by giving them greater support or through more imaginative marketing.

Even if this is not the case and the potential of these products is limited, their retention may be justified because they complement more profitable items and customers expect the manufacturer, producer or supplier to offer a complete product line. It also has to be remembered that a Lorenz curve represents a 'snapshot' of the situation at a particular point in time. No account is taken of the future position of these products. That is, the top performing products of today may, in the longer term, fall into decline whilst other products achieving only moderate sales could be the 'star performers' of the future.

The Lorenz curve may show a spurious concentration due to the capturing of data at a single point in time when, in reality, there are random fluctuations in period-to-period buying. Several perspectives should be taken when conducting an analysis of this type. It may be the case that a certain product, or group of products, is assigned to a low category when the criterion is 'sales volume' but would fall into a higher category when the criterion used is perhaps 'profit contribution'.

Efficiency Control

If the profitability analysis reveals that the company is earning poor profits in connection with certain products, territories or markets, the question is whether there are more efficient ways to manage the sales force, advertising, sales promotion and distribution in connection with these poor performing entities.

Sales Force Efficiency

Hartley provides the following key indicators of sales force efficiency in their territory:

— average number of calls per salesperson per day
— average sales call time per contact
— average revenue per sales call
— average cost per sales call
— percentage of orders per 100 sales calls
— number of new customers per period
— number of lost customers per period
— sales force cost as a percentage of total sales.

Advertising Efficiency

Difficult as it is, the marketer should try and track the following:

— advertising cost per thousand buyers reached overall, for each media category, and each media vehicle
— percentage of audience who noted, saw/associated, and read most for each media vehicle
— consumer opinions on the advertisement content and

effectiveness before/after measures of attitude towards the product
- — number of inquiries stimulated by the advertisement
- — cost per inquiry.

Sales Promotion Efficiency

Track should be kept of each sales promotion campaign and its impact on sales:

- — percentage of sales sold on the offer
- — display cost per $ sales
- — percentage of coupons redeemed
- — number of inquiries resulting from the demonstration.

Distribution Efficiency

This will enable the marketer to search for economies in distribution. Measures are mainly taken through statistical/ operational research methods:

- — inventory control
- — warehouse location
- — transportation methods
- — optimum routing, scheduling, loading, unloading.

Monitoring and control enables marketing management to address two vital questions: are resources being used effectively and is there a better way of using them? In answering these questions much waste can be removed from marketing activities and functions.

References

Aaker, D.A., *Strategic Market Management*, John Wiley & Sons, New York, 1988, pp. 10-11.

Hartley, R.F., *Sales Management*, Houghton, Mifflin, Boston, 1979.

Mockler, R.J., "Developing The Science Of Management Control", *Financial Executive*, December 1967, pp. 84-93.

Pearce, J.A. and Robinson, R.B., *Formulation And Implementation Of Competitive Strategy*, Irwin, Homewood, 1982.

12

Marketing Extension

Working with farmers, your main marketing task should be to provide them with the necessary information and contacts to allow them to increase their earnings through better marketing. This involves helping them to:

— select profitable crops and improve production techniques;

— improve sales and achieve better prices;

— reduce costs and losses.

Production Techniques of Crops

You need to know which crops generate better profits and how production choices, such as variety, production timing and product quality, can affect the profitability of individual crops. To do this you must know the products produced in your area and how they are marketed. This information can be gathered by talking to farmers and traders individually or by meeting with them as a group. Individual interviews make it easier to gather confidential commercial information. They also make it easier for less confident farmers and those with lower status to express their views.

On the other hand, gathering information from a group of farmers is effective and also very useful in helping farmers to understand their own problems and opportunities. In the majority of cases your work will involve you in finding ways of improving the marketing of existing products. However, there may be the opportunity for farmers to diversify into new products and you also need to be in a position to identify market opportunities for these.

Improving Sales

From speaking to farmers, you should be able to learn what they consider to be their main marketing problems and what ideas they have for solving those problems. You can improve farmers' sales by working with them to improve their access to buyers and markets and by helping them to understand which products have expanding demand. You also need to know the expected prices for products and how prices change during the season. This will help farmers negotiate better prices by being better informed.

Improving sales and prices requires an understanding of the market. At a local level, this comes from talking to buyers, traders and transporters. Initially, you may be nervous about talking to business people. However, traders generally enjoy talking about their business and become very helpful if they feel this assistance will eventually lead to an increase in their turnover. Carrying out market research in this way is a powerful tool for improving marketing. Once you start talking directly to the trade and understand how the market works, you can realise how valuable this information is to farmers and how much better equipped you are to help them.

With some support and help, farmers can also carry out their own market research. Once they have been helped to start finding out about the market for themselves they gain confidence and quickly feel able to do the work on their own. A farmer group can select between four and six farmers to carry out market research. You can advise them on interviewing techniques, provide them with checklists of questions in their own language and let them observe you doing market research interviews.

Reducing Marketing Costs

You need to be aware of typical marketing costs and work with farmers to reduce those costs, such as by encouraging them to share transport or buy inputs in bulk. Good post-harvest advice can help improve quality and reduce wastage - both factors affect profit.

Information for Farmers

Farming Area

You need to find out the strengths and weaknesses of your area. This includes identifying:

- — major crops grown, when they are harvested and their particular characteristics;
- — costs of producing these crops;
- — typical prices that farmers receive, how the prices change depending on buyer and time and what premiums for quality are given, if any;
- — farmers' skills and their problems;
- — businesses that transport, store, process and pack agricultural products;
- — relative importance of the different local markets and traders;
- — levels of existing trade and the possibility of growth;
- — leaders in the farming community;
- — assistance that farmers believe they require to help them market their products.

The purpose of gathering this information is for you to thoroughly familiarise yourself with both the problems and the opportunities of your area. It is very important to speak to farmers. In particular you must ensure that you meet medium- and small-scale farmers and not just large farmers.

Farmers generally have a good understanding of their problems and are delighted to have an opportunity to talk. At this stage your role is to listen and learn. You should try to understand how they might react to new ideas and which farmers are likely to be most receptive to the idea of trying out new activities. At the end of this information gathering you should have a clear idea of the crops, the marketing system, the individuals and the problems of the area. You should also have some idea of possible solutions that are worth investigating.

Market Research

Market research requires two main activities: firstly, finding out about how the market works and, secondly, finding out what products the market demands.

Finding out about how the market works involves understanding:

— the channels through which products pass;

— who the important people and companies are;

— how they do their business and who they currently buy from;

— their interest in trading with farmers from your area;

— who they sell to.

Finding out what products the market demands involves understanding:

— Product specifications, varieties, colour, size, grade, quality and packing;

— Prices, price patterns, variations according to season, quality and supply;

— Supply, volumes, competing suppliers and seasonality;

— Preferences of customers and consumers;

— Opportunities for additional production to be marketed.

Gathering Information about Market

Interviews must be held with a cross-section of the farming community and with the small local businesses that are involved in agricultural marketing. Gathering information about the market involves talking to the important businesses in the marketing chain, such as buyers who travel from farm to farm, transporters, other traders, wholesalers, processors, retailers, exporters and, less often, importers and even consumers. It should involve visiting local retail and assembly markets and, if applicable, major wholesale markets. Interviews should be carried out face-to-face but, when long distances are involved, telephone interviewing could be used if the people being interviewed are willing to cooperate over the phone.

To help gather information in a systematic way and to ensure that all the important questions are asked, it is useful to have a questionnaire or, at least, a checklist of questions. The following paragraphs briefly describe these questionnaires.

Farmer questionnaire: The first part covers questions to the farmer about the farm business and concentrates on gathering basic data needed. It asks such questions as how large the farm is, whether it has irrigation and what equipment the farmer has. It asks what major crops are grown, which ones are marketed and which are mainly for home consumption, Finally, it examines how the selling is normally done and asks what the farmer's major problems are.

The second part of the questionnaire concentrates on individual products, with questions on yields, costs, prices, packaging, transport and marketing arrangements. All of this is important information needed to build up knowledge about the crops and other agricultural products and to be able to calculate the costs and possible returns. It is not advisable to gather detailed production data on more than two products from each grower, as the process of data collecting can be very time consuming.

Trader questionnaire: The first part of the questionnaire in Annex 2 covers questions to the trader about his or her business. The second part covers the most important agricultural products traded by that trader. It is not advisable to gather detailed data on more than two products per trader.

Interview Programme

The most difficult part of carrying out an interview programme is the first interview. For example, you may feel nervous about talking directly to the private sector. It helps to have tested the questionnaire before starting the full interview programme. This will establish whether the wording of questions need to be changed and give you a chance to practice. Interviewing a small-scale farmer or a shopkeeper is a good way to start. It helps you to become comfortable with the process and to gain skills in interviewing.

When interviewing a group of farmers it is important to be well organised. Normally it is necessary to visit or send a message in advance, at least a day before, to arrange for the farmers' group to meet you at a specific place and time. You should speak to the farmers as a group to:

— explain the purpose of the survey;
— ask the farmers to outline the main crops that they grow and the problems they are experiencing.

When the meeting is finished you should thank the group and ask them if there are any additional points that they want to make, especially farmers who have not previously spoken. When interviewing agribusinesses, traders and retailers the process is similar except that they are generally contacted and spoken to individually. This interviewing process involves:

— introducing yourself;
— explaining at the beginning why gathering the information is important and that this should be to the long-term advantage of the person being interviewed;
— explaining how much time it will take;
— starting by making the interviewees comfortable, often by encouraging them to explain how they started and developed their business;
— asking the noncontroversial questions first;
— keeping sensitive questions until towards the end of the interview;
— sharing information to encourage the interviewees to exchange their knowledge. For example, you could tell

them about the production potential of farmers in your area;

— confirming the answer if there is any doubt as to what the person being interviewed means;

— writing down as much as possible on the questionnaire form while the interviewee is talking;

— thanking interviewees for their time, ideas and help;

— writing up the questionnaire properly and reading it to ensure your full understanding of what was said;

— interviewing a wide selection of farmers, traders and businessmen to be able to gather the ideas and opinions of a wide range of people.

Interview Findings

Interview findings should be written up, in note form, as soon as possible. Use a table to compile the quantitative data. Let the data and the interview findings build up a picture of the farming sector and the rural resources. This should cover:

— the farm sizes and incomes;

— the products they produce;

— how farmers market their products;

— the important local agribusinesses supplying inputs and those involved in crop marketing;

— the differences in crops, markets and income between areas;

— typical costs of production and incomes for the main crops;

— farmers' problems, the solutions that they would like to see and the opportunities for developing the commercial aspects of their farming businesses.

For the major products that you ask questions about, you can learn:

— typical volumes and values of product sold;

— quality preference in terms of variety, appearance, size, taste, packing, grading;

— post-harvest practices, shelf life, storage opportunities;
— differences in demand according to time of year, day of the week and whether influenced by festivals such as Diwali, Christmas, Lunar New Year or Ramadan;
— other competing suppliers, their quality, seasonality and price characteristics;
— trends in consumer demand and opportunities for additional supplies;
— typical prices and marketing costs.

As a result of conducting interviews you should have an understanding of the marketing chain and then be able to advise farmers on:

— the different marketing channels for major products and their relative importance;
— who the important businesses involved in agricultural marketing are and how/where they can be contacted;
— the different companies that growers can work with, how they like to do business with farmers and their trading and business interests;
— the likely costs of marketing, including transport, packaging, storage and commission charges;
— prices and how and why they change.

It is essential for farmers to know where and how they will sell their products before they start to grow them.

Improving Agricultural Marketing

Getting Information Across to Farmers

Talking directly to farmers, traders and others makes it possible to gather information needed to improve agricultural marketing. Knowledge of the range of products produced, seasonality of crops and approximate costs of production can help farmers to understand their marketing possibilities and thus increase farm income. This first requires a careful analysis of the collected information and then an effective method of presentation of that information to farmers. Discussions with groups of farmers can be conducted using information presented on boards or flip charts. Some of the informations are briefly described below.

Crop Calendars

A crop calendar can be used to compare those periods when an area is able to supply produce with the periods when market prices are likely to be high. It can also be used to compare the seasonality of an area's production with that of a competing producing area. For example, farmers on the island of Mindanao in the southern Philippines have compared their crop calendar with that of competing vegetable farmers in Northern Luzon province, in order to identify periods when they have a production advantage.

Cost of Production Data and Sales Price

Cost of production data and sales price figures can be used to draw up crop budgets. These can then be used to advise farmers on the potential profitability of different crops. Banks and credit institutions may also find the data useful in working out production loan requirements. The yields that farmers claim to achieve can be very variable. Sometimes they don't know what their yields are. Yields on research stations are usually much higher than farmers' yields and must not be used for calculating crop budgets. Yields can be estimated by weighing the harvest from a known area of the field and then calculating the yield for a hectare. However, this is only useful when the research is being carried out at harvest time. Farmers can be asked to record yields in order to make future crop budget calculations possible.

Maps of Production Location

Maps of production locations help extension workers and farmers to understand whether there are 'clusters' where particular products are produced. These maps are also useful for discussions with traders and can be used to identify locations where farmers could group together in order to sell to traders. Maps of alternative markets, distance from producers, size and whether their prices are good are also useful. They help producers to think about the options they have for selling their products.

Marketing System Descriptions

Simplified diagrams showing the flow of products to markets are also a useful tool to help farmers understand the alternative ways that they can sell their products. Using different thicknesses of lines helps show which channels are the most important.

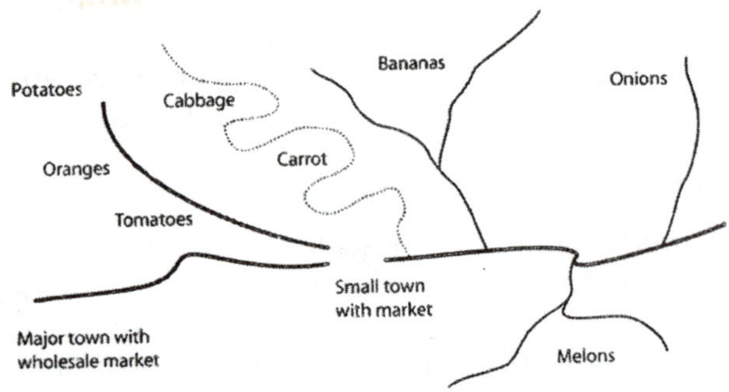

Figure 1. Map of a production area

Figure 3 shows the different marketing channels that vegetables can move through. As in Figure 2 the relative importance of the different channels has been estimated and is approximately indicated by the thickness of the lines.

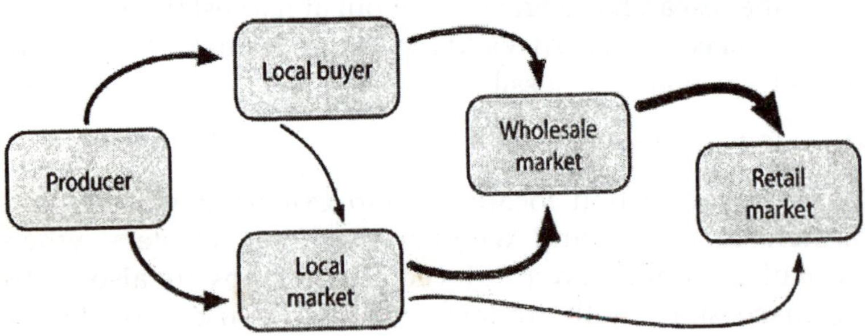

Figure 2. Market channels

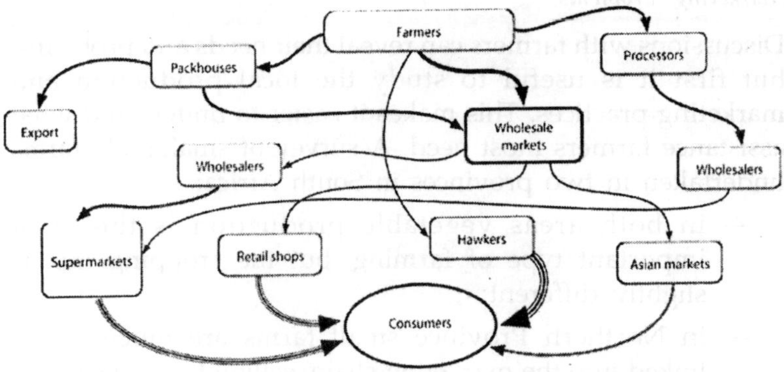

Figure 3. Marketing channels for vegetables, South Africa

In South Africa wholesalers are independent businesses who buy in bulk and sell on to the major retailers. Agents sell product on farmers' behalf in the wholesale (national produce) markets and receive a commission. Pick-up operators are small-scale mobile traders, driving small trucks, who buy both in the field and at wholesale markets and sell to hawkers, who sell fresh produce from stalls in small markets and on the streets.

In 2002, sales through both supermarkets and via the informal sector were increasing, while sales through the wholesale markets were falling, although they remained the single most important outlet in terms of volume. Sales to the traditional processing sector were flat but there was growth in more progressive types of processing such as snacks, ready-to-eat meals, sauces and convenience foods, as well as in exports.

Information on Traders

One way of increasing the volume and value of transactions in the marketing chain is by improving the communication between the people in it. Farmers' requirements are often quite simple. They mainly want to know who would like to buy their products. Such information is not complex and lists of addresses and telephone numbers can be compiled with some short notes on each trader.

Marketing Problems

Discussions with farmers can reveal their needs and problems, but first it is useful to study the local production and marketing practices. This makes it easier to understand what assistance farmers most need. A survey of small-scale farms undertaken in two provinces in South Africa:

— in both areas vegetable production is the most important type of farming, but the cropping mix is slightly different;

— in Northern Province small farms are much better linked into the marketing chain, selling to hawkers and at open markets. In Eastern Free State farmers mainly sell to individual consumers;

— Northern Province producers hire transport or use their own, but Eastern Free State growers mainly rely on selling directly from their farms;

— Eastern Free State growers are generally nearer to markets but complain about buyers demanding produce on credit and not paying, as well as the level of theft;

— Both areas believe that marketing could be improved by new physical markets and look forward to the expansion of supermarkets that would buy directly from farmers.

The importance of the constraints identified varied from area to area, transport of produce was clearly considered to be the major one. The second most important constraint was said to be the limited number of traders and the absence of competition between them. However, this raised the question of why there were so few traders. Was it because they did not have the necessary resources, knowledge and interest, or was it because there was little demand for the products the farmers grew.

Farmers always complain about poor prices and this is a predictable finding of any field research. Inadequate prices may reflect high marketing costs or a lack of demand. It may be possible to improve prices by lowering the unit costs of marketing and promoting more competition between buyers, by improving negotiating by farmers and by organising access to new market opportunities. During the survey in Mozambique farmers often described traders as unreliable. By this they meant that the traders who visited were inconsistent and unpredictable and there was no certainty as to whether they would visit and what prices they would offer. This may indicate a wish on the part of farmers to develop more regular and reliable trade.

Trader Fact Sheets

In addition to Trader Fact Sheets, Product Fact Sheets can be prepared to give specifications of the products demanded by the market, along with indications of the seasonal price and supply patterns. The purpose of the fact sheet is to provide producers and suppliers with the critical information they need in order to make correct decisions on the products they produce and sell.

The information presented in Product Fact Sheets can be developed during trader interviews. It should include information on:

— varieties, appearance, taste;
— grading and quality standards;
— seasonality and supply patterns;
— typical prices and price patterns;
— packaging;
— sales trends.

Helping Farmers to Make Decisions

Extension workers sometimes try to "push" farmers into accepting recommendations. However, when decisions about what to grow or how to sell are imposed this rarely leads to success. Farmers do not feel that the decisions are theirs, they are not committed to them and they feel a lower sense of responsibility. If things do go wrong it is easy for farmers to blame the person who persuaded them to do the "wrong" thing.

Helping farmers to make their own decisions is a more difficult and slower process but, in the long run, it will be more successful than trying to tell farmers what to do. When groups of farmers take on "ownership" of their plans they are more enthusiastic, show more determination to overcome problems and take greater pride if their plan proves successful. They are much more able to overcome problems in the future and to actively seek solutions for themselves. To make decisions, farmers must be well informed.

They need to know what choices they have. They will have to discuss what they can do to improve their marketing and agree on what to do and on who is responsible for the individual tasks. Your role is to guide this process. The ways in which you can help farmers to decide on what needs to be done to improve their incomes depends on what stage they have reached in their marketing development.

Farmers Meeting

Decisions on what to do are generally made at farmers' meetings, which you can organise. These should last between two and three hours. Invitations need to be sent in advance. In the time available only two or three major topics can be discussed. Decide the topics to be discussed and draw up an agenda. The most successful meetings maximise the number of farmers actively joining in the discussion. The meeting arrangement is important.

Clustering the active participants together helps encourage discussion. If women play an active role in farming you need to ensure that they have a full opportunity to express their views. After the normal formalities, such as prayers, you should explain the purpose of the meeting and the agenda. Asking people to introduce themselves has the dual function of helping outsiders to learn or remember people's names and getting people used to speaking to a group. Meetings should normally involve a combination of presentations and led discussions. Your approaches to organising a farmer meeting could include:

— discuss topics that both help farmers to understand their existing situation and identify their opportunities and constraints;
— encourage farmers to think of ways to improve their own marketing;
— focus on practical issues;
— use audiovisual presentations wherever possible;
— use traders and others to inform farmers about how the market works;
— ensure that each topic discussed follows logically from the last;
— provide farmers with the information they need to make decisions;
— use case studies and examples from elsewhere;
— anticipate the marketing problems that farmers will identify and be able to offer different solutions;
— finish the meeting with a clear understanding of what the next steps are, who is responsible for them and when they will be carried out.

Meeting Content

You can make short presentations on the results of your market research. Factual presentations need to be kept simple and information provided should make a particular point or illustrate an issue. Short presentations by farmers or traders can be very useful. An effective method of helping people who are unused to talking in public is for you to interview them.

Encourage farmers to participate by asking them to provide information and to indicate what they see as their problems and their opportunities. Questions from other participants should be encouraged. The meeting should be a place where ideas can be discussed and where support and agreement is gained.

Discussion topics could include:

— comparisons of production and marketing costs between different farmers;
— identification of the major crops produced and those that are sold and are the most profitable;
— advantages and disadvantages of alternative markets;
— identification of problems and possible solutions;
— identification of potential new products;
— how to find new markets.

Offering Options

During discussions a number of issues and problems will emerge. Farmers may suggest possible solutions, but will often not be aware of the range of ways that problems can be handled or opportunities exploited. You can make suggestions regarding alternative solutions to farmers' marketing problems. Often, farmers identify different markets or marketing strategies that they would like to develop. Being aware of these options is useful in order to explain to farmers some of the implications of using different marketing channels.

Towards the end of the meeting the "next steps" need to be agreed upon. It is useful at this point to summarise the main points discussed, the points agreed and the options that have been considered as the next steps. Improving marketing is often a long process. It is unlikely that marketing problems will be solved in one farmers' meeting. The best outcome is often to agree on the next actions to take to help solve the problems. This must take into account what must be done and who will do it. A timetable needs to be prepared, so that everybody understands their roles and responsibilities.

Solve Marketing Problems

When organising farmer meetings you must have a good idea of what can be done to solve marketing problems. Solutions that farmers propose must be realistic and achievable. Normally, achievable solutions are those the farmers work on themselves. "Solutions" that are less likely to be achievable or sustainable in the long run are those that require an outside body, such as the government or an NGO, taking responsibility for marketing the produce. It is often tempting for those working with farmers to become involved directly in marketing, for example to use government vehicles or those of an NGO or a development project to transport farmers' produce.

In the long run this has many disadvantages. It is unrealistic to expect government or other vehicles to carry out this activity. Once started it is difficult to stop and stopping will disappoint farmers who become dependent on the service. From the outset it is important to establish business relationships that can continue without external support. It is much better for farmers to work with a local transport company or with established traders than to rely on subsidised support from development agencies. Governments have often tried to help farmers by guaranteeing to buy produce at fixed prices. Although this may help individual farmers in the short term, in the long term it is a very expensive policy.

Farmers will increase their production if they know that there is a guaranteed price and market. This production far exceeds market demand and therefore has to be thrown away. Sometimes, processing or storage are seen as the solution for marketing problems caused by surplus production. They are not. Raw material supply for processing should mostly involve contract production, to ensure the right volumes are available throughout the processing season.

A factory cannot be justified on the basis of occasional surpluses. Such investments must only be made when there is a firm market for the processed product and a reliable raw material supply. Long-term storage of horticultural produce has only limited usefulness, especially in situations where there is oversupply. Overcoming surpluses is difficult, but it is more likely to be achieved through better market information and through farmers carrying out the market-planning activities discussed in this guide.

Running a successful business requires different skills from those of being a civil servant. Government-run trading operations are rarely successful businesses. As they are not profitable, they are not sustainable and, in the long term, create more problems for farmers than they solve. Staff often come under pressure from well-connected farmers to buy substandard produce, which cannot then be sold. Farmers, particularly those who are a long way from the market, often ask for their transport costs to be subsidised.

This is an expensive policy and not sustainable, and when the subsidies are withdrawn it leaves the growers worse off than they were before because they planned their farming activities on the basis of subsidies, not on the basis of market demand and their ability to supply that demand profitably. Grading reduces the volumes marketed and increases costs, but puts up prices. Introducing grading standards needs to be considered with care. Standards are best based on the grading already being carried out by traders.

Farmers need to be aware of these and be able to follow them, but governments should not try to impose standards not required by the trade. Any standards introduced need to be supported by the trade and consumers must be prepared to pay for the additional cost. Marketing systems have often developed over generations. Any changes need to be carefully considered so that they work with the system, not against it. In most cases, your role is to help farmers work within the existing systems, or try to make small changes to those systems.

References

Coleman, Eliot., "The New Organic Grower," *A Master's Manual of Tools and Techniques for the Home and Market Gardener*, 2nd Edition, Chelsea Green Publishing, Lebanon, NH, 1995.

George, A.P., Nissen, R.J. & Brown, B.I., "The custard apple," *Queensland Agricultural Journal*, September-October: 287-297, 1987.

Nennich, T. and D. Hoffbauer., "Very Early Sweet Corn Production," *Presented at NE Sustainable Farming Association (SFA)Conference*, February 2004, Duluth, MN, 1987.

13

Liberalisation and Agricultural Marketing

The prolonged economic recession which began in the late 1970's accelerated the rapid deterioration in the economic condition of many developing nations in the form of an ever widening gap in their balance of payment accounts. Many LDC governments reacted by implementing 'curative' measures that actually fuelled inflation. These included increased borrowing, restricting access to foreign exchange, the extension of price controls, increased import tariffs and control of imports through licensing requirements. On occassion, such measures were pursued independently but on others they were part of IMF sponsored economic stabilisation programmes.

By the early 1980's it was apparent that stabilisation measures on their own would not solve the problem and alternative approaches were sought. The World Bank was first to conceive an economic structural adjustment programme (ESAP). Soon most international funding agencies were insisting that borrowing governments implement ESAPs. A key element of all structural adjustment programmes has been the reform or liberalisation of markets, including agricultural and food markets. The World Bank first applied the term structural adjustment to describe its programme of policy-based lending which began in the early 1980s.

The objectives of structural adjustment programmes are not confined to restoring macro-economic balance but are also intended to stimulate economic growth. Structural adjustment involves improving the structure of production by allocating resources in accordance with their opportunity cost rather than on any other basis. The argument in support of this approach is that resource allocation efficiency is maximised, increasing the value of current output and improving the prospects for the rate of growth over time and avoiding the need for subsidies and taxes in support of the production structure. In addition to increased allocational efficiency, structural adjustment is concerned with improvements in both operational and economic efficiency.

Operational efficiency is increased when unit costs of production are minimised through efficient management and the adoption of the appropriate technology. Economic efficiency is the consequence of a high level of allocational efficiency plus a high level of operational efficiency and ensures that consumers' needs are satisfied at prices which reflect the minimum sustainable cost of production.

Whilst and improved structure of production, through increased allocational and operational efficiencies, is the central platform of structural adjustment, structural improvements in practice have also included diversification of the economy. That is, by broadening the base of economic activity the flexibility of the structure can be improved and so the economy is better able to withstand external shocks such as a fall in the world prices of certain commodities, adverse weather conditions that impact on particular crops or substantive changes to trading conditions applied by economic blocs like the European Union.

The in-built inflexibility of LDC economies meant that the external shocks of the 1970s had a far greater impact than they would have had if these economies had a broader base. The challenge for those charged with developing structural adjustment programmes is to find designs capable of simultaneously stimulating economic growth whilst protecting the population from excessive levels of hardship during the course of the programme. In addition, ESAPs endeavour to make the domestic economy more flexible so that it is better able to cope with changes in the world economy. Overall the objectives of ESAP are to:

- — restore equilibrium in the balance of payments
- — reduce the fiscal deficit to a manageable size
- — bring down inflation
- — improve long term employment prospects
- — increase investment and
- — lead to sustained growth.

In order to achieve these objectives policy makers must:

- — identify an agenda of reforms in policies and institutions
- — develop a sequence of measures which is technically consistent and politically sustainable and
- — negotiate these policies between governments and the lending agencies.

The objectives themselves are at the macro-economic level. In most instances they are attempted through policies designed to manipulate supply rather than demand. These policies are directed towards reducing spending overall and redirecting demand towards domestically produced goods. The expectation was that most countries that instigated structural adjustment programmes would have completed them within three years. Both the duration of individual programmes and the extent to which the Bank would be involved in policy-based lending were woefully miscalculated.

Some structural adjustment programmes have extended over eight years or more, and many are in their second and third phases. Moreover, the World Bank's involvement in funding these programmes has continued to increase, rather than diminish, and the Bank has publicly conceded that structural adjustment is:

> "..not a one-shot effort..but reflects the need for macro-economic and sector policies to be continuously appraised and modified."

All of this points to the fact that a knowledgeable and

respected institution like the World Bank is still learning from experience about the processes of structural adjustment. It should not therefore be surprising that other lending institutions, the international donor community, government ministers, policy makers and others involved in the development, implementation or administration of structural adjustment programmes are on a learning curve and as yet have no firm understanding of what constitutes 'best practice' with respect to ESAPs.

Macro-economic Stabilisation Programmes

Whereas the World Bank has been the principal sponsor of ESAPs, which focus on the supply side of economies and impact indirectly on the demand side, the IMF has been the champion of economic stabilisation programmes. These operate to stimulate the demand side of the economy and have an indirect effect on the supply side of the economy. Stabilisation policies work to reduce a country's expenditure levels to match its current resources. They do not directly lead to higher growth rates but rather provide the economic stability necessary before increased growth can be a real prospect. Attwood explains the objectives of macro-economic reform, thus:

> "Macroeconomic reform involves creating a conducive climate for investment, addressing the imbalances in public expenditure, reducing the fiscal deficit, increasing parastatal efficiency and appropriate debt management."

The policy instruments typically employed in the pursuit of economic stabilisation are:

- — exchange rate policy
- — fiscal policy and
- — monetary policy

Thus, for example, export performance (demand) might be improved because the reforms could result in a devaluation of the local currency (exchange rate policy), and/or higher levels of investor confidence due to inflation being contained as government brings its own spending under control (fiscal policy) and interest rates are allowed to rise to their economic level (monetary policy).

During the earliest round of ESAPs there was a degree of specialisation between the IMF, which handled demand management measures, and the World Bank, which focused on supply management measures. However, during the 1980s the IMF and World Bank began to develop programmes for an

> "..orderly adjustment of both macro-economic and structural imbalances so as to foster economic growth while bringing about a balance of payments position that is sustainable in the medium term."

This move was initiated by the World Bank in 1980 when it introduced its Structural Adjustment Loan (SAL) programme. In the mid-1980s, the IMF launched its Structural Adjustment Facility and its Enhanced Structural Adjustment Facility (SAF and ESAF). These are longer term concessional lending instruments which closely resemble the policy-based lending facility of the World Bank. Countries wishing to take advantage of SAF or ESAF must first develop a Policy Framework Paper, covering the short to medium term and the government has to jointly agree this with the IMF and the World Bank.

There is much debate about the sequencing of reform measures. Discussion tends to centre around the ordering of structural adjustment vis stabilisation, liberalisation of domestic vis international markets, and the sequencing of measures intended to liberalise specific markets. There appears to be a widespread consensus that the liberalisation of domestic markets particularly those in the agricultural sector should precede attempts to liberalise international trade. It is argued that success in liberalising domestic markets would help establish a more robust and flexible economy, one better able to compete in international markets. A central objective of structural adjustment has been to remove distortions in the economy resulting from government intervention and central control over markets. A secondary objective has been to improve the management of those activities that remain the responsibility of the state in the post-market liberalisation period.

Role of State in Liberalised Markets

Countries undertaking market reforms have had to face the vexing question of what to do about government agricultural marketing institutions. Most of these parastatals have accumulated very large debts and deficits, and have, therefore, been an enormous drain on their treasuries. In some cases, the poor financial performance has been due to mismanagement and operational inefficiencies, but in others government has placed on the parastatal social responsibilities such as the management of the strategic grain reserve and developmental roles involving promoting the interests of smallholder farmers.

In general, these social and developmental responsibilities cannot, by their nature, be profitable activities. Hence, the dilemma of governments seeking to reduce public expenditure, a large part of which has in the past been spent on financing agricultural marketing parastatals, but who cannot afford to allow social and developmental objectives to be abandoned in blind pursuit of liberalised markets. In some cases, governments have disbanded their agricultural marketing parastatals whilst others are seeking to restructure these marketing institutions. The efficient allocation of resources is central to all structural adjustment programmes. This does not preclude the participation of the state in agricultural production and marketing activities.

Historically, however, government involvement in many areas of economic activity has proved to be allocationally and operationally inefficient. It has been argued that government structures are not flexible enough to react to changing opportunity costs. Moreover, resources are often allocated on the basis of political considerations and operational inefficiencies arise from the absence of incentives. As a result, structural adjustment has also involved reducing the direct role of the state in marketing.

Reforming Agricultural Marketing Parastatalsa

In broad terms, there are four alternative courses of action which can be taken with respect to the restructuring of agricultural marketing parastatals, these being:

- — abolition of the parastatal, passing its essential functions to the private sector and/or non-government organisations (NGOs)
- — transformation of the parastatal into a non-commercial organisation carrying strategic food reserves and stabilising prices
- — transform the parastatal into a fully commercial enterprise, operating as a market oriented, profit making concern and
- — transform the parastatal into a fully commercial enterprise, operating as a market oriented and profit making concern within a competitive marketplace.

The issue of privatisation is not a single option, but a policy direction which itself involves a range of possible options. The options discussed here need not be considered as being mutually exclusive. It is conceivable that several elements could be combined within a single reform programme. For instance, once the relevant market(s) have been liberalised, it would be possible to contract out the management of a parastatal and at the same time privatise non-core assest and/or functions whilst retaining public ownership of the parastatal. Other combinations are equally possible. The parastatal could be divided into several strategic business units (SBUs). For example, a Livestock & Meat Marketing Board could be divided into the following business units:

- — procurement and fattening
- — animal procurement advisory service
- — auction management
- — animal health and development advisory services
- — abattoir services
- — meat grading and packaging and

— meat marketing services.

In many senses each of these business units operates in different, although related, markets, as SBUs could each be a cost and profit centre. Once organised in this way they can be treated independently of one another. Thereafter, a number of opportunities arise due to the flexibility which such a major reorganisation would create. Depending upon circumstances, some could be privatised, some might be the object of joint ventures, other could remain in public ownership but their management be privatised in an attempt to increase efficiencies whilst reducing government expenditure and others might remain as government owned and managed public enterprises.

Privatisation of Agricultural Marketing Parastatals

An agricultural marketing board, or any other form of parastatal marketing organisation, can be commercialised and/or privatised. The process of commercialising an agricultural marketing parastatal involves management in establishing return-on-investment, turnover and profit targets. In order to achieve these targets the parastatal is expected to adopt a market orientation. In addition, the commercialised parastatal would be expected to raise funds on the financial markets of the private sector and pay interest at the market rate rather than rely upon public funding.

Privatisation takes the additional step of transferring ownership of the parastatal out of the public sector and into the custody of private investors. The transfer of ownership can be effected in a number of ways. Shares in the enterprise can be floated on the stock exchange or can be sold to special interest groups such as management, employees or suppliers. The restructuring of a public enterprise involves two key preliminary steps:

- — transformation into a genuinely viable commercial enterprise, earning a realistic return on capital and with a balance sheet fully aligned to trading results.
- — transformation of the enterprise's special legal status

into that of a normal commercial institution with no special trading rights or privileges conferred by statute.

An initial step might be to appoint a Board of Directors as Zimbabwe did with its four agricultural marketing boards. These independent directors can then be asked to exercise their collective judgement as to how the enterprise can be made more efficient and better meet customer needs.

There then has to be a significant degree of deregulation of the markets which these enterprises serve, with more autonomy for the marketing boards, especially in pricing. Another priority is to deal with the accumulated debts of parastatals, where these exist. Before the processes of commercialisation or privatisation can commence there are usually a series of obstacles to be overcome.

Accumulated Deficits

Boards which are in a relatively strong financial position are far better placed to undertake restructuring than those carrying large, accumulated deficits. The dilemma faced by policy makers is to decide how to handle these deficits. If they are simply written off by the government then this provides the parastatal with 'free' capital, an unfair advantage over potential competitors and provides no evidences of the organisation's future viability to prospective investors. Even where there is no intention to privatise the parastatal, the provision of free capital runs contrary to the spirit of transforming an organisation into a fully commercialised enterprise.

Source of Finance

Many marketing boards carry large deficits and need fresh injections of cash. However, the magnitude of there deficits usually discourages commercial lending institutions from supporting them. International donor agencies are a possible alternative source of funds but their rules of operation often prevent them from providing concessionary loans to the private sector, even recently privatised parastatals; these could however be available to a commercialised parastatal.

Tax Liabilities

Potential investors would be concerned about the liability of a restructured marketing board to corporation tax. A commercial company which makes losses over a period of time can usually offset these against profits made in other years, for the purposes of assessing its tax liabilities. How governments treat the losses made by marketing boards prior to privatisation will have a significant bearing on how they are perceived by potential investors.

The magnitude of the losses are such that if the accumulated losses were written off against future profits, it might be a very long time before the enterprise paid any tax. On the other hand, if no allowance is made for these losses then the marketing board constitutes a most unattractive investment.

Developmental Roles

Marketing boards, and other types of parastatals, frequently have development roles, that is, activities and projects whose aim is to lead to the long term development of a sector of agriculture, a section of the population and/or a region of the country. For instance, a parastatal may be charged with helping convert subsistence farmers into cash crop farmers, or helping small scale farmers penetrate a dairy market dominated by large, commercial farms.

Problems arise when the board has development responsibilities but no provision has been made for an adequate system of financing. In principle, the problem is easily solved in the case of commercialised, but not privatised, parastatals. That is, non-viable development activities should be separately identified and financed by government. The difficulty is that the accounting systems used by many parastatals are simply not capable of accurately separating out commercial from non-commercial activities or their attendant costs. Where the intention is to privatise the parastatal it is unlikely that prospective stakeholders would accept a development role unless the particular activities could be carried out at a profit.

Even then, private investors would usually want to reserve the right to withdraw from an activity, if they identify alternative opportunities which offer a higher return on investment. Another complication is the fact that governments tend to have wide-ranging political, social and economic objectives, many of which are likely to transend some of the aims of parastatals restructuring. This makes it difficult to deal with the restructuring or reform of an agricultural marketing parastatal in isolation from an array of confounding development issues.

Prevailing Legislation

The restructuring or reform of marketing boards and other parastatals will invariably involve the amendment or repeal of a substantial body of legislation relating to a board and the products for which it has been responsible. Rarely is this a simple matter of withdrawing the prevailing legislation. In the case of agricultural products, legislation relates to a number of different issues economic, public health, research funding, etc. Whilst the processes of deregulation may focus on the economic and marketing issues, the public health measures cannot be swept away along with defunct rules and practices which related to controlled markets.

Rather, it is likely that public health aspects will have to be reinforced and strengthened since deregulation often means that the number of market participants will increase in number. Similarly, the need for industry-wide funding of research and the provision of industry-wide services remains unaltered. It is therefore necessary to review the whole corpus of legislation which directly or indirectly relates to the marketing board concerned, to decide the parts which can be repealed, those which should be retained and those which need to be amended. This process might involve the Ministry, the Office of the Attorney General, Parliament, a Cabinet Committee and then, perhaps, the Head of State.

Each of these participants is likely to have a wide-ranging portfolio and agriculture is but one of them. Not surprisingly, therefore, effecting the necessary regulatory changes can take a considerable time, even when the government and the management of the parastatals are wholly committed to change. All too often, the time scale for legislative changes is underestimated by those who develop restructuring programmes. The legislative issue is not of itself a major constraint, but the volume of work involved takes time. As in all aspects of government business, the passage of new legislation through the system will have to take its place with other new legislation before it can be passed into the law of the land. This inevitably affects the rate of progress of the restructuring of any government parastatal.

Accumulated Deficits

Government capital investment in agricultural marketing parastatals often takes the form of irredeemable interest-bearing loans. The interest rate is usually highly favourable to the parastatal, compared to the rates prevailing on the open money markets. In most instances the government does not actually receive the interest due on parastatal deficits. Converting debt to equity improves the look of the balance sheet since debts must be repaid and at a specific point in time whilst equity belongs to the owners of the business and they only receive payment whenever the enterprise makes sufficient profits to pay out a dividend.

A highly geared enterprise is generally perceived to be more of a financial risk for investors than one which largely depends on shareholder funds and retained earnings to finance its operations. Where governments of developing countries have considered exchanging their outstanding loans to parastatals for equity, it is often solely with an eye to reducing or eliminating the interest payments of a beleaguered marketing board. This, however, is unsatisfactory where the enterprise is supposed to be of a commercial character.

If little or not return is paid on the capital sums outstanding to government then this treats capital as a 'free good', which it is not. This is neither good in the campaign to engender 'commercial attitudes' within a former parastatal nor in the context of creating a 'level playing field' for emerging competitors who do not have access to free capital. Where governments provide 'free capital' to privatised parastatals it is an admission of failure to run the business as a commercial concern.

Since equity capital carries higher risks than loan funds, over several years shares should earn a higher return, otherwise no equity investment would be made. There may however be a case for writing off capital investments which were based on wrong assumptions or wrong policies in earlier years. For instance, investments may have been made in establishing poultry enterprises in rural years areas in anticipation of the electrification of those districts or villages. If for whatever reasons, that electrification has not taken place, those production units will be unviable and it would be best to write them off. A debt-equity swap would, at best, be self-delusion and at worst, would be concealment of a futile kind.

Private Sector Participation in Marketing

In many cases the donors or lending institutions have made market liberalisation and encouragement for increased private sector participation part of the conditions attached to their structural adjustment loans. In some instances, the reform or abolition of a loss-making agricultural marketing parastatal has also been part of the agreement between the lender and the loan recipient. Experience of implementing these reforms has been varied. In some cases, private sector participation has developed very quickly whilst in others, the process has been extremely slow. Much depends upon the stage of development of the private sector at the time market liberalisation measures are launched.

In some countries, strong 'informal' or parallel marketing channels have co-existed with the formal channel throughout the period of administered pricing and "controlled" marketing of agricultural products. When these markets are deregulated the process of transferring 'informal' marketing functionaries into the formal sector tends to occur quickly. The entrepreneurs already exist and they have accumulated a certain amount of capital from their past marketing activities. On the other hand, where governments have been successful in suppressing informal marketing activities, the experience and culture of entrepreneurship and risk-taking may have been lost, or at least significantly diminished. In these cases, private sector participation in deregulated markets is a much slower process.

The Grain Market Board (GMB) held both a monopsony and a monopoly with respect to the staple food of the country, white maize. The GMB supplied large-scale millers located in the urban centres of Zimbabwe. A parallel channel did exist with unlicensed traders buying and selling grain and small-scale millers, using hammer mill technology, providing a service to customers. However, this illegal trade was conducted on a very small scale and the bulk of the grain passed through the formal single channel comprising the GMB and urban millers who used industrial roller milling technology.

The Zimbabwean Government paid subsidies to the GMB both in order to keep consumer prices down and to ensure a steady supply of the country's staple food. Prices to the farmers for maize were determined by the government rather than by market forces. Whilst in years of normal rains Zimbabwe can grow enough grain to feed itself and can even export white maize, the total amount of grain handled by the GMB was showing a discernible fall as the large-scale commercial farmers began to grow alternative and more profitable crops.

As trade in maize was deregulated, the number of custom millers increased substantially. A number of production millers also came into being. Production millers buy, mill, bag and brand maize grain using hammer mill technology. Market liberalisation brought many more players into the marketing system, giving growers a choice of market for their product. There is now more competition for the farmers' maize. Consumers have also benefited. They now have a wider range of products from which to choose. Price sensitive consumers can now buy grain direct from growers, or the GMB, and take it to a custom miller. The straight-milled maize is the cheapest of the options, available. Alternatively the consumer can buy the more refined product of the production miller who dehulls the grain before milling. This is more expensive than straight-run meal but not so expensive as the highly refined meal produced by roller mill technology. The increase in the level of competition has also manifested itself in the form of marketing promotions.

Prior to market liberalisation the active promotion of maize meal was virtually unheard of in Zimbabwe. The large-scale millers were assured of a sizeable demand for their product. After all, it is the staple food of the country and they were the sole suppliers. In the post-liberalisation period advertising expenditure on roller meal brands has increased substantially and in-store promotions are increasingly common.

Private Sector Participation in Agricultural Markets

Initially, the World Bank attached great importance to increasing the efficiency of parastatals as a means of bringing about market reforms. After all, agricultural marketing parastatals typically represented a sizeable burden upon the governments of LDCs and were characteristically inefficient. However, in due course the Bank began to see greater potential in the liberalisation of markets and the privatisation of marketing institutions. Marketing reforms have tended to follow a pattern.

In most cases, the first step has been to enfranchise private traders and actively encourage them to participate in markets from which they were previously excluded. The next step has been the removal of price controls. Marketing subsidies and parastatal subventions are then removed before the final act of market reform, i.e. the lifting of controls on international trade in agricultural products.

Scarborough and Kydd suggest that the following are necessary in order to promote an efficient private sector:

- — encouraging and policing competition
- — promoting the wider availability of information
- — maintaining appropriate quality standards
- — strengthening the legal system to ensure enforceability of contracts
- — providing an adequate transport infrastructure
- — undertaking spatial planning to allow appropriate access by marketers and consumers to central places
- — supporting the development of credit
- — research into the technological problems in storage and processing experienced by the private sector and
- — training in technical and managerial aspects of marketing, processing and storage.

Prior to liberalisation government actions were perhaps the most significant impediments to private sector trade development. Although market liberalisation has, in most instances, changed government policy towards the private sector, the relationship between the state and commercial enterprises remains critical in determining the likelihood of success of any privatisation initiatives.

The state effectively sets the rules of the game within which the private sector operates, and if these rules are too restrictive, or if they change too frequently, then private sector participation may well be inhibited. Here, consideration is given to some of the potential impediments to private sector participation in agricultural markets. As shall be seen, many, but not all, of these impediments are within the direct control of government.

Policy Implementation

Even when government is committed to encouraging private sector participation in agricultural marketing, the bureaucracy which implements policy changes may be less committed. Years of market controls and licensing may have created large vested interests in an underpaid civil service, which may see the spectre of retrenchment in deregulation measures. It is therefore not impossible that government policy is undermined at the implementation stage. In the past, many LDC governments have been openly hostile to the private sector and so any trust established between the two parties is likely to be fragile. On the side of the private sector, bureaucratic delays will almost certainly be interpreted as an absence of real commitment, on the part of government, to free market economics and a suspicion that market liberalisation measures might be reversed at any time.

Administration of Licensing

A common post-liberalisation regulation is the requirement for traders to be licensed. This has been a feature in Malawi, Mali, Senegal, Uganda, Zambia and Zimbabwe, among others. Licences allow some residual control over the private sector; licences can be refused to traders suspected of unfair trading practices and can enable the state to collect marketing information. In some cases, the administration of trader licensing has presented prospective traders with few difficulties. In Malawi, for example, merely have to pay a registration fee and provide evidence of ownership of a seized weighing scale.

In contrast, Uganda has used licence fees as an overt tax on traders; and in Senegal, traders dealing in more than 200 kg of grain have to obtain a licence, and an authorisation to collect a specific product. Authorisation is only given after the trader has shown proof of a minimum balance in his/her bank account. The administration of licences has been inconsistent. Sometimes the bureaucracy involved in applying for licences imposes substantial costs on traders in time, bribes and fees. At the beginning of a liberalisation process, licensing regulations may not be well publicised, or may change, leading to uncertainty among traders.

Quantitative Restrictions

Traders are sometimes limited to transporting loads of a specified amount. This can impose costs on traders, as there may be economies of scale, which increase the efficiency of the marketing system. Quantitative restrictions can be imposed in a variety of ways. For example in Zimbabwe, even though a maize marketing liberalisation programme had been implemented, the Grain Marketing Board (GMB) refused to sell maize in quantities less than 50 kgs. This effectively prevented very small traders, without transport, from participating in the maize marketing system. Even if the prospective Zimbabwean trader can afford to hire a truck, he/she probably will not be able to purchase enough grain to make up an economic load.

Uncertain Regulations

Regulations, rather than direct intervention measures, can be the principal instrument of government policy. If regulations are too rigid then parallel or 'informal' markets may re-emerge. This has happened in both Senegal and Uganda. Moreover, access to the legal system, where this becomes necessary, has to be both quick and inexpensive. The uncertainty surrounding the regulations which are to apply to the private sector can also prove an impediment to private sector participation in agricultural marketing.

During the early stages of market liberalisation, changes to regulations may occur fairly frequently and this unsettles would-be investors in the agricultural marketing system. This can happen because the impact of liberalisation is difficult to predict, and as government monitors the process it may feel it necessary to tighten or relax the regulations surrounding the private sector as time passes.

Price Regulation

In order to retain a measure of control over food prices some governments have continued to impose price regulations in the post-market liberalisation era. These frequently take the form of floor and ceiling prices. These can have a substantial impact upon private trade. Private traders require a return on the resources which they invest in the marketing process. They will concentrate on those areas where marketing activities are most profitable, usually collection of grain near urban consuming centres, and ignore more distant markets where the information is poorer. This is certainly what happened in Malawi and Tanzania. Where government set narrow price bands within which the private sector must operate, these patterns are reinforced.

Smith recommends that government seeks to reduce the number and breadth of regulations to a minimum consistent with orderly production and marketing. He cites the example of the frequent requirement to obtain licences to trade and the need for separate permits for each commodity or groups of commodities in which traders wish to deal. Very often it is necessary to register the premises within which trade is to take place, and there may be restrictions on the quantities which can be traded and the times and forms of trading.

Very often the reasons for many of these regulations have long since forgotten but traders remain on the statutes of the country. There are thus many instances where a simplification and reduction of regulations, and their consistent application, would remove a deterrent to private sector activities.

Public and Private Sector Agricultural Marketing

In many countries, liberalisation has allowed for the co-existence of public sector agricultural marketing institutions. The public sector institutions may perform a market stabilising function, as say a buyer-of-last-resort, they may be the conduit through which food aid is released on to the market or they may manage the Strategic Grain Reserve. Problems arise when public sector bodies benefit from support which is not extended to the private sector. For example, subsidies on inputs, such as fuel, may only be available through public sector agents. Similarly, public and private organisations may not have equal access to credit and finance.

Many state bodies have historically had easy access to finance, often at subsidised terms, and without regard to the profitability of their operations. This has two negative effects on the private sector: it reduces the public sector's costs of operations, giving it an unfair competitive advantage, and it reduces the capital available for investment in private sector agricultural marketing operations. Tanzania's private sector became the dominant grain marketing force in 1990 when it was decided that parastatals and co-ops should only have access to credit on commercial terms. Neither of these parties was considered a commercially viable agency so they could not obtain the funds they needed to carry on their marketing activities at the same level as in the past.

Public sector marketing organisations have often enjoyed preferential access to foreign exchange. Input and output markets are often interlinked through credit arrangements. Where farmers rely on credit from marketing agents to buy imported inputs, private traders who have difficulty in acquiring these imports, may be disadvantaged in dealings over output trading. They may also have difficulty in obtaining access to fuel and transport, spare parts in particular, if they cannot compete for foreign exchange.

In many countries, exporters are prohibited from retaining foreign exchange earnings but must convert it to local currency at official exchange rates. This has sometimes led to flourishing cross-border parallel markets. This caused the Ghanaian government to institute a foreign exchange retention system, in the post-liberalisation period, whereby cocoa exporters could keep a proportion of the foreign exchange they earned, thereby reducing the incentive for smuggling. A similar scheme operates in Tanzania where 35% of export earnings can be retained to purchase production inputs.

Inadequate Infrastructure

A major problem for traders in many countries is the low investment in infrastructure. In Africa, poor roads and inadequate storage facilities contribute to high marketing costs and commodity losses. In Uganda, some traders claim that the number of trips they can make have decreased to a fifth of what they could make ten years ago because of large increases in transport times and costs. Most small traders rely on public transport, or hiring space on trucks. Access to transport and ownership of trucks is often the basis for local monopolies in the transport sector, which increase traders' costs.

The problem is all the more acute where foreign exchange shortages compel government to restrict the import of trucks and spare parts. Adequate storage facilities can reduce crop losses and thereby food marketing costs. These often tend to be lacking in local markets, where a high proportion of grain trading takes place. Local market organisation is often the responsibility of local government. In some instances, market fees may be inadequate to maintain the market structure, or may be diverted to other areas of government expenditure. The absence of storage facilities also discourages traders from holding grain over time. This in turn prevents the development of private sector arbitrage which can moderate seasonal price fluctuations.

Credit Constraints

Most small traders have restricted access to formal credit markets, and tend to borrow from informal sources. These can be extremely expensive sources of funds and often lock the borrower into a never-ending cycle of debt. Commercial lending institutions are neither used to, nor motivated to lend to small-scale marketing enterprises. Financial institutions prefer to lend in large amounts to large, established enterprises operating in high profit markets. Complete liberalisation of financial markets can actually lead to a shortage of capital for investment in agriculture since it tends to be a low profit sector of the economy.

Lack of access to credit and finance prevents small traders from expanding. The quantities of commodities bought and sold, the amounts stored and transported and the ability to exploit economies of scale are all restricted by poor access to credit. Problems are bound to arise in the agricultural marketing systems of countries which have implemented market liberalisation programmes if the financial system cannot be reoriented to service a large number of small private sector marketing agents as opposed to a few very large public sector organisations.

Marketing Information

With long established private sector marketing systems, informal networks usually exist to provide traders with information on market conditions, prices and the creditworthiness of other parties. Conversely, where suppression of the private sector has been effective, in the past, the marketing information system tends to be underdeveloped. This was the case in Malawi where traders remained unaware of price differentials between markets and were unable to exploit opportunities for profitable market arbitrage which would also have increased market efficiency. Where there have in the past been strong parallel markets, information systems may exist but access to them may not be extended to post-liberalisation market entrants.

Macroeconomic Environment on Private Traders

In particular, private sector participation is affected by exchange rate policy, economic stabilisation measures and the level and nature of economic aid.

Exchange Rate Policy

To improve the balance of payments, exchange rate devaluation is usually implemented. Devaluation increases the cost of imports, and with it many agricultural marketing costs are increased e.g. packaging/bags, fuel and transport costs, agricultural inputs and imported foods. Where the private sector is involved in the marketing of imports, government needs to acknowledge where price increases are due to devaluation rather than the result of privatisation. Equally, where the private sector is operating under controlled prices, the allowance for marketing margins accommodates increases in cost due to devaluation.

Stabilisation Policy

Stabilisation programmes usually mean improved budgetary control through stricter monetary control, reductions in expenditures and tax increases. Each of these is likely to impact on both traders' costs and revenues. Austerity measures invariably reduce demand for most products and at the same time traders can find that they result in substantial increases in interest rates, licence fees, market fees, sales taxes, etc. The danger is that traders can be driven back into informal markets where some of these costs can be avoided.

Distributing Aid

Structural adjustment programmes normally attract an increased inflow of aid from donors wishing to support the reforms. Much of the additional aid will be in the form of foreign exchange but some will be food aid or fertiliser aid. The way in which this aid is distributed can impact seriously on the development of the private sector. For instance, the private sector needs access to foreign exchange on the same basis as the public sector and co-operative agencies. Food and fertiliser aid distribution can have a more disruptive effect on private trade if it is not carefully timed.

An influx of cheap food can reduce prices and cause considerable losses for private traders who have stored food grains. A system of distributing aid through auctions has worked well in Somalia and could work elsewhere. Governments have to be careful in accepting aid projects which compete with potential private sector initiatives. These might be, for example, projects to build processing plants or storage facilities. Government has to be clear where it wants to encourage private sector investment. Governments can seek assistance from international donors on behalf of the private sector. Help can be sought to improve transport facilities or access to credit, or to fund training in technology, technical competence or business skills.

Improve Private Sector Performance

There are a number of areas in which government can lend

support to the development and expansion of the private sector.

Policy Statements

The state has to make clear its view of the role of the private sector in agricultural marketing system, i.e. it must have clear objectives with the respect to the marketing system. It is not enough to simply lift existing restrictions on the functions of the private sector. A positive role should be developed for it. The government's policy has to be announced in unambiguous public statements, which make clear the extent of market deregulation.

It is equally important that the extent of the future involvement of the public sector in the agricultural marketing system be clearly articulated. If the public sector is allowed to enter the market, it must be known under what conditions, at what prices, and for what purpose this will occur. If a Strategic Grain Reserve is held then the trigger for grain release must be known to the private sector. Otherwise, uncertainty about the likely effect of government policy on market conditions will prevail.

Regulatory Framework

All to often in structural adjustment programmes the need for supporting legislation is either underestimated or neglected altogether. Government can provide a set of stable regulations which would:

— clearly lay out the rights and obligations of consumers, producers and traders, underpinned by a carefully constructed contract law
— establish an acceptable system of weights and measures and perhaps a product grading system
— clearly specify the kind of exchanges that are legal, between which parties, and the constraints placed upon the place of exchange and
— the designation of an inspectorate to enforce the rules and regulations.

Training Programmes

Many of the entrepreneurs who come into a liberalised market will lack the basic knowledge and skills to ensure that their businesses can survive the periodic adverse economic conditions. Some may be technically proficient but know little about financial management or marketing; others may possess the basic entrepreneurial skills but have very limited levels of technical know-how. If government wishes to establish a private sector capable of growth and development then training programmes will be required. This does not necessarily mean that government has to provide or even fund the training. It may mean, instead, that government facilitates the training.

Infrastructure

Investment in roads, market places and storage facilities can reduce marketing costs and thereby increase levels of commercialisation. This might involve investing in new facilities and/or rehabilitating existing facilities. Where public sector marketing boards have under-utilised capacity, particularly in storage, this should be made available to the private sector, either through divestiture or through leasing arrangements.

Marketing Information Systems

The provision of market intelligence removes a barrier to market entry. Larger and longer established organisations, including marketing parastatals, have usually developed intelligence gathering systems over time. They have little motivation to share their information with smaller enterprises. In fact, to do so would lose them an important competitive advantage. This being the case, a government sponsored marketing information system would improve market transparency and help small-scale enterprises compete more effectively with larger organisations.

Transport Shortages

Transport shortages are a common complaint among private

sector agribusinesses. This is especially true of small-scale businesses located in rural areas. Perhaps the best government can do is to give transportation a high priority within its foreign exchange allocation so that more vehicles, spares and fuel can be brought into the country. Emphasis should be placed on increasing the number of vehicles in the possession of the private sector.

Credit

Since poor access to credit and other forms of finance are a major obstacle to the private sector, especially the small-scale operator, government may have no choice but to get involved in establishing appropriate lending schemes. These may be financed from the Treasury, through special funds provided by international donors or through savings and credit schemes initiated by the private sector itself. Alternatively, government can encourage commercial banks to set special loan schemes targeted at various sub-sectors of agriculture and agribusiness. Due to the inherent risks in agriculture, and in dealing with small businesses with very limited resources, lending institutions will probably require some form of government underwriting of these schemes.

References

Campbell, D., "Community-controlled economic development as a strategic vision for the sustainable agriculture movement," *American Journal of Alternative Agriculture* (12)1: 37-44, 1997.

Flora, C.B., "Sustainable agriculture, the structure of agriculture and rural communities," In *Alternative Farming Systems and Rural Communities*, proceedings of the annual meeting of the Institute for Alternative Agriculture, March 1992, pp. 39-48.

Lockeretz, W., "Comparative local economic benefits of conventional and alternative cropping systems," *American Journal of Alternative Agriculture* 4(2): 75-83, 1989.

Langè, T., "The complexities of globalization: the UK as a case study of tensions within the food system and the challenge to food policy," *Agriculture and Human Values* 16(2): 169-185, 1999.

Bibliography

Abbott, J.C., *Agricultural Marketing Enterprises for the Developing World*, 1987, pp. 152-157.

Ashby, B.H., *et al.*, *Protecting Perishable Foods During Transport by Truck*, HBK-669. USDA, AMS, September, 1987.

Atlantic Mutual Companies, *Buyers Guide To Marine Cargo Insurance*, New York, NY, 1990.

Bird, E. R., G.L. Bultena, and J.C. Gardner (Eds.)., *Planting The Future: Developing an Agriculture that Sustains Land and Community*, Walthill, Nebraska: Center for Rural Affairs, 1995.

Campbell, D., "Community-controlled economic development as a strategic vision for the sustainable agriculture movement," *American Journal of Alternative Agriculture* (12)1: 37-44, 1997.

Cassell, Clark C., *The World is Your Market - An Export Guide for Small Business*, Edited by William Delphos. Braddock Communications, Washington, DC, 1990.

Coles, R.C. and Beharrell, B., "Packaging Innovation in the Food Industry," *British Food Journal*, 92, 1992, pp. 21-32.

Dupree, H.K. ad J.V. Huner, *Transportation of Live Fish*, Pages 165-176 *in* H.K Dupree and J.V. Huner, editors., Third Report to Fish Farmers. U.S. Fish and Wildlife Service, Washington, D.C, 1984.

Feenstra, G., "Local food systems and sustainable communities," *American Journal of Alternative Agriculture* (12)1: 28-36, 1997.

Flora, C.B., "Sustainable agriculture, the structure of agriculture and rural communities," In *Alternative Farming Systems and Rural Communities*, proceedings of the annual meeting of the Institute for Alternative Agriculture, March 1992, pp. 39-48.

Friedheim, Amy, *Ocean Liner Freight Rates and Services*, USDA, AMS, May 1991.

Fuell, L. D., D. C. Miller, and M. Chesley, *Dictionary of International Agricultural Trade*, USDA, FAS, June 1988.

Gill, C.O. & Phillips, D.M., The efficiency of storage during distant continental transportation of beef sides and quarters, *Food Res. Int., 26 (4)*: 239-245, 1993.

Hardenburg, R. E., A. E. Watada, C. Y. Wang, *The Commercial Storage of Fruits, Vegetables, and Florist and Nursery Stocks*, HBK-66. USDA, ARS, September 1986.

Johnson, S.K., *Transport of Fish and Crustaceans in Sealed Containers., Inland Aquaculture, Handbook*, Texas Aquaculture Association, College Station, TX. A1504-A1509, 1988.

Koc, M. and K. Dahlberg., "The restructuring of food systems: trends, research, and policy issues," *Agriculture and Human Values* 16(2): 109-116, 1999.

Kotler, P., "Marketing Management: Analysis, Planning and Control," 6th edition, (Ed) New Jersey, Prentice-Hall International Inc., 1988, p.71.

Lange, T., "The complexities of globalization: the UK as a case study of tensions within the food system and the challenge to food policy," *Agriculture and Human Values* 16(2): 169-185, 1999.

Levy, D., "A Lobster Tale: The Collective Marketing of Brazilian Seafood," In: *Successful Agribusiness Management*, Gower Publishing Company Ltd, 1985, pp. 116-121.

Lockeretz, W., "Comparative local economic benefits of conventional and alternative cropping systems," *American Journal of Alternative Agriculture* 4(2): 75-83, 1989.

Maretzki, A. and C. Anderson (project co-directors)., *The Northeast Network: Food, Agriculture, and Health Policy Education*, Ithaca, New York: Cornell University, 1991.

McCarthy, *Basic Marketing: A Managerial Approach*, 9th edition, Homewood III.: Richard D. Irwin, 1981.

Piper, R.G., *et al., Fish Hatchery Management*, U.S. Fish and Wildlife Service, Washington, D.C. 517pp, 1982.

Index